# THE DEVELOPING ROLE OF ISLAMIC BANKING AND FINANCE: FROM LOCAL TO GLOBAL PERSPECTIVES

# CONTEMPORARY STUDIES IN ECONOMIC AND FINANCIAL ANALYSIS

Series Editors: Robert J. Thornton and
J. Richard Aronson

Recent Volumes:

| | |
|---|---|
| Volume 83: | Foreign Direct Investment in the United States, Edited by W. L. Casey |
| Volume 84: | Colombia: An Opening Economy? Edited by C. M. Callahan and F. R. Gunter |
| Volume 85: | The Irish Economy in Transition: Success, Problems and Prospects, Edited by J. R. Aronson, V. Munley and R. J. Thornton |
| Volume 86: | Asia Pacific Financial Markets in Comparative Perspective: Issues and Implications for the 21st Century, Edited by J. A. Batten and T. A. Fetherston |
| Volume 87: | Developments in Litigation Economics, Edited by P. A. Gaughan and R. J. Thornton |
| Volume 88: | European Responses to Globalization: Resistance, Adaptation and Alternatives, Edited by Janet Laible and Henri J. Barkey |
| Volume 89: | Globalization: Perspectives from Central and Eastern Europe, Edited by Katalin E. Fabian |
| Volume 90: | Privatization in Transition Economies: The Ongoing Story, Edited by Ira W. Lieberman and Daniel J. Kopf |
| Volume 91: | Personal Injury and Wrongful Death Damages Calculations: Transatlantic Dialogue, Edited by John O. Ward and Robert J. Thornton |
| Volume 92: | Moving Beyond Storytelling: Emerging Research in Microfinance, Edited by Todd A. Watkins and Karen Hicks |
| Volume 93: | The Impact of the Global Financial Crisis on Emerging Financial Markets, Edited by Jonathan A. Batten and Peter G. Szilagyi |
| Volume 94: | Derivative Securities Pricing and Modelling, Edited by Jonathan A. Batten and Niklas Wagner |

CONTEMPORARY STUDIES IN ECONOMIC AND FINANCIAL ANALYSIS VOLUME 95

# THE DEVELOPING ROLE OF ISLAMIC BANKING AND FINANCE: FROM LOCAL TO GLOBAL PERSPECTIVES


EDITED BY

**FOUAD H. BESEISO**

*Economic Future Center for Consultancy and Strategic Studies, Amman – Jordan*



Emerald

United Kingdom – North America – Japan
India – Malaysia – China

Emerald Group Publishing Limited
Howard House, Wagon Lane, Bingley BD16 1WA, UK

First edition 2014



**British Library Cataloguing in Publication Data**
A catalogue record for this book is available from the British Library

ISBN: 978-1-78350-817-4
ISSN: 1569-3759 (Series)

# CONTENTS

# LIST OF CONTRIBUTORS

| | |
|---|---|
| *Asif Akhtar* | Department of Business Administration, FMSR, A.M.U., Aligarh, India |
| *Mohammad Mahbubi Ali* | Research Affairs Department, International Shri'ah Research Academy for Islamic Finance (ISRA), WILAYAH PERSE KUTUAN, Kuala Lumpur, Malaysia |
| *Fouad H. Beseiso* | Center of Economic Future for Consultancy and Strategic Studies (Founder and Executive Chairman), Amman, Jordan |
| *Nesrine Bouzaher* | University Mohamed Khider, Biskra, Algeria |
| *Dababrata Chowdhury* | School of Business, Leadership and Enterprise, University Campus Suffolk (UCS), Suffolk, England |
| *Mohammad Dolatabadi* | Information Technology, Tehran, Iran |
| *Mohammad Faisal* | Department of Business Administration, FMSR, A.M.U., Aligarh, India |
| *Lotfollah Forouzandeh* | Economic and Social Department, Payame Noor University, Tehran, Iran |
| *Tarek Kandil* | Faculty of Commerce and Business Administration, Helwan University, Ain Helwan, Cairo, Egypt |
| *Sabrina Kerdoudi* | Mohammed Khider University, Economic Department, BP 145RP BISKRA, Algeria |

*Aishath Muneeza* — Deputy Minister, Ministry of Islamic Affairs, Republic of Maldives

*Okba Necira* — University Mohamed Khider, Biskra, Algeria

*Ayomi Dita Rarasati* — School of Civil Engineering and Built Environment, Faculty of Science and Engineering, Queensland University of Technology, Queensland, Australia

*Asad Rehman* — Department of Business Administration, FMSR, A.M.U., Aligarh, India

*Eric Too* — School of Management & Marketing, Faculty of Business & Law, Deakin University, Australia

*Bambang Trigunarsyah* — Department of Construction Engineering and Management College of Environmental Design, King Fahd University of Petroleum and Minerals, Dhahran, Saudi Arabia

*Hajer Zarrouk* — Department of Finance and Economics, Emirates College of Technology, UAE; PS2D, FSEG, University El Manar Tunis, Abu Dhabi, United Arab Emirates

# ABOUT THE EDITOR

**Professor Fouad H. Beseiso**

Former Central Bank Governor and Minister. A Banking and Financial Economist with accumulated Monetary, Financial and Economic experience supported by many years of work in the field of Arab, Islamic Regional and International Banking, finance and development. In 1994 Prof. Beseiso was appointed as the first Governor and Founder of the Palestinian Central Bank (Palestine Monterey Authority – PMA) and performed his mission within seven years. Currently Prof. Beseiso who founded the Economic Future Center for consulting and strategic studies (Amman) and the Economic Future Center for consulting and financial studies (Palestine) is the Executive Chairman of these centers. Prof. Beseiso attended as a keynote Speaker in the International Conference on Islamic Finance organized by Emerald Publishers Group International and Abudhabi University Knowledge Group in Abudhabi on April 14–16, 2013. Prof. Beseiso's presentation was on "The Role of Central Banks in Shaping the Future of Global Islamic Banking."

Prof. Beseiso's Economic, Academician skills are centered around Middle East Islamic Economics and Finance, Crisis Management and Strategic Planning, Monetary Economics – Mainly Central Banking & Development Banking, Human Development and Governance.

His academic activities in 2002–2010 included many Jordanian, Arab, and International Universities: Professor of International Economy, PhD Program, University of International Islamic Sciences, Economics, Public Finance, Banking, Financial and Business Sciences.

*Consultancies*
Many consultancies have been performed to many banks on strategic planning, development, managing failure prevention, merging, and performance evaluation, and Consultancy Missions were accomplished while working with UN-ESCWA as a Senior Regional Senior Adviser.

*Training Seminars*
Supervised many training programs and seminars for Arab Financial Institutions' Senior Management through Economic Future Center which he founded.

*Professional Memberships*
Membership in many professional societies, national, regional, and International.

*Banking and International Awards and Prizes*:
Man of the Year 2002, The American Biographical Institute, U.S.A.
World's Most Respected Experts, International Directory of Experts and Expertise, American Biographical Institute, U.S.A.
Arab Banks Union Prize for Most Respected Bankers.

*Publications, Researches, and Studies*
Manual on The Management of Economic Financial and Banking Crisis (The Conceptual and Practical Basis), published by Arab Banks Union (2010).
Two researches on the Economics of Environment and Sustained.
Section 1 Conceptual Framework of Environmental Economics and Management.
Governance and Pragmatic Approach for Integrating Sustained Environment into Human Development-Regional Case (ESCWA).
"The Arab Economy of Palestine under the British Mandate, 1920–1948" (Beirut – Palestinian Encyclopedia – 1990).
"Pragmatic Approach to Arab Gulf States Development Co-operation" (Beirut – Arab Unity Studies Centre – 1984).
"The Israeli Economy – Motivations for War and Peace" (Amman – Dar Al-Jalil – 1984).

"The Arab Boycott of Israel and Its Economic Impact" (Amman – Central Bank of Jordan – 1971).
Many other published and unpublished researches and articles on the Economy of Jordan, Palestine, Israel, The Arab Gulf States, Middle East, Arab Economic co-operation and Economic Crisis.

# INTRODUCTION

This volume is designed to constitute a scientific and practical illustration for the contemporary developing role of Islamic Banking and Finance components including Islamic Banking, Non-Islamic Banking Finance (Takaful, Financial Markets Products) with particular relevance and stronger analytical focus directed to country, regional emerging markets, and International case studies with their derived lessons related to the challenges and success determinants.

This volume's main contribution is centered around highlighting extensively on a vital stage of the Islamic Finance developing role that reflects the lessons of its experience, current state as well as the future determinants of effective inclusion of Islamic finance into the global financial and banking system.

This volume is the product output of many inputs and contributions of many eminent scholars and practitioners presented their research papers to the International Conference on Islamic Banking and Finance which was initiated and organized by Emerald Publishing Group International and held in Abu Dhabi, UAE, on June 24–26, 2012.

The planned topics of the conference aimed at reviewing, analyzing the current Islamic finance developments (conceptually and practically), and defining the determinants of future role in the national, regional, and international development and financial stability, mainly in a world of periodic economic and financial crisis.

The progressive emergence of open, dynamic, globalized discussions on the Islamic Finance Issues as supported by its persistence growth motived Emerald to publish this volume as a contribution to the holistic approach to globalized Islamic Finance.

The presented papers to the conference were subjected to more in-depth scientific research review with a solid commitment to world standardized rules and guidelines and updating reflecting the course of joint discussions and serious dialogue between scholars on both conceptual and pragmatic aspects of Islamic Banking and Finance, particularly with relation to their contribution to development and stability of economic and financial system within national, regional, and international context.

The conceptual and practical review of this volume contributions resulted in dividing the issues into three parts: Part I centered around The Regulatory and Developing Role of Islamic Banking, including the central banks' regulatory and challenging role, Shari'ah required governance Islamic banking regional role, and impacts of international financial crisis (mainly in MENA region). Thus, Part I explores the required efforts to be made to gradually replace informal markets with organized and regulated ones and to enhance the overall development of the financial sector and its real economic and social contribution.

Part II is dedicated to The Developing Role of Non-Islamic Banking Finance, and the Islamic Financing of Infrastructure projects and how to maximize this role, directing attraction to financial markets with their Islamic financial instruments and products. It illustrates the roles of Islamic Stockbroking as well as Islamic Insurance (Takaful) which is based on an analytical research of emerging markets and their success factors.

Part III sheds intensive scientific lights on Determinants of Effective Islamic Finance Contribution – Country Case Studies, including mergers and acquisitions' impacts on financial performance in England, defining how the field studies can help decision makers to identify the major factors that may shape the attitude of customers toward Islamic banks (India case study). Fundamental basis of strategic effective direction for the privatization process in Iran is analyzed.

This volume is designed to include an institutional and reference base through Annexes section which constitutes an integral part for the research papers included in the volume and serves as institutional and information base on Islamic banking and finance which is thought to be responding to a particular need for all those interested in the issues of Islamic banking and finance.

This volume has been structured aiming at contribution to the strategic vision of the Islamic Finance International Institutions as well as to be main source of intensive lightening on the Islamic finance mission based on development of a dynamic, comprehensive, and innovative Islamic financial services industry, which closely supports real economic activities and is well integrated within the international financial system characterized by the rapidly changing global market, technological and regulatory environments (as clearly reflected in the strategic document of IFSB (Annex 2: http://ifsb.org/docs/10_yr_framework.pdf).

Consequently, this volume aimed at a fruitful contribution while defining how public policies, governance, legal framework, and field studies' lessons can help decision makers to identify the major factors that may shape the attitude of both Islamic Financial Institutions and customers toward safe and sound services and through defining main determinants for successful, strategic inclusion of the Islamic Financial System into the real sustained development nationally, regionally, and internationally.

Final acknowledgement note should value the International Publishing and conferences initiatives within defined priorities responding to the Economic, Monetary, and Financial Issues continues to be performed by Emerald Group orchestra and its sincere team of management and professionals including Ms. Valerie Robillard, the Publisher, and Ms. Tansy M. Fall, Managing Editor, who provided appreciated assistance and valuable advice to me during the whole stage of producing this volume.

Professor Fouad H. Beseiso (PhD)
*Volume Editor*

# PART I
# THE REGULATORY AND DEVELOPING ROLE OF ISLAMIC BANKING

# CENTRAL BANKS' ROLE IN SHAPING THE FUTURE OF ISLAMIC BANKING

Fouad H. Beseiso

## ABSTRACT

Purpose – *This chapter's goal is to define the kind of seeds to be planted for moving forward in the safe and stable drive toward a leading central banking role directed at achieving a sustained Islamic banking and finance development within the global financial system. The system witnessed the input of Islamic banking with its fruitful contribution as a feasible banking structure in both implementing agreed reforms and shaping the next steps directed toward crisis prevention and crisis resolution.*

Approach and methodology – *The adopted approach is based upon scientific conceptual basis as well as the practical experience related to the central banking role and Islamic banking evolution. This chapter will define the strategic role of Central Banks and highlight the conceptual basis governing the leading role of central banks as well as the practical basis derived from our central banking and Islamic banking experience.*

Contribution – *In light of the conceptual and practical basis for enabling an efficient and effective role of Central Banks as a regulatory body in*

**The Developing Role of Islamic Banking and Finance: From Local to Global Perspectives**
**Contemporary Studies in Economic and Financial Analysis, Volume 95, 3–30**

**ISSN: 1569-3759/doi:10.1108/S1569-3759(2014)0000095009**

*shaping the future of the Islamic Financial System. Legal, institutional and managerial strategic determinants for this role have been defined.*

*The analytical work of this chapter crystallises in a pioneering initiative the main determining factors governing the role of central banks as the main regulatory body for Islamic banking, and how this role could be effective in affecting the future role to be played by the Islamic banks in the global financial system. Also, to this end, the integrated required role by central banks, public policies, multilateral institutions and Islamic banks are illustrated.*

Findings – *Energy and cooperative hard work and commitment from all players, including the regulators of Islamic banks supported by public policies, international and multilateral institutions and members of the Islamic banking family is thought to be the main determining factor for transforming the Islamic banking family into one that will make the Islamic people and all humanity – through the global financial system – live with more stability, welfare and happiness.*

**Keywords:** Central banking; Islamic banking; strategic planning; crisis and risk management; banking technology

## INTRODUCTION

This chapter defines the kind of required seeds for moving forward in the safe and stable drive toward a leading central banking role to achieve a sustained Islamic banking and finance development within the global financial system. The system witnessed the input of Islamic banking with its fruitful contribution as a feasible banking structure in both implementing agreed reforms and shaping the next steps directed toward crisis prevention and crisis resolution.

This chapter will define the strategic role of central banks and highlight the conceptual basis governing the leading role of central banks as well as the practical basis which has resulted from three decades of experience, including our central banking and Islamic banking experience. This research, while defining the main role of central banks as the leading regulatory body for emerging and fast-growing Islamic banking sector, ends with defining the integrated determining factors for achieving stability, sustained growth and effectiveness for the Islamic banking sector.

Institutions offering Islamic financial services constitute a significant and growing share of the financial system in several countries.

Since the inception of Islamic banking about three decades ago, the number and reach of Islamic financial institutions worldwide has risen from one institution in one country in 1975 to more than 300 institutions operating in more than 75 countries.

The entire banking systems of Sudan and Iran are based on Islamic finance principles. In Pakistan, the transformation of the financial system to be compliant to Islamic *Shariah* principles has been planned. Some countries have licensed Islamic banks alongside conventional banking such as in Malaysia, Indonesia, Bangladesh, Jordan, Egypt and Oman. This is applied either by independent Islamic banks, or Islamic windows or branches belonging to the conventional banks, or by establishing Islamic subsidiaries.

Global financial institutions, such as Citibank, offer instruments conforming to Islamic *Shariah* principles in several countries. Offshore financial centres have attracted some Islamic banking services for cross-border activities (Sundararajan & Luca Errico, 2002) (http://kantakji.com/fiqh/Files/Markets/y144.pdf).

Although Islamic banks are concentrated in the Middle East and Southeast Asia, they are also niche players in Europe (see Annex 4) and the United States.

## CENTRAL BANKS' ROLE FOR ISLAMIC BANKING GOVERNANCE

The main question is how, in adopting the proposed conceptual and pragmatic approach to central banking role in organising and supervising the Islamic banking, can we construct a new solid base for a new system of Islamic banking governance and surveillance which can strengthen our capacity for more financial sector developmental input into the sustained development, and strengthen the sector capacity to prevent crises and advance countries' shared objectives of stability, development and prosperity in order to set a dynamic and sustainable future path for the Islamic finance services.

At this early stage of analysis, we should appreciate the leading role and innovative contributions by the entrepreneurs and institutions who initiated the investment in Islamic banking and the regional and international financial institutions including international Islamic banking, that have played a leading role in building the institutional basis for the Islamic banking sector growth, while achieving successful take-off and strengthening their role within the international financial system, despite the modest contribution but with continued growing role in the international financial circles. We value also the role of regional and other international institutions, research and training centres, all of which have contributed to the Islamic banking operations and progress within adopted standards and best practices in parallel with international best practices.

A number of multilateral institutions have been created recently to provide assistance to governments and supervisory authorities to help them understand Islamic banking and to issue standards and best-practice guidelines for this industry. These organisations include the Islamic Financial Services Board (IFSB), Accounting and Auditing Organisation for Islamic Financial Institutions (AAOIFI) (Annexes 1 and 2), and the Islamic Development Bank (ISDB). These are in addition to the International Monetary Fund (IMF), Arab Monetary Fund (AMF) and other bodies such as the Bank for International Settlements (BIS). The concerned authorities should engage in dialogue with the local interlocutors of this industry, to promote an open and fluid exchange of information and ideas (Solé, 2007).

The establishment of the IFSB in 2002 as an international prudential standard-setting body to promulgate the international regulatory and supervisory standards for Islamic financial institutions is aimed towards achieving this objective. In this regard, the IFSB has already made progress in developing the prudential standards on the capital adequacy and risk management framework. In addition, the IFSB has been working on developing standards on corporate governance (Annex 2).

At present, some countries, to achieve safe banking activities mainly for capital adequacy with relation to asset management risks, have adopted the Basel 2 and the latest 3 Accord standards in their regulatory and supervisory framework for their Islamic banking industry. However, these standards, issued by BIS, did not adequately address the requirements of Islamic banking operations and transactions, resulting in gaps in the standards.[1]

> The implementation of Basel III requirements poses both challenges and opportunities for Islamic financial institutions, which will have to devote significant efforts and resources to meet the new international standards Therefore, these developments should be taken into account with respect to the capital treatment and risk associated for the different types of Islamic financial contracts to truly reflect their features and characteristics. (http://www.bnm.gov.my/index.php?ch = 9&pg = 15&ac = 145)

## ISLAMIC BANKING CONCEPT

The Islamic banking system and activities are based on Islamic law (*Shariah*) which mainly differs from the conventional banking system in the financing activities on profit-and-loss sharing arrangements (PLS) or the purchase and resale of goods and services to form the basis of contracts. Also, Islamic law prohibits usury, which is called *riba*.

> In PLS modes, the rate of return on financial assets is not known or fixed prior to undertaking the transaction. Islamic law also generally prohibits trading in financial risk (which is seen as a form of gambling). In addition, Islamic law prohibits investing in businesses that are considered haram (such as businesses that sell alcohol or pork, or businesses that produce un-Islamic media). (http://www.imf.org/external/np/ms/2012/031412.htm)

Islamic banking at least in theory, unlike conventional banking, is committed in its financing activities mainly to the viability of the project and the profitability of the operation, but not the size of the collateral.

> Good projects which might be turned down by conventional banks for lack of collateral would be financed by Islamic banks on a profit-sharing basis. It is especially in this sense that Islamic banks can play a catalytic role in stimulating economic development. In many developing countries, of course, development banks are supposed to perform this function. Islamic banks are expected to be more enterprising than their conventional counterparts. (http://www.islaam.net/main/display.php?part=full&category=7&id=261)

Under Islamic rules arrangements, Islamic banks should have a strong risk management to meet the requirements of PLC principal, and for not all projects attract investors who are committed to *Shariah* principles. Here the IFSB plays an effective role in formulating and issuing standards governing financing activities, as well as covering the cross-border supervision issues including the home-based supervisor issue.

## INTERNATIONAL ISLAMIC BANKING

The Islamic finance industry still lacks global scale. Professor Rodney Wilson of the Institute for Middle Eastern and Islamic studies at Durham University in the United Kingdom estimates Islamic banking assets for less than 0.5% of the world's total. And worldwide *sukuk* debt outstanding amounts to perhaps 100 billion U.S. dollars (USD)? This is just 0.1% of the global bond market (Imam & Kpodar, 2010). However, all indicators and waves of attraction spreading globally show a rapidly growing percentage contribution in the international financial system.

## SUSTAINED GROWTH WITHIN FINANCIAL GLOBALISATION

Many developments in the global financial system and the principles governing the international economic, financial and trade relations, as well as the institution of many multilateral agencies, paved the way to create motivating forces for better competition, wider markets for financial services and diversity of available Islamic financial products. The global financial developments and creative banking technologies showed their impact on the developments in the Islamic financial activities. The multilateral Islamic institutions proved through their active contribution to be a precondition for creating effective regulations and basic norms for supervising Islamic banks by their central banks. IFSB and AAOIFI are the best examples of proposing principles of the regulatory central banking guiding services and call for adopting the best international standards and practices, as reflected in Annexes 1 and 2.

All of these developments constitute a determining favourable basis for ensuring an effective environment for the growing role of the Islamic finance system as an effective participatory contributor to the whole global financial system.[2]

The focus should be now directed on the main question: why is the central banking role so important? The case for central banking's effective role rests primarily on the need to promote the construction of the legal, organisational and risk management, and to create a supervisory framework, responding to the basic determinants for the successful developmental mission of Islamic banks.

## EFFECTIVE REGULATORY AND SUPERVISORY FRAMEWORK

### *International Conventional Framework*

Islamic regulatory and supervision principles are not separated from the international conventional framework, mainly as central banks are originally responded to this international formulated basis – with some differences – as issued by the *Bank for International settlements (BIS)*.

The BIS, which services world central banks, could be considered as the main important international counterpart for the IFSB, which plays its role as the servicing body for the Islamic central banks.

BIS since its inception has played a vital role as an international central bank, providing many services related to banking supervision, risk management, and financing central banks and governments with short-term liquidity during financial crisis, and it offers a wide range of financial services designed to assist central banks and other official monetary institutions in the management of their foreign-exchange reserves.

In the field of banking supervision and risk management, the Basel Committee is the primary global standard-setter for the prudential regulation of banks and provides a forum for cooperation on banking supervisory matters. Its mandate is to strengthen the regulation, supervision and practices of banks worldwide with the purpose of enhancing risk management and financial stability (http://www.bis.org/bcbs/about.htm).

As an example of its effective role, the Basel Committee on Banking Supervision issued on 18 December 2013 a progress report on banks' adoption of the Committee's *Principles for effective risk data aggregation and risk reporting*, which were published in January 2013.

> The Principles aim to strengthen risk data aggregation and risk reporting practices at banks to improve their risk management practices and decision-making processes. Firms designated as global systemically important banks (G-SIBs) are required to implement the Principles in full by 2016.
>
> To facilitate consistent and effective implementation of the Principles, the Committee agreed to a coordinated approach for national supervisors to monitor and assess banks' progress. The first step of this coordinated approach was to issue a "stocktaking" self-assessment survey completed by G-SIBs, other large banks and supervisors during 2013. (http://www.bis.org/press/p131218.htm)

In the management of their foreign-exchange reserves, some 140 customers, including various international financial institutions, with 4% of the global foreign-exchange reserves have been invested by central banks with the BIS. BIS financial services are provided out of two linked trading rooms: one at its Basel head office and one at its office in Hong Kong SAR.

> The Bank continually adapts its product range in order to respond more effectively to the evolving needs of central banks.
>
> The BIS extends short-term credits to central banks, usually on a collateralized basis. From time to time, the BIS also coordinate emergency short-term lending to countries

in financial crisis. In these circumstances, the BIS advances funds on behalf of, and with the backing and guarantee of, a group of supporting central banks. (http://www.bis.org/banking/index.htm)

## *Islamic Banking Framework*

The banking system could not exercise its activities effectively and achieve sustained growth unless it performs its programs, policies, and activities within the framework of effective legal and institutional infrastructure. This effective infrastructure as a precondition could not exist without the vital role played by central banks as the main motivator for sustained growth in the banking and financial system. Coordinating their role with the other national and international players of public economic and financial policies always should be important.

Central banks should have real vision and belief in the mission of supporting Islamic banks and own the capacity to perform their mission within the international regulatory standards that provide the opportunity for a major improvement in the management and effectiveness of Islamic banks. They must, however, be accountable and transparent, avoiding the risk of becoming planners without serious performance with the result of many numbers and reports for prestigious media and popularity but with few real results.[3]

> The further development of Islamic finance requires for it to be endowed with the right pre-requisites that will ensure the evolution of an intermediation system that is viable, resilient and sustainable. Of essence, is the timeliness to develop an Islamic financial industry that is comprehensive and sound that promotes financial stability and growth through the robustness of its regulatory framework, the dynamism of its interconnected markets, the strength of its financial infrastructure and the responsiveness and sophistication of its products and services? (http://www.bnm.gov.my/index.php?ch=9&pg=15&ac=145)

Some argue that it is, in fact, the central bank which is the obstacle to Islamic banks' progress. The author of this chapter, with central banking experience within its regional context, believes that this issue seems to be determined by the degree of commitment by governors of central banks, and political will pertaining to Islamic finance values and basis.[4] Despite the rapid growth of Islamic finance in the last few years, many supervisory authorities and practitioners are unfamiliar with the Islamic banking mission, principles and requirements for sustained growth within the dual financial system (conventional and Islamic).

## CRISIS AND ISLAMIC BANKING

In light of lessons from frequent crises which had a drastic impact on banks including Islamic banks, central banks should be very careful within their strategic direction to run a system through which an early warning system with related required indicators should be built, and to work efficiently, with better crisis and risk management and established measures to deal with crises (Beseiso, 2010a).

### *The Role of Central Banks in Crisis Management*

Growing numbers of non-Muslims are turning to Islamic banking as customers motivated by the created environment of turmoil in the Western banking system increasingly see the Islamic sector as a safe haven.

> The Birmingham-headquartered Islamic Bank of Britain said it had seen significant growth in non-Muslim customers since the onset of turbulence on financial markets as Islamic banks, bound by strict religious principles, are largely seen as insulated from the credit crisis. (http://www.birminghampost.net/birmingham-business/birmingham-business-news/other-uk-business/2008/10/03/non-muslims-turn-to-islamic-bank-as-a-safe-option-65233-21962049/)

Islam's prohibition on the charging or paying of interest – *riba* – as well as rules on the kinds of investments they can make are among the reasons Islamic banks are coming through the crisis safer.

Islamic Bank of Britain head of marketing Steven Amos said:

> Our core business will always be Muslims but the numbers of non-Muslims are really picking up.
>
> We've had massive interest and it's down to the number of reasons why we're insulated from the credit crunch.
>
> There were two reasons for the credit crunch. The first is liquidity – banks' lending to each other on the money markets – but Islamic banks do not borrow or lend on money markets because interest is not allowed. (*Ibid.*)
>
> The second reason Islamic banks are insulated is to do with assets – everything has to involve an underlying asset or service and if you are going to trade in an asset you have to own it first. (*Ibid.*)

A potentially important part of the Bank's crisis prevention means is acting as a precautionary line of defence to be made readily available against arising problems from contagion. The key insight underpinning it was the need to incentivise good policy. It confirms the principle of using central banks to help safeguard a strong policy framework in the face of turbulence in capital markets (*Ibid.*).

Second, enhancing transparency is critical to strengthening crisis prevention, helping to ensure that vulnerabilities are addressed at an early stage and strengthening the accountability of the central banks. Greater transparency would not only benefit Islamic banks, but strengthen financial sector public confidence in public policies and operations (*Ibid.*).

## RISK MANAGEMENT FRAMEWORK

Strengthened capacity and qualitative standards of risk management are considered of urgent priority, emerging from an objective which has been motivated by periodic risks, instability in the financial markets and the latest deep international financial and economic crisis. This capacity of risk management should be integrated within the improved corporate governance.

> Sound risk management practices will minimize adverse consequences faced by financial institutions during periods of uncertainty. Robust internal controls to provide qualitative standards are also necessary to complement the quantitative analysis of risk to provide a check and balance in the overall risk management practices.
>
> Effective risk management systems are central to supervisory efforts. The risk management system in Islamic institutions needs to be able to address the unique characteristics and attributes associated with Islamic financing operations. Involving financial contracts and instruments gave rise to other risks besides credit risk including market and operational risks. (http://www.bnm.gov.my/index.php?ch=9&pg=15&ac=145)

## CAMELS MODEL[5]

The Camels model is an effective indicator for evaluating key banking assets and activities as the model relates to the capital adequacy, kind of assets, management efficiency, achieved earnings, liquidity position and sensitivity to the market operations. (For a detailed review of the banks' risks, including the role of the Camels model, refer to Sundararajan and Errico (2002), IMF working paper, pp. 4–15.)

## STRATEGIC PLANNING FOR CENTRAL BANKS

Approaching various determinants for effective regulatory system to lead sustained growth of Islamic banking requires – in our belief – the central banks' adoption of a strategic planning approach.

Key phases of the strategic planning cycle are planning, documentation, implementation and monitoring (Fig. 1).

With long-term direction and goals, it is unlikely that action will be focused on goals achieved. Effective planning helps banking institutions (BIs) including the Islamic sector to identify what makes them distinctive and what they have in common with other BIs, and therefore it helps to maintain their individuality.

Generating ideas falls into three categories – undertaking new activities, making improvements, and discontinuing selected activities (http://www.centralbanking.co.uk/conferences/archv/2004/PDF/hr041broch.pdf; http://www.bis.org/review/r050225f.pdf).

Strategic planning is the part of the strategic management process that is concerned with identifying the institution's long-term direction. It is a continuous, cyclical activity with three main phases: planning; researching and analysing strategy and plans, generating ideas and choices documentation; and documenting the plans.

Implementation and monitoring – taking action to achieve the agreed goals, and monitoring progress or non-achievement in order to adapt to the future strategy.

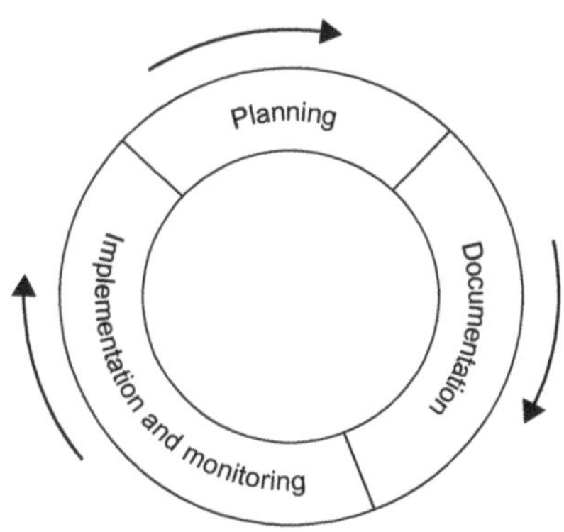


*Fig. 1.* The Strategic Planning Process. *Source*: http://www.hfrp.org/publications-resources/browse-our-publications/strategic-planning-process-steps-in-developing-strategic-plans. See also Beseiso (2010a, 2010b), pp. 510–514.

## BASIS FOR PLANNING AND TERMINOLOGY (REFER TO ANNEX 3)

## ISLAMIC BANKING – MENA REGION

The global financial crisis has demonstrated the growing popularity of Islamic banking, which is increasingly regarded as more trustworthy and stable than its conventional banking counterparts. With figures to support this, a recent report by Ernst & Young expects MENA's Islamic banking industry to reach $990 billion by 2015. In light of its increasing significance, Forbes Middle East has created a sub-ranking of Islamic banking in the MENA region. Detailed research led by an in-house team revealed total Islamic banking assets exceeding $293 billion across 18 banks.

## CENTRAL BANKS PRIORITISED INTEGRATED MISSION FOR ISLAMIC BANKING: FINANCIAL SYSTEM – DEVELOPMENT AND GROWTH

Many conceptual and empirical studies resulted in highlighting the role of an effective, efficient, and well-developed financial system as a determining factor for achieving economic and social growth. The sustained development of a financial system is determined to a large extent by the conceptual and practical role played by central banks. IMF concepts and empirical studies shed light on this fact in the following:

> The theoretical argument for linking financial development to growth is that a well-developed financial system performs several critical functions to enhance the efficiency of intermediation by reducing information, transaction, and monitoring costs. A modern financial system promotes investment by identifying and funding good business opportunities; mobilizes savings; monitors the performance of managers; enables the trading, hedging, and diversification of risk; and facilitates the exchange of goods and services. These functions result in a more efficient allocation of resources, a more rapid accumulation of physical and human capital, and faster technological progress, which in turn feed economic growth. (http://www.imf.org/external/pubs/ft/med/2003/eng/creane/)

### *Effective Regulatory and Supervisory Infrastructure*

As mentioned before, central banks' supervisory and regulatory role in creating the effective infrastructure for the banking system is crucial for enhancing the capacity of the banking role in achieving sustained growth.

Dr. Zeti Akhtar Aziz, Governor of the Malaysia Central Bank (Bank Negara Malaysia), defined in her presentation to the 3rd Annual Islamic Finance Summit organised by Euro money the basis for effective institutional building of the Islamic financial system as follows:

> A well-developed financial infrastructure is an effective legal, regulatory and supervisory framework which would underpin the stability of the financial system. The regulatory and supervisory function is an indispensable and vital component of the financial infrastructure. For the Islamic financial system, this framework also needs to be consistent with the requirements of the Shariah principles, including the establishment of a Shariah council, which provide assurance that the strategic direction, the formulation of policies and the conduct of financial transactions are in compliance with the *Shariah* principles. (http://www.bnm.gov.my/index.php?ch= 9&pg=15&ac=145)

She added:

> The legal framework should also deal with supervisory issues, including the relevant regulatory agencies involved in the supervision of Islamic financial institutions and encompass the licensing and conduct of Islamic banking business. The relevant agencies should have clear responsibilities and objectives to ensure effective financial supervision.
>
> While the conventional banking system is guided by the Basel core principles which outlines the minimum requirements for the supervisory regime, these principles need to be reviewed, as mentioned before, from the perspective of Islamic banking, taking into account the unique characteristics and risks involved in Islamic banking and its products and services. A fundamental issue is the setting of prudent and appropriate minimum capital adequacy requirements for Islamic banks. (*Ibid.*)

### *Greater Transparency and Disclosure of Information*

Transparency and disclosure are essential principles governing the bank of banks (central bank) in approaching its successful mission, particularly in a rapidly changing and competitive environment. While the comprehensive and timely availability of financial information will increase market discipline, the disclosure of information needs to be complemented with the ability of the market players to analyse and appropriately interpret the information.

## RISK MANAGEMENT

Recent and continuing international financial crises and risks created a priority to build a financial sector infrastructure framework which must effectively combine strong regulation and market discipline to reinforce financial stability.

> The recent crisis has shown that markets cannot be exclusively relied on to rein in excesses. A broader perspective of regulation that looks beyond individual institutions is also essential to identify the build-up of system-wide risks. Equally, financial institutions need to consider how to meaningfully include such system-wide perspectives in their approach to managing risks in their respective institutions. (http://secure.bnm.gov.my/index.php?ch = 9&pg = 15&ac = 430)

Islamic banking principles and activities bases, which are different from the conventional banking products and services due to restriction applied through required conformity to Islamic religious principles, are outlined in the *Qur'an* and Islamic *Shariah* laws. Such commitment necessitates adopting particular measures to manage special risks arising from Islamic banking services. Risks which were defined according to Basel 3 issued by the Bank of International Settlements (BIS) also are applicable to the Islamic banks' case. Consequently, Islamic banks are required to adopt strategic managerial plans to build effective and efficient capacity to manage risks and to deal with challenges that arise.

> The risk management infrastructure needs to be instituted in charge of the identification, measurement, monitoring and control of all inherent risks present in all the various types of financing. The respective risks in the Islamic financial instruments therefore need to be fully explored and quantified to provide for their effective assessment and management. (http://www.bnm.gov.my/index.php?ch = 9&pg = 15&ac = 145)

Continued abnormal developments leading to deepening uncertainties and greater volatility in financial markets have required greater attention to building more robust risk management capabilities.

> In the area of Islamic banking, the requirement to manage the risks becomes more important because of the unique peculiarities in the contracts. Basel II has, to a certain extent, incorporated some aspects in the identification of risks, in particular the credit, market and operational risks that can be assimilated by the Islamic banks in terms of its product offering, However, further refinement will have to be done by the Islamic financial specialists to assess the appropriateness of the capital definition in particular as outlined by the Basel committee. One of the considerations that need to be addressed in assessing the risks associated with the Islamic bank is with regard to the capital charge on its investment accounts. (*Ibid.*)

This is an area that is being addressed by the Islamic Financial Services Board in the drafting of the standard on the overall risk management framework for the Islamic financial community that takes into account this unique requirement of Islamic banking (*Ibid.*).

New hedging products which are scarce in the market need to be developed in the quest for compatible risk-mitigating products.

> In accordance with the Islamic principles the *Shariah* has allowed the Ummah to undertake juristic reasoning based on contemporary analysis and logical inference. Indeed, the development of new hedging products is something that the Islamic financial community can look forward to. In conventional banking, these instruments are used to mitigate risk. Indeed the Islamic financial community will soon develop such products for this purpose. (*Ibid.*)

## SHARIAH EFFECTIVE FRAMEWORK

There is intensive descriptive literature about Islamic finance, but there has been relatively little empirical work on Islamic banking and financial stability, particularly with relation to the leading role to be played by central banks as regulators for this sector, an area of increasing interest as Islamic banking grows. One of the central issues toward developing a dynamic Islamic financial industry is the *Shariah*.

> The *Shariah* should always be viewed as an enabler to innovation and creativity, rather than a constraint. Efforts, therefore, need to be enhanced to fully appreciate and maximize the true potential and wisdom of the *Shariah*. The collaboration among the *Shariah* scholars, practitioners, researchers and regulators to undertake in-depth studies and research to create new products will provide the fundamental foundation towards the development of a dynamic Islamic financial system. (*Ibid.*)

## QUALIFIED AND COMPETENT SHARIAH EXPERTISE

One of the main challenges facing sustained growth of Islamic banking and finance relates to the required expertise quantitatively and qualitatively; the requested expertise covers a wide range of talents and competences which respond to all service needs, including the most needy activities such as strategic crisis and risk management, legal issues, long-term financing, which is not always available and is reflected by Islamic banks' refuge to less risky and easier-to-administer activities directed to short-term financing.

Consequently, given the rapid global growth of Islamic finance, the continued creation of *Shariah* expertise is a prerequisite to build a pool of qualified and competent *Shariah* talent, as well as to accord more emphasis on extensive *Shariah* research in Islamic finance. Many initiatives have been taken in establishing research academies and institutions. This rising need requires the establishment of an institutional framework for continued cooperation between them and the operational sector (*Ibid.*).

## LEGAL FRAMEWORK

The legal infrastructure needs to comprise both effective regulatory and substantive laws covering all activities and services, as well as appropriate regulations to establish the basis for effective and efficient banking services, and to deal effectively with problem banks and resolve the disputes relating to Islamic financial transactions. Indian central banking experience as an example reflected how the legal framework played a vital role in the growing application of banking technology.

In the Palestinian case, we initiated a legal framework that enabled us to establish a sound banking system and enabled banks to face continued occupation risks; continued consultations with the banking sector contributed to the success on this direction.

## DEVELOPMENT OF FINANCIAL MARKETS

Targeting the institutional building of Islamic financial markets is considered a top priority and constitutes a vital determining factor for achieving sustained growth, as well as a more dynamic and responsive institutional framework for Islamic finance. Persistent building of the Islamic financial markets should include its key components comprising Islamic equity and debt capital market, and the Islamic money market which would act as a platform to provide a ready source of short-term funding and investment. Financial instruments and interbank investment will allow surplus banks to channel funds to the deficit banks, thereby maintaining the funding mechanism necessary to promote stability in the system.

The Islamic financial system also needs to include the capital market to provide an alternative source of financing, as well as to create broader and more diverse Islamic financial instruments for investors. The equity and bond markets will provide a more balanced allocation of financial and economic resources.

This would result in a more efficient distribution of risks within the system, thus creating stability in the system. The equity and bond markets would also provide an avenue for raising long-term capital.

> With a wider spectrum of instruments in the market, fund managers would be able to manage their portfolios better and spread their risk according to their desired risk tolerance, thereby contributing toward greater stability. The Islamic money market will also facilitate the conduct of monetary policy. (http://www.bnm.gov.my/index.php?ch = 9& pg = 15&ac = 145)

Complementing these financial markets is the development of non-bank Islamic financial institutions (the main topic for Part II of this volume). *Takaful*, or Islamic insurance, provides risk protection for its policyholders and serves as an important mobiliser of long-term funds. In addition, development financial institutions, savings institutions and housing credit institutions need to be developed to meet the diversified customer demands. These specialised institutions will meet the different requirements of the economy (*Ibid.*).

## ISLAMIC BANKING AND TECHNOLOGY

Islamic banking achieved great success as proved by their capacity to lessen the dangers of international crisis and their continued growth with relation to conventional banking. Islamic banking has been reaching a stage which could be described as "a mature growth phase" (http://www.path-solutions.com/website/islamicbanking.php), while being at the same time subject to fierce compaction, challenges on regional and

> unpredictable pressures from the multitude of new regulations to risk management, the islamic banking industry has no option but to consider strategic choices and address operational fundamentals and regulatory and Sharia compliance to capture untapped market opportunities. (*Ibid.*)

For all above mentioned considerations technology has become a determining factor for their sustained growth.

Islamic banking is entering a mature growth phase in its life cycle, as mentioned earlier. With increasing competition, more product development and better customer value is being delivered. But in a growing industry such as Islamic banking, where Islamic banks are facing a variety of challenges and unpredictable pressures from the multitude of new regulations to risk management, customer retention and cost of legacy systems, the industry has no option but to consider strategic choices and address operational fundamentals and regulatory and *Shariah* compliance to capture untapped market opportunities.

As the level of competition increases, Islamic financial institutions may have few alternatives to capitalise on opportunities presented by the latest technologies to remain competitive.

Practical experience and empirical studies illustrated a strong relationship between information technology (IT) and sustainable growth of banks; this is why banks are focusing on improving the performance and optimum utilisation of IT systems. Most IT initiatives are today derived from business objectives.

> Creating synergy between IT and operations to ensure sustainability will be a key driver in the future success of the financial services sector. The benefits of technology such as scale, speed and low error rate are also reflecting in the performance, productivity and profitability of banks, which have improved tremendously in the past decade. (http://mcgladrey.com/Bulletins/The-four-pillars-of-mobility-success-developing-a-successful-strategy)

Technology initiatives have been taken by banks in the areas of financial inclusion, mobile banking, electronic payments, IT implementation and management, managing IT risk and business innovation. While some areas have gained sufficient traction, others are still evolving. Technology has today been an integral component of all banks' activities and the main condition for increasing competitiveness. In the future, technology will play a stronger role as a business driver in all functional areas of the banking business (*Ibid.*).

Regulatory initiatives from the central bank also have played a large role in the developing banking technology.

Electronic payments through credit and debit cards are emerging as a fast-growing segment, as customers can easily use them and enjoy their convenience.

> The banking sector is projected to grow at a strong pace over the next decade and will need to strongly leverage the IT infrastructure to acquire and service the customer base and risk management. (*Ibid.*)

The conventional core banking software has been developed in light of the developed applications, which are based on fixed interest and defined calculation methods. In the Islamic banks and financial institutions that apply *Shariah* principles, fixed interest rates are prohibited and the profits are not known until the maturity date of the business contract/investment is made. The sharing of profit can vary from one form of financing to another. This also may vary in different jurisdictions and between banks, too:

> From a technical point of view, Islamic banking IT solutions might benefit from the developed conventional banking solutions while require adaptation to Islamic principles and software must be flexible, user friendly while constantly taking into consideration global best practices and processes accessible, scalable, compatible (able to run in different platforms and operating systems), highly secure with preventive features and have automated implementation with modern and reliable database technology. (http://www.sailanmuslim.com/news/a-glimpse-into-islamic-banking-software-systems-by-mr-muath-mubarak/)

With the latest developments in technology, Islamic banking software should be able to swiftly migrate or adapt to the advanced technology as and when necessary, while constantly taking into consideration global best practices and processes.

> Many software systems for the banks were developed with heavy development costs, after a number of years of research and development with equal amounts of testing. The Islamic finance industry is seeing everyday a new IFI. New start-up institutions will find it difficult to afford this strategic investment at the initial stages in order to build a robust IT platform with rich functionality. (*Ibid.*)

Trained professionals with in-depth knowledge about Islamic finance and continued training programmes are a determining factor for success in the field of Islamic banking technology.

> The IT team especially cannot enjoy the liberty of implementing IT systems like in conventional banks. In IBS each and every matter has to go through a Shariah Supervisory Board (SSB) to obtain the necessary approvals. Furthermore, Islamic banking systems require more information disclosure. This transition or system implementation in an Islamic bank will easily consume a minimum of six months and above depending on the complexity of the implementation project. (*Ibid.*)

In an interview with Muscat Daily, Thamer al Harbi, regional sales manager – Middle East, Temenos, spoke about the technological requirements and challenges that banks will face when launching Islamic banking in Oman.

The following text contains questions and answers in connection with this issue:

*What are the technological challenges that Omani banks may face while starting Islamic banking?*

Most Omani banks selected their system and had set up their technological infrastructure many years ago without any consideration about Islamic banking as it was not offered in Oman earlier.

The main challenge that most of the banks will face in the beginning is how to expand into Islamic banking with minimum investment and minimum operational cost. The biggest technological challenge would be to implement a robust software system, which will enable them to compete in this market as fast as possible.

As we have seen in other markets, customers will decide which bank they have to choose for services within the first six months of the launch of Islamic banking in Oman. At the time of the launch of the service in Oman, there will be tough competition among banks to win over new customers in this new line of business. So the challenge is how quickly banks can introduce Islamic products in the market.

*From the technology point of view, will it be easy for the two upcoming full-fledged Islamic banks to compete with existing banks offering the service?*

Definitely, from a technology point of view, it will be easy to start and manage a full-fledged Islamic bank compared to conventional banks with Islamic windows.

For conventional banks, the challenge is bigger as they are not using a technology that enables them to expand into this new sector. These banks need to acquire completely new systems and integrate it to provide services which will incur additional cost. It is going to be same thing which we had seen in other markets.

When commercial banks think of offering Islamic banking windows they require to keep conventional banking practices, such as accounting, funds and technology, completely separate from Islamic offerings.

Gulam Ali Khan, Islamic banking calls for technology change

© Muscat Daily 2011, Dec 24 2011.

http://www.muscatdaily.com/Archive/Business/Islamic-banking-calls-for-technology-change/(language)/eng-GB

## PLAYERS AND PRINCIPLES GOVERNING THE ISLAMIC BANKING FUTURE

The emerging Islamic banking and finance sector has been a fact, achieving a noticeable, sustainable growth rate within the global system and aspiring toward higher levels of inclusion globally, as well as a stronger role on a national and regional basis.

Islamic global banking's future is determined by three main forces which include the central banks, international and multilateral institutions, public policies and the concerned banking and financial institutions that constitute the main family of the Islamic financial sector.

The role to be played effectively by these three main forces is governed by certain bases which have been provided from recent economic, banking and financial experience including international, regional crisis and risks.

For central banks as the main regulatory body, the prioritised activities will involve a number of important conceptual and practical bases for the financial sector, beginning with including their main role in the development of the financial sector as a means not only to enhance the growth and development potential, but also to reinforce a strong foundation for financial stability. Motivating the banks to acquire the latest technologies was illustrated earlier in this chapter.

Regulations directed mainly to crisis and risk management and supporting strategies to Islamic financial include an agenda

> Which seeks to empower all individuals, irrespective of income level, economic activity or geography, to have the means and opportunity to undertake financial transactions, generate income, accumulate assets and to financially protect themselves against unexpected adverse events. (*Ibid.*)

One of the main challenges facing the emerging role of central banks as being in charge of Islamic monetary policy and regulating Islamic banking and finance require the adoption of Islamic *Shariah* rules in exercising their monetary policy tools such as discount rates. Many proposals have been initiated to face this challenge (http://www.islaam.net/main/display.php?part=full&category=7&id=261).

### *Greater Cooperation among the Regulators*

Strengthened cooperation between regulators will constitute a strong joint institutionalised consultancy forum which will create opportunities to exchange views and define the best-practice policies, practices and regulations, as well as the best solutions to the arising joint risks and crises.

This required joint cooperation necessitates regulators to continuously exchange views and share information between themselves as well as with stakeholders on key issues and developments faced in their own financial jurisdictions.

Thus, greater cooperation among the banking regulators would ensure that the Islamic financial system is directed by stronger and more efficient regulatory authorities, resulting in fewer vulnerabilities and abuses. In this respect, sharing of information among the regulators including across borders is important, especially in a more complex and liberalised global environment. In this regard, central banks should play their vital role to facilitate the integration of the Islamic financial system as a viable component of the global financial system.

This mission has many components, including: Basel 3 and the Islamic finance perspective, initiating an active role in reforming IMF and the international financial system (Lin, Fardoust, & Rosenblatt, 2012), integration between Islamic financial sectors among Islamic countries (Investment Conference for Islamic Countries, 2011) and integration within the global realm that can contribute to greater global financial stability and enhance the prospects for a more balanced global growth (Beseiso, 2010b).

### *International and Multilateral Institutions' Role*

Sustained dialogue and consultations between international multi-country institutions, whether specialists in the overall banking and finance for the international conventional system such as IMF, BIS, or specialists in Islamic banking and finance such as IFSB, AAOIFI (Annexes 1 and 2) proved to constitute an effective contribution to the whole development process of Islamic banking, as mentioned earlier.

In the most recent crisis and in the continued challenging environment, it is important to focus on the implementation of international prudential standards and sound risk management practices in Islamic financial institutions to ensure the financial stability and integrity of the financial system. Accordingly, greater mutual respect to global *Shariah* principles for Islamic finance would also contribute to the orderly global development of Islamic finance, thus sustaining the overall viability and soundness of the Islamic financial system as it becomes an integral part of the international financial system.

Issues such as effective central banking regulation and supervision, managing crisis and financial risks, developing international Islamic financial and monetary markets, human capital development and required expertise applied to governance and ethics are considered a priority for building up the solid base for future successful Islamic finance inclusion into the national, regional and global system. Thus the concerned authorities first should engage in dialogue with the local interlocutors of this industry, and second, with the international and multilateral institutions, to promote an open and fluid exchange of information, ideas and required solutions to arising problems and challenges.

### *Role of Banking and Finance Sector in Shaping Their Future*

One of the basic challenges facing the Islamic banking inclusion into the financial national and international system is their concentration on the short-term financing activities. Islamic banks are expected to be more enterprising than their conventional counterparts. In practice, however, Islamic banks have been concentrating on short-term trade finance, which is the least risky.

> Part of the explanation is that long-term financing requires expertise which is not always available. Another reason is that there are no back-up institutional structures such as secondary capital markets for Islamic financial instruments. It is possible also that the tendency to concentrate on short-term financing reflects the early years of operation: it is easier to administer, less risky, and the returns are quicker. The banks may learn to pay more attention to equity financing as they grow older. (http://www.islaam.net/main/display.php?part = full&category = 7&id = 261)

*Mudaraba* and *musharaka* constitute, at least in principle if not in practice, the twin pillars of Islamic banking. However, most Islamic banks are seen to give priority as mentioned earlier to the short-term trade financing, which is weakening the main mission and developmental role of Islamic banking. The inclusion of other financing instruments including *Mudaraba* and *musharaka* would be a basic contribution to the future sustainable growth of Islamic banking (*Ibid.*).

Effective bank governance is fundamental to support financial sector soundness. Although the central banks have issued corporate governance guidelines for bank directors, a clear governance framework is needed to safeguard the banks' financial integrity. IMF consultation missions encouraged the central banks to adopt the newly evolving international principles on governance standards for banks and recommended conducting bank governance diagnostics in the context of the forthcoming Financial Sector Assessment Programs (http://www.imf.org/external/pubs/ft/med/2003/eng/creane/):

> better positioned financial institutions to withstand the destabilizing episodes emanating from external shocks, the rethinking of business models in the light of a re-assessment of risk and return expectations, a reflection on fundamental value systems that ultimately shape individual actions, with greater premium placed on responsible and ethical behavior. (http://secure.bnm.gov.my/index.php?ch = 9&pg = 15&ac = 430)

The Islamic banking and finance sector could meet its growth and development goals in a manner that avoids the turbulences that will undermine its future prospects.

At the same time, lessons provided by crisis require Islamic banks to be committed to strategic management principles including governance, which will significantly strengthen their liquidity funding positions in order to support orderly credit intermediation processes.

Technological progress as referred to earlier should be part of the strategic management.

> To execute a serial of ambitious plans so as to improve business agility, achieve increased performance and help generate significant savings, Islamic financial institutions should partner with a leading Islamic banking software provider with the expertise to help them transform their business quickly, safely and cost effectively. (http://www.path-solutions.com/islamicbanking.php)

### *Public Policy Role*

Public policy is very important for the financial services sector while aligning itself with the defined objectives directed to a longer term sustainable growth.

Public policies are mandated to formulate strategies to develop countries' economies and their financial systems within well-developed legal, economic and institutional systems. Most emerging economies have strengthened their economic and financial systems following the Asian financial crisis which erupted during the 1990s. They improved their fiscal and external debt positions, and reformed their banking sectors. This has supported their economies, enabling capacity during the recent global financial turmoil.

The global financial crisis and the Asian financial crisis have provided us with many important lessons that should form the basis for the development of a sound economic and safe financial policy framework. Such a framework must effectively integrate both strong regulation and market discipline to reinforce financial stability.

Countries' legislative, executive and jurisdiction authorities play a vital role in strengthening the institutional arrangements and the capacity to safeguard financial stability.

## CONCLUDING REMARKS

This chapter aims to define the kind of seeds for moving forward in the safe and stable drive toward a leading central banking role, achieving a sustained Islamic banking and finance development within the global financial system. The system which witnessed the input of Islamic banking with its fruitful contribution as a feasible banking structure in both implementing agreed reforms and shaping the required capacity for crisis prevention and crisis resolution.

To reach its defined objective on highlighting the strategic role of central banks, the research shed light on the conceptual basis governing the leading role of central banks, as well as the practical basis derived from our central banking and Islamic banking experience. The road ahead calls for greater institutionalised cooperation and tighter coordination among the different members of the Islamic finance family. A joint initiative initiated by central banks and regional and international financial institutions is needed to ensure that the joint strategic direction and imperative programs are successfully implemented.

The role of central banks would be achieved effectively if created within the framework and foundations of a newly created socio-economic and social system for sustained human development based upon lessons from the Arab and international financial crisis and what is called in the region the Spring Revolutions in Arab countries (Beseiso, 2011).

While ending this research, an important general determining factor for the effective role of the whole financial system (including Islamic) should be realised with relation to the public policies governance and stability role as mentioned by IMF:

> There is agreement that macroeconomic stability is critical for the growth of financial sector services. Countries should adopt appropriate macroeconomic policies, encourage competition within the financial sector, and develop a strong and transparent institutional and legal framework for financial sector activities. In particular, there is a need for prudential regulations and supervision, strong creditor rights, and contract enforcement. (http://www.imf.org/external/pubs/ft/med/2003/eng/creane/)

With central banks' commitment, energy and hard work of both the regulators of Islamic banks and members of the Islamic banking family supported by wise public policies within human development system, life could be inspired to a joint strategic plan, based upon approaching both the challenge in the Islamic banking industry and performing its mission in building the sustained basis for steering the development of an Islamic financial system toward one which is more dynamic and responsive to a safe and sound national, regional and global financial system.

## ABBREVIATIONS AND ACRONYMS

**AAOIFI** Accounting and Auditing Organisation for Islamic Financial Institutions

| | |
|---|---|
| **BIS** | Bank for International Settlements |
| **Camels** | CAMELS stand s for Capital, Assets, Management, Earnings, liquidity and Sensitivity to market risk corresponding to various aspect of financial soundness |
| ***Halal*** | lawful |
| ***Haram*** | unlawful in Islamic *Shariah* |
| **IBs** | Islamic Banks |
| **IFIs** | Islamic Financial Institutions |
| **IFSB** | Islamic Financial Services Board |
| **ISDB** | Islamic Development Bank |

| | |
|---|---|
| *Muḍārabah* and *Mudareb* | A *Muḍārabah* is a contract between the capital provider and a skilled entrepreneur – *Mudareb* whereby the capital provider would contribute capital to an enterprise or activity, which is to be managed by the entrepreneur as the *Muḍārib* (or labour provider). Profits generated by that enterprise or activity are shared in accordance with the terms of the *Muḍārabah* agreement whilst losses are to be borne solely by the capital provider unless the losses are due to the *Muḍārib's* misconduct, negligence or breach of contracted terms. |

| | |
|---|---|
| **PLS** | Profit-and-loss sharing arrangements |
| ***Riba*** | Interest |
| ***Rab al Mal*** | Owner of the capital |
| ***Shariah*** | Islamic law |

## NOTES

1. This issue has been discussed in many conferences, including The Arab Banks Union, IFSB conferences: http://www.ifsb.org/event_detail.php?e_id = 194

2. In Annexes 1 and 2 some illustrations are mentioned with their important consultative regulatory role.

Annex 1 illustrates part of (AAOIFI) activities such as: full text of accounting, auditing and governance standards for Islamic financial institutions,1421H (2000). The full address of the Institution is as follows: P.O. Box 1176, Manama, Bahrain. Tel.: (+973)244496, Fax: (+973)250194, e-mail: aaoifi@batelco.com.bh, Website: www.aaoifi.org

3. Many strategic development plans which had been formulated by developing countries proved to be just prestigious media documents which lacked the strong political well and serious performance.

4. The author of this chapter had the opportunity as the Founder and first Governor of Palestine Monetary Authority to attend and participate in several meetings and discussions about Islamic banking with governors through the Arab Banks Union and the annual meetings of the council of Arab Central Banks and Monetary Authorities Governors organised by Arab Monetary Fund.

5. CAMELS model is a measure of the relative soundness of a bank and often is calculated by some supervisory authorities on a 1 to 5 scale with 1 representing the strongest performance (http://kantakji.com/fiqh/Files/Markets/y144.pdf).


## ACKNOWLEDGEMENT

This chapter was originally prepared to constitute the main conceptual and practical base for the author contribution-presentation as a keynote speaker in the conference on Islamic Finance held in Abu Dhabi (24–26 April 2013). This chapter has been revised to serve as an introductory conceptual and practical base for this volume. I should acknowledge the value of the professional scientific review of my research paper done by Mrs. Tansy M. Fall, managing editor with Emerald, the publisher of this volume.


## REFERENCES


Beseiso, F. H. (2010a). Manual on the management of economic financial and banking crisis – The conceptual and practical basis, Arab Banks Union.

Beseiso, F. H. (2010b). The available opportunities for Islamic financial system as alternative for the current international system. A research paper presented at the conference on Recent International Economic and Financial Crisis from Islamic Perspective, Organised by the University for International Islamic Sciences and International Institute for Islamic Thought, Amman, December 1–2.

Beseiso, F. H. (2011). The role of sustained Arab human development and economics of happiness in shaping socio-economic and political system for the Arab post revolutions era. 12th conference on the Political Economy of the Current Socio-Economic and Political Changes in the Arab Countries, Arab Economic Research Society, Cairo.

Imam, P., & Kpodar, K. (2010). Islamic banking – Good for growth? *Finance & Development*, *47*(4). Retrieved from http://www.imf.org/external/pubs/ft/fandd/2010/12/imam.htm

Investment Conference for Islamic Countries. (2011). *Islamic chamber of commerce and industry and Omani chamber of commerce*, Le Royal Amman Hotel, May 21.

Lin, J. Y., Fardoust, S., & Rosenblatt, D. (2012). Reform of the international monetary system: A jagged history and uncertain prospects. Policy Research Working Paper, Vol. 1 of 1 no. WPS 6070, May 15.

Sundararajan, V., & Errico, L. (2002). *Islamic financial institutions and products in the global financial system: Key Issues in risk management and challenges ahead.* IMF Working Papers, WP/02/192, November. Retrieved from http://kantakji.com/fiqh/Files/Markets/y144.pdf

Solé, J. (2007). Islamic banking makes headway. *IMF Survey Magazine*, IMF Research, IMF Monetary and Capital Markets Department, September 19.

## ELECTRONIC SOURCES (WEBSITES)

http://books.google.jo/books?hl=ar&lr=&id=9FtK7n6r_dwC&oi=fnd&pg=PA3&dq=IMF+Finance+and+development+Magazine+,+Islamic+Banking&ots

http://kantakji.com/fiqh/Files/Markets/y144.pdf

http://mcgladrey.com/Bulletins/The-four-pillars-of-mobility-success-developing-a-successful-strategy

http://secure.bnm.gov.my/index.php?ch=9&pg=15&ac=430

http://www.aaoifi.org

http://www.imf.org/external/np/ms/2012/031412.htm

http://www.bnm.gov.my/index.php?ch=9&pg=15&ac=145

http://www.birminghampost.net/birmingham-business/birmingham-business-news/other-uk-business/2008/10/03/non-muslims-turn-to-islamic-bank-as-a-safe-option-65233-21962049/

http://www.bis.org/banking/index.htm

http://www.bis.org/bcbs/about.htm

http://www.bis.org/press/p131218.htm

http://www.bis.org/review/r050225f.pdf

http://www.imf.org/external/pubs/ft/med/2003/eng/creane/

http://www.centralbanking.co.uk/conferences/archv/2004/PDF/hr041broch.pdf

http://www.muscatdaily.com/Archive/Business/Islamic-banking-calls-for-technology-change/(language)/eng-GB

http://www.imf.org/external/pubs/ft/fandd/2010/12/imam.htm

# *SHARI'AH* GOVERNANCE APPLICABLE TO ISLAMIC BANKS IN MALAYSIA: EFFECT OF ISLAMIC FINANCIAL SERVICES ACT 2013

Aishath Muneeza

## ABSTRACT

Purpose – *This chapter aims to explore the* Shari'ah *governance rules applied in the Malaysian Islamic banking arena and the effect of Islamic Financial Services Act 2013 on it.*

Design/methodology/approach – *This is a legal exploratory study primarily focused on library research.*

Findings – Shari'ah *governance is a concept that has been developed and applied gradually in Malaysia and the new Islamic Financial Services Act 2013 has taken it to the next level. However, this does not mean that it has resolved the problems in* Shari'ah *governance that existed before the enactment of the act.*

**The Developing Role of Islamic Banking and Finance: From Local to Global Perspectives**
**Contemporary Studies in Economic and Financial Analysis, Volume 95, 31–44**

**ISSN: 1569-3759/doi:10.1108/S1569-3759(2014)0000095010**

Originality/value – *Islamic Financial Services Act 2013 is a new statute that repealed Islamic Banking Act 1983. As such, not many have reviewed this new piece of legislation. This chapter will give insight into the evolution of* Shari'ah *governance as part of corporate governance of Islamic banks in Malaysia and will help explain the most recent developments in this arena along with the challenges.*

**Keywords:** Banking; Islam; Malaysia; *Shari'ah* governance

## INTRODUCTION

*Shari'ah* governance can be considered as part and parcel of corporate governance principles. The objective of *Shari'ah* governance is to ensure that application and adherence to the principles or tenets of *Shari'ah* are not compromised at any cost. The prefix attached to the phrase "Islamic banking" mandates it to comply with the principles of *Shari'ah* that are mainly derived from the Quran (the Holy Book) and the Sunnah (Prophet SAW's[1] traditions). There are many other sources of Islamic law too. Public interest (*maslahah*), equity (*istihsan*), and custom (*uruf*) are also considered among the secondary sources of Islamic law (See Kamali, 2007).

The principles applicable to *Shari'ah* governance are in one sense universal, as the primary rules of it will be common to all, irrespective of the jurisdiction in which it is applied. However, the secondary rules of it might differ from jurisdiction to jurisdiction depending on and considering the variable factors in the respective jurisdictions. One example of this is that in all jurisdictions that apply *Shari'ah* governance principles, there must be a *Shari'ah* supervisory or an advisory body formed of competent scholars who can advise on *Shari'ah*-related matters. The basic qualification of these *Shari'ah* advisers or scholars is that they must be well-versed in *Shari'ah*. However, in different jurisdictions, the name of these *Shari'ah* advisory bodies may differ and even the specific qualifications of the scholars sitting in these bodies also might differ, depending on the customer and public interest of the respective jurisdiction.

Malaysia is a country which is considered a role model for Islamic banking. One reason for this is because it has enacted a number of legislations and best practices that Islamic banks should adopt. Likewise in the arena of *Shari'ah* governance of Islamic banks, it also has adopted a number of rules that are widely accepted in the world today, which are worth researching.

The first form of *Shari'ah* governance principles that was adopted in Malaysia was embedded in the Islamic Banking Act (IBA) 1983. The requirement to form an in-house *Shari'ah* Committee in each Islamic bank laid the foundation for *Shari'ah* governance in the country. Subsequently, the *Shari'ah* governance principles were developed gradually by learning and correcting the mistakes from the practice. This attitude in Malaysia proved to be viable and successful and showed the world that *Shari'ah* governance can be regulated.

The latest development in Malaysia regarding Islamic banking is that in July 2013, it repealed IBA 1983 and adopted a new law called Islamic Financial Services Act (IFSA) 2013. This new piece of legislation also brings a new revolution to the existing practices of *Shari'ah* governance in the sense that it makes mandatory things that were not obligated before. Some of the best practices that have been followed are now part of the law, strengthening the application of *Shari'ah* governance, the backbone of Islamic banking.

This chapter will give insight into the theory of *Shari'ah* governance with reference to corporate governance. It will also analyze the development of *Shari'ah* governance in Malaysia with special reference to the problems facing it. Not only this, but the chapter also will discuss the effect of IFSA 2013 on *Shari'ah* governance.

## *SHARI'AH* GOVERNANCE WITH REFERENCE TO CORPORATE GOVERNANCE

It is hard to find a comprehensive or a universal definition for corporate governance. The OECD[2] Principles of Corporate Governance 2004[3] of defines corporate governance as the system through which companies are directed and controlled. *Shari'ah* corporate governance simply refers to the corporate governance affairs which are conducted in concert with Islamic law. *Shari'ah* governance[4] is just one part of the broad principle of *Shari'ah* corporate governance. But the reason why most of the literature that deals with *Shari'ah* corporate governance only focuses on *Shari'ah* governance is because, in the beginning of the development of *Shari'ah* corporate governance, *Shari'ah* supervisory boards[5] were the only component that were added to the existing conventional corporate governance structures. It is imperative to understand that over time, *Shari'ah* governance has expanded to form a full-fledged term of *Shari'ah* corporate governance that includes

*Shari'ah* auditing, *Shari'ah* review, *Shari'ah* research, *Shari'ah* compliance, *Shari'ah* risk management, etc., compelling the author to call it *Shari'ah* corporate governance, rather than just *Shari'ah* governance.

## GRADUAL DEVELOPMENT OF *SHARI'AH* GOVERNANCE IN MALAYSIA

The development of *Shari'ah* governance for Islamic banks in Malaysia began with the introduction of Islamic banking to the country in 1983. The first initiative is stipulated in IBA 1983, in which the establishment of an in-house *Shari'ah* Committee in each full-fledged Islamic bank is compulsory.[6] Later on, the Central Bank of Malaysia Act (CBMA) 1958 was amended to create a *Shari'ah* Advisory Council at the Central Bank Level.[7] Section 16B of the Central Bank of Malaysia Act 1958 states the following:

> The Bank may establish a *Shari'ah* Advisory Council, which shall be the authority for ascertainment of Islamic law for the purposes of Islamic banking business, takaful business, Islamic financial business, Islamic development financial business, or any other business which is based on *Shari'ah* principles and is supervised and regulated by the Bank.[8]

The main objective of these committees and the council is to play the role of watchdog in promoting *Shari'ah* compliance in all of Islamic banking. This is the beginning of *Shari'ah* corporate governance in Malaysia.

The role, qualification, and regulatory matters related to *Shari'ah* Committee were not clearly stated in the Islamic Banking Act 1983 or in any other law.[9] Hence, there was a need to have some kind of guideline to complement the legislation and further elaborate it. BNM/GPS1 is the guideline that was enacted by the Central Bank of Malaysia to explain how *Shari'ah* corporate governance works within Islamic financial institutions. But it shall be noted here that the term "*Shari'ah* corporate governance" was and is not used in any laws of the country; instead, the laws of the country use the term "corporate governance for Islamic Financial Institutions."

*Shari'ah* corporate governance in Malaysia at that time was not problem free. The problems encountered in this arena include the absence of the definition of *Shari'ah* corporate governance; the position or the rank of *Shari'ah* Committee within the Islamic bank organizational structure is not expressly mentioned; and *Shari'ah* audit, review, and research are not mandatory or emphasized.

Then came the Corporate Governance Guidelines for Licensed Islamic Bank (GP1-i) that were formulated to advance the espousal of effectual and high standards of corporate governance practices by Islamic banks and Islamic bank holding companies, and these set out extensive principles and minimum standards and specific requirements for sound corporate governance. It adopted the definition of corporate governance given by the Finance Committee Report on Corporate Governance, February 1999, which is as follows:

> Corporate governance is defined as the process and structure used to direct and manage the business and affairs of the institution towards enhancing business prosperity and corporate accountability with the ultimate objective of realising long-term shareholder value, whilst taking into account the interests of other stakeholders.[10]

The principles enshrined in the guidelines are based on the concepts of responsibility, accountability, and transparency, with greater emphasis on the function of the board and the management. There are 14 principles laid down by the guideline.

Corporate matters other than those related to the *Shari'ah* Committee of Islamic banks are regulated by the conventional laws of the country; that is, by the Companies Act 1965. However, certain guidelines were formulated by the Central Bank, Bank Negara Malaysia to sustain and build *Shari'ah* corporate governance in Malaysia.

The year 2009 was a landmark year in Malaysia for *Shari'ah* corporate governance. This is because the old Central Bank of Malaysia Act 1958 was repealed and the new Central Bank of Malaysia Act 2009 was enacted. It was gazetted on September 3, 2009 and came into effect on November 25, 2009. The significance of this new Act is that the Act has a dedicated part on the operation of *Shari'ah Advisory Council (SAC)* which is operated at Bank Negara or Central Bank level. Also section 27 of CBMA acknowledges the existence of dual banking systems in Malaysia. Some people say that this Act has solved all the issues related to SAC in the arena of *Shari'ah* corporate governance in Malaysia. But a deeper analysis on the matter would prove otherwise. This new Act has created some new issues in the arena to which adequate answers are needed.

To solve the existing problems in the *Shari'ah* corporate governance of Islamic banks and other Islamic financial institutions in Malaysia, a new *Shari'ah* governance structure was introduced by Bank Negara; that is, the *Shari'ah* Governance Framework of 2011. The *Shari'ah* Governance Framework (SGF) for Islamic financial institutions (IFIs) supersedes the Guidelines on the Governance of *Shari'ah* Committees of IFIs introduced

***Table 1.*** Impact of SGF Resolving the Incumbent Conflicts.

| *Shari'ah* Governance Conflict before SGF | Has SGF Solved the Conflict? |
|---|---|
| Definition of *Shari'ah* governance is absent | There is no precise definition, but the main requirements which shall be reflected in a good *Shari'ah* governance framework is mentioned:<br>"A sound and robust *Shari'ah* governance framework is reflected by effective and responsible board and management, an independent *Shari'ah* Committee that is both competent and accountable, supported by a strong internal *Shari'ah* research capacity, and monitored through active *Shari'ah* review, *Shari'ah* audit and *Shari'ah* risk management process." |
| The position or the rank of *Shari'ah* Committee within the Islamic Financial Institutions is not expressly mentioned | "The board, upon consultation with the *Shari'ah* Committee shall approve all policies relating to *Shari'ah* matters and is expected to ensure that such policies are implemented effectively." This proves that *Shari'ah* committee has an effective role in the IFIs. However, the actual rank of it is not clear; but what is known is that in all *Shari'ah*-related matters, it has the ultimate say in the organization. |
| *Shari'ah* Audit is not compulsory and the qualification of *Shari'ah* auditors need to be enacted | *Shari'ah* audit is defined and it is mandatory to do *Shari'ah* audit. The qualification of the auditor also is mentioned.<br>*Shari'ah* audit refers to "the periodical assessment conducted from time to time, to provide an independent assessment and objective assurance designed to add value and improve the degree of compliance in relation to the IFI's business operations, with the main objective of ensuring a sound and effective internal control system for *Shari'ah* compliance."<br>"The function shall be performed by internal auditors, who have acquired adequate *Shari'ah*-related knowledge and training." |
| The minimum requirements in *Shari'ah* reports need to be amended | It is amended under the new framework as following:<br>"In the name of Allah, the Beneficent, the Merciful<br>In compliance with the letter of appointment, we are required to submit the following report:<br>We have reviewed the principles and the contracts relating to the transactions and applications introduced by the ABC Islamic Financial Institution during the period ended. We have also conducted our review to form an opinion as to whether the ABC Islamic Financial Institution has complied with the *Shari'ah* principles and with the *Shari'ah* rulings issued by the *Shari'ah* Advisory Council of Bank Negara Malaysia, as well as *Shari'ah* decisions made by us. |

| | |
|---|---|
| | The management of ABC Islamic Financial Institution is responsible for ensuring that the financial institution conducts its business in accordance with *Shari'ah* principles. It is our responsibility to form an independent opinion, based on our review of the operations of the ABC Islamic Financial Institution, and to report to you.<br>We have assessed the work carried out by *Shari'ah* review and *Shari'ah* audit which included examining, on a test basis, each type of transaction, the relevant documentation and procedures adopted by the ABC Islamic Financial Institution.<br>We planned and performed our review so as to obtain all the information and explanations which we considered necessary in order to provide us with sufficient evidence to give reasonable assurance that the ABC Islamic Financial Institution has not violated the *Shari'ah* principles.<br>In our opinion:<br>1. the contracts, transactions and dealings entered into by the ABC Islamic Financial Institution during the year ended that we have reviewed are in compliance with the *Shari'ah* principles;<br>2. the allocation of profit and charging of losses relating to investment accounts conform to the basis that had been approved by us in accordance with *Shari'ah* principles; (where appropriate, the opinion paragraph shall also include the following matters:)<br>3. all earnings that have been realized from sources or by means prohibited by the *Shari'ah* principles have been considered for disposal to charitable causes; and<br>4. the calculation of *zakat* is in compliance with *Shari'ah* principles.<br>We, the members of the *Shari'ah* Committee of ABC Islamic Financial Institution, do hereby confirm that the operations of the ABC Islamic Financial Institution for the year ended have been conducted in conformity with the *Shari'ah* principles." |
| *Shari'ah* risk management is not emphasized | It is mandatory to use *Shari'ah* risk management ("the *Shari'ah* risk management control function shall form as part of the IFI's integrated risk management framework").<br>"*Shari'ah* risk management is a function to systematically identify, measure, monitor and control of *Shari'ah* non-compliance risks to mitigate any possible of non-compliance events. The systematic approach of managing *Shari'ah* non-compliance risks will enable the IFI to continue its operations and activities effectively." |
| The legal liabilities of the *Shari'ah* scholars are unknown | This matter is not dealt with in SGF. However, the Common law principles could be applied to tackle this problem. |
| The role of *Shari'ah* committee is only supervisory | The role of *Shari'ah* committee may be no more supervisory; if the changes are successfully adopted: |

**Table 1.** (*Continued*)

| *Shari'ah* Governance Conflict before SGF | Has SGF Solved the Conflict? |
|---|---|
| | "The board is ultimately accountable and responsible on the overall *Shari'ah* governance framework and *Shari'ah* compliance of the IFI, by putting in place the appropriate mechanism to discharge the aforementioned responsibilities. The board is also expected to perform diligent oversight over the effective functioning of the IFI's *Shari'ah* governance framework and ensure that the framework commensurate with the size, complexity and nature of its business."<br>"The board, upon consultation with the *Shari'ah* Committee shall approve all policies relating to *Shari'ah* matters and is expected to ensure that such policies are implemented effectively.<br>The board may consider appointing at least one (1) member of the *Shari'ah* Committee as a member of the board that could serve as a 'bridge' between the board and the *Shari'ah* Committee. The presence of a director with sound *Shari'ah* knowledge would foster greater understanding and appreciation amongst the board members on the decisions made by the *Shari'ah* Committee."<br>"In the event the management becomes aware that certain operations are found to be carrying out business(es) which is(are) not in compliance with *Shari'ah*, or against the advice of its *Shari'ah* Committee or the rulings of the SAC, the management shall:<br>(i) immediately notify the board and *Shari'ah* Committee as well as the Bank of the fact;<br>(ii) immediately cease to take on any new business related to the *Shari'ah* non-compliant business; and<br>(iii) within thirty (30) days of becoming aware of such non-compliance or such further period as may be permitted by the Bank, furnish a plan to rectify the state of non-compliance with the *Shari'ah*, to be duly approved by the board and endorsed by the *Shari'ah* Committee." |

*Source*: Muneeza, Hassan, and Wisham (2011).

by Bank Negara Malaysia in 2004. SGF has changed the previous *Shari'ah* governance structure in the sense that it has increased the number of *Shari'ah* advisory committee members from three to five; the minimum qualification of a *Shari'ah* scholar sitting in the *Shari'ah* Advisory Committee is a Bachelor's degree in *Shari'ah*; and the detail procedures and process of *Shari'ah* risk management, *Shari'ah* audit, *Shari'ah* research, and *Shari'ah* review are discussed more than in the previous guidelines. The success of this governance framework is yet to be tested. It is hoped that the new framework would prove to be a blueprint for the global industry of Islamic banking.

Table 1 illustrates the extent to which SGF has solved the *Shari'ah* governance conflict existing under the previous structure.

## EFFECT OF ISLAMIC FINANCIAL SERVICES ACT 2013

The latest development in Islamic banking in Malaysia that took place is the repeal of IBA 1983 and BAFIA 1989 by introducing IFSA 2013[11] and FSA 2013. IFSA 2013 repealed IBA 1983 and the *Takaful* Act 1949,[12] while FSA 2013 repealed BAFIA 1989, the Exchange Control Act 1953, the Payment Systems Act 2003, and the Insurance Act 1984.[13]

IFSA 2013 provides for the regulation and supervision of Islamic financial institutions, payment systems, and other relevant entities, and the oversight of the Islamic money market and Islamic foreign exchange market to promote financial stability and compliance with *Shari'ah* for related, consequential, or incidental matters.[14] IFSA 2013 consists of 291 sections with 16 schedules. This legislation is a comprehensive legal framework to regulate Islamic finance in Malaysia and compared to IBA 1983, the scope of this legislation is wider. The most significant change that are found in IFSA 2013 in relation to Islamic banking is that the definition of Islamic banking business[15] is changed and detailed provisions on *Shari'ah* governance with audit on *Shari'ah* compliance[16] is introduced. Furthermore, by virtue of section 138 of IFSA 2013, a financial ombudsman scheme is introduced. A financial ombudsman scheme is defined as a scheme for the resolution of disputes between an eligible complainant and financial service provider regarding financial services or products.[17] This type of dispute resolution outside the court would definitely create more legal certainty among the stakeholders of Islamic banking.

Table 2 illustrates the *Shari'ah* governance aspects dealt with in IFSA 2013 and the effect of each of the changes.

**Table 2.** *Shari'ah* Governance in IFSA 2013.

| *Shari'ah* Governance Matters | Explanation | Effect |
|---|---|---|
| Imposes a duty on Islamic banks to follow *Shari'ah*[a] | It is expressly stated that if the Islamic banks become aware of any non-compliance activity conducted by it, it shall immediately notify the Bank Negara and its *Shari'ah* Advisory Council; immediately stop such activity; and within thirty days of becoming aware of such non-compliant activity shall submit Bank Negara a plan to rectify such non-compliance.[b] | *Shari'ah* compliance becomes a legal duty of each and every Islamic bank. |
| *Shari'ah* matters are those matters that are decided by the Shari'ah Advisory Council of Bank Negara Malaysia[c] | It is expressly states that for the purpose of IFSA 2013, compliance with any ruling of the *Shari'ah* Advisory Council of Bank Negara is deemed to be in compliance with *Shari'ah*. Not only this, but Bank Negara Malaysia has the power to specify standards on *Shari'ah* matters with the advice from its *Shari'ah* Advisory Council.[d] | The decision of *Shari'ah* Advisory Council of Bank Negara Malaysia is binding on all Islamic banks and these decisions need to be followed and adhered to. If not, the activity of the Islamic bank will become non-*Shari'ah* compliant. It shall be observed that the definition to religion Islam or *Shari'ah* is not found in IFSA 2013. |
| Establishment of *Shari'ah* Committee[e] | It is mandatory to establish a *Shari'ah* Committee in every Islamic bank. | In-house *Shari'ah* governance matters are handled via these *Shari'ah* Committees. |
| Appointment of *Shari'ah* Committee members[f] | All *Shari'ah* scholars appointed to a *Shari'ah* Committee shall adhere to the fit and proper requirements or disqualifications of a member of *Shari'ah* Committee and they can only be appointed after getting prior approval from Bank Negara. | Uniform standard is introduced |
| Duties of *Shari'ah* Committee and *Shari'ah* Committee Members[g] | Minimum duties are stated and these are the statutory duties. | Duties of *Shari'ah* committees and the members of *Shari'ah* Committees are set by Bank Negara. |
| Termination of membership from *Shari'ah* Committee[h] | The instances in which the services of members of *Shari'ah* Committees are specifically stated in IFSA 2013. | *Shari'ah* Advisers is a profession and their professionalism standards are laid down by a statute. |

| | | |
|---|---|---|
| Information to be provided to *Shari'ah* Committee[i] | The institution, directors, officer, or controller of Islamic banks are legally compelled to provide any document or information on its/his capacity to provide the *Shari'ah* Committee and intentionally false or misleading information shall not be provided. | It is a legal duty for Islamic banks to provide information to *Shari'ah* committee now, if not they can be punishable under IFSA 2013 for non-compliance with the Act. |
| Qualified Privilege and Duty of Confidentiality[j] | It is expressly stated that a member of *Shari'ah* Committee shall not be liable for a breach of duty of confidentiality between members and the Islamic banks in respect of any reporting made to Bank Negara or the discharge of any of his/her duties or functions or any of the obligations that has been discharged in good faith. It is also stated that they cannot be sued in any court for defamation for any statement made without malice in discharging his/her duties. | Statutory privilege is given to in-house *Shari'ah* committee members and the legal duty of confidentiality is introduced expressly. |
| Audit on *Shari'ah* compliance[k] | Bank Negara may require any Islamic bank to appoint any person as it may approve and the remuneration of such person appointed shall be borne by the Islamic bank. | *Shari'ah* compliance audit becomes compulsory if Bank Negara requires the Islamic bank to do it. |

[a]Section 28 (1), IFSA 2013.
[b]Section 28 (3), IFSA 2013.
[c]Section 28 (2), IFSA 2013.
[d]Section 29, IFSA 2013.
[e]Section 30, IFSA 2013.
[f]Section 31, IFSA 2013.
[g]Section 32, IFSA 2013.
[h]Sections 33 and 34, IFSA 2013.
[i]Section 35, IFSA 2013.
[j]Section 36, IFSA 2013.
[k]Sections 37 and 38, IFSA 2013.

It is imperative to note that though positive changes are seen from IFSA 2013 and the effect of it on *Shari'ah* governance is good, there is an immediate need to define what *Shari'ah* or the religion of Islam is. The need for this arose because it is imperative for the Islamic banks to know what the acceptable juristic views are that shall be followed by those in the jurisdiction of Malaysia. Furthermore, a yardstick needs to be developed to regulate the remunerations of *Shari'ah* scholars sitting on the *Shari'ah* advisory bodies. The need for this persists, as this is a crucial area when the independence of *Shari'ah* scholars sitting in these advisory bodies is discussed.

## CONCLUSION

To conclude this chapter, it can be stated that *Shari'ah* governance is the backbone of every Islamic bank and it is vital to regulate *Shari'ah* governance for the coherence of Islamic banking industry. Malaysia has taken a gradual approach in developing *Shari'ah* governance. The latest development of *Shari'ah* governance in Malaysia is found in the new IFSA 2013, which went into effect from June 30, 2013. IFSA 2013 has brought positive changes and has legalized a number of *Shari'ah* governance principles in the form of statutory duties. This is indeed a remarkable move. It is anticipated that the success and the practicality of the changes enumerated in IFSA 2013 will be evident once it is practically followed. But for now, all that can be said is that IFSA 2013 will bring revolutionary changes to *Shari'ah* governance aspects and the whole world can learn from this experience in Malaysia.

## ABBREVIATIONS

| | |
|---|---|
| **AAOIFI** | Accounting and Auditing Organization for Islamic Financial Institution |
| **BAFIA** | Banking and Financial Institutions Act |
| **BNM/ GPS1** | Guidelines on the Governance of *Shariáh* Committee for the Islamic Financial Institutions |
| **CBMA** | Central Bank of Malaysia Act |
| **IBA** | Islamic Banking Act |

| | |
|---|---|
| **IFI** | Islamic Financial Institutions |
| **IFSA** | Islamic Financial Services Act |
| **OECD** | Organization for Economic Cooperation and Development |
| **SAC** | *Shari'ah* Advisory Council |
| **SAW** | Sallalallah Alaihi Wasallam |
| **SC** | *Shari'ah* Committee |
| **SGF** | *Shari'ah* Governance Framework |
| **SSB** | *Shari'ah* Supervisory Board |

## NOTES

1. SAW: Sallallahu Alayhi Wasallam (peace be upon him).
2. Organization for Economic Cooperation and Development.
3. The OECD Principles of Corporate Governance provide best practice recommendations on corporate governance. They are used extensively worldwide as a benchmark for standard setting and identifying best practices.
4. Islamic Financial Services Board's Guiding Principles on *Shari'ah* Governance Systems for Institutions Offering Islamic Financial Services defines "*Shari'ah* governance system" as the set of institutional and organizational arrangements through which an institution offering Islamic financial services oversees *Shari'ah* compliance, that is, that Islamic banking products and operations are in accord with *Shari'ah* principles (IFSB, 2009).
5. The Governance Standards issued by Accounting and Auditing Organization for Islamic Financial Institution (AAOIFI) defines a *Shari'ah* board as: "an independent body entrusted with the duty of directing, reviewing, supervising the activities of Islamic Financial Institutions for a purpose of *Shari'ah* compliance and issuing legal rulings pertaining to Islamic banking and finance" (AAOIFI, 2005).
6. Section 3 (5) of the Islamic Banking Act 1983: For the conventional Banks offering Islamic banking services, section 124 (3) compels them to seek advice from the *Shari'ah* Advisory Council established at Bank Negara Level.
7. Section 16B of Central Bank of Malaysia Act 1958.
8. Section 16B of Central Bank of Malaysia Act 1958.
9. The legal requirement of *Shari'ah* scholars sitting in SAC is evident from Section 16B (2) of the CBMA, which states that the members of the SC shall be persons who possess knowledge or experience both in *Shari'ah* and also in banking, finance, law or any other related discipline. The responsibilities of the SAC are mentioned in Section 16B (4) of the CBMA which expressly states that "the *Shari'ah* Advisory Council shall have such functions as may be determined by the Bank and shall determine its own procedure."
10. See Corporate Governance Guidelines for Licensed Islamic Bank (GP1-i).
11. IFSA will be enforced from June 30, 2013.

12. See the definition of "Repealed Acts" in section 2 of IFSA 2013.
13. See the definition of "Repealed Acts" in section 2 of IFSA 2013.
14. See preamble of IFSA 2013.
15. See section 2, IFSA 2013, section 2 of IFSA 2013 defines "Islamic banking business" as accepting Islamic deposits on current account, etc., accepting money under an investment account, and provisions of finance and as such other business prescribed under section 3 of the Act.
16. See sections 30–38, IFSA 2013.
17. Section 133, IFSA 2013.

## REFERENCES

AAOIFI. (2005). *Governance standard for IFIs, No. 1, Sharia Supervisory Board (SSB): Appointment, composition and report*. Bahrain: AAOIFI.

IFSB. (2009). *Guiding principles on Shari'ah governance systems for institutions offering Islamic financial services*. Kuala Lumpur: IFSB.

Kamali, M. H. (2007). *Principles of Islamic jurisprudence*. Selangor: Ilmiah Publishers.

Muneeza, A., Hassan, R., & Wisham, I. (2011). *Islamic banking under the Malaysia law*. Kuala Lumpur: A.S. Nordeen Publications.

OECD. (2004). *Principles of corporate governance*. Paris: OECD.

## STATUTES & GUIDELINES

Banking and Financial Institutions Act, 1989 (Act 372)

Central Bank of Malaysia Act, 1958 (Act 519)

Central Bank of Malaysia Act, 2009 (Act 701)

Companies Act, 1965 (Act 125)

Corporate Governance Guidelines for Licensed Islamic Bank (GP1-i)

Financial Service Act, 2013 (Act 758)

Guidelines on the Governance of *Shariáh* Committee for the Islamic Financial Institutions (BNM/GPS1)

Islamic Banking Act, 1983 (Act 276)

Islamic Financial Services Act, 2013 (Act 759)

*Shari'ah* Governance Framework 2011

# THE IMPACT OF THE INTERNATIONAL FINANCIAL CRISIS ON THE PERFORMANCE OF ISLAMIC BANKS IN MENA COUNTRIES

Hajer Zarrouk

**ABSTRACT**

Purpose – *The financial crisis at the end of the past decade resulted in downturns in stock markets and the collapse of many large banks around the world. It encouraged economists worldwide to consider alternative financial solutions. Attention has been focused on Islamic finance as an alternative model. This study examines the performance of Islamic banks in 10 Middle Eastern and North African (MENA) countries over the period of 2005–2010.*

Methodology/approach – *It is an intertemporal analysis where it compares the profitability, liquidity, risk and solvency, and efficiency of 43 Islamic banks before and after the financial crisis.*

**The Developing Role of Islamic Banking and Finance: From Local to Global Perspectives**
**Contemporary Studies in Economic and Financial Analysis, Volume 95, 45–69**

**ISSN: 1569-3759/doi:10.1108/S1569-3759(2014)0000095011**

Findings – *The results show that the financial crisis negatively affected the performance of Islamic banks. The profitability and liquidity of Islamic banks in Gulf Cooperation Council (GCC) countries decreased drastically after the crisis. Islamic banks in non-GCC countries were efficient and more profitable compared to GCC countries. However, they took excessive risk during and after the financial crisis. The chapter concludes that Islamic financial institutions are not immune from the effects of the global recession.*

Originality/value – *The financial crisis has led to a greater recognition of the importance of liquidity risks. Reinforcing regulations and setting up a strong liquidity management framework are needed to improve the Islamic financial industry.*

**Keywords:** Financial crisis; Islamic bank performance; MENA countries

## INTRODUCTION

Islamic finance is one of the fastest growing segments of the global financial industry. There are over 300 *Sharia'* compliant financial institutions worldwide in more than 75 countries (El Qorchi, 2005). According to the recent reports by Ernst & Young (2012, 2013), Islamic banking assets with commercial banks globally are valued at US$ 1.54 trillion in 2012 and set to cross US$ 1.7 trillion in 2013. In the Middle Eastern and North African (MENA) region, the volume of Islamic banking assets raise to 416 billion USD in 2010. Zahar and Hassan (2001) suggested that Islamic banks are set to control 40–50 percent of Muslim savings by 2009/10. It is too big to be ignored. Several factors have contributed to the strong growth of Islamic institutions, such as the high demand of many Islamic countries for *Sharia'*-compliant products; progress in strengthening the legal and regulatory framework for the Islamic financial industry; increasing demand from conventional investors for diversification purposes; and the capacity of the Islamic industry to create a number of financial instruments that meet most of the needs of corporate and individual investors. Furthermore, an increase in oil prices during 2004–2007 resulting in higher investable surplus, and the boom in real estate market in a number of GCC countries during the same period may enhance the growth of Islamic banks in this region (Salman, 2012).

The establishment of modern Islamic financial institutions started three decades ago. This refers to a system of banking, which operates in accordance with the rules of *Sharia'*, the legal code of Islam. The main differentiating factors of the Islamic banking system are the sharing of risk and the prohibition of "riba" (usury/interest). Grais and Pellegrini (2006) noted that Islamic banks would (i) not engage in interest-based debt transactions, (ii) not conduct a purely financial transaction disconnected from real economic activity, (iii) not participate in a transaction where there is the exploitation of any party, and (iv) not participate in activities regarded as harmful to society.

Currently Islamic banking is a growing worldwide phenomenon. There are at least 70 countries that have some Islamic financial services, and almost all major multinational financial institutions are offering these services. The countries of the Gulf Cooperation Council (GCC) have the largest Islamic banks. The market share of the Islamic finance industry in the banking systems of the GCC countries at end-2008 was in the range of 11–35 percent, compared with 5–24 percent in 2004. Imam and Kapdar (2010) highlighted the determinants of diffusion of Islamic banking across the world.

The recent global crisis, unprecedented in modern history, has brought to the forefront wide ranging issues concerning global financial stability. More specifically, specialists and academics have taken note of the strong growth in Islamic banking. The current global environment has renewed the focus on the viability and resilience of the Islamic banking industry. Governor Zeti Akhtar Aziz of the Central Bank of Malaysia, at "The Meeting of the Central Banks and Monetary Authorities of the OIC Member Countries" on October, 2009, noted that the strengths of Islamic finance due to the close link between financial transactions and the real economy and the built-in dimensions of governance and risk management, have contributed to its resilience. In the same way, the Governor Durmuş YIlmaz of the Central Bank of Turkey argued that during the global crisis, the Islamic financial industry has demonstrated significant resilience. He stressed that these Islamic institutions offer services that limit excessive leverage and disruptive financial innovation, thereby ensuring macroeconomic stability. In fact, many conventional banks have been exposed to the type of assets associated with most the losses. This view is further supported by Parashar and Venkatesh (2010) that Islamic banks are less susceptible to financial crisis.

However, the fundamental elements of Islamic finance, such as asset baking and risk sharing, have shielded Islamic banks from the impact of the crisis.

This chapter is an addition to the growing literature that studies the resilience of Islamic banks. The majority of the literature (Bader Mohamad,

Ariff, & Hassan, 2008; Hassan & Bachir, 2003; Samad, 1999; Samad & Hassan, 2000; Beck, Demirgue-Kent, & Merrouche, 2013; Shehzad, 2013; Siraj & Sudarsanan, 2012) compared Islamic banks to conventional banks. This study is an intertemporal analysis where it compares the performance of Islamic banks before and after the global financial crisis in order to evaluate the hit Islamic banks had. Hence, it considers the Islamic banks in MENA countries. It uses data covering 2005–2009 for 44 Islamic banks in 10 countries: Bahrain, Kuwait, Qatar, Saudi Arabia, the United Arab Emirates (UAE), Turkey, Egypt, Yemen, Sudan, and Jordan. To assess the impact of the crisis, this study focuses on the performance of Islamic banks in MENA countries. However, to control heterogeneity across countries, the analysis considers two groups: Islamic banks in GCC region and those in non-GCC region. The key variables used to assess the impact on performance are profitability, liquidity, risk and solvency, and efficiency ratios.

The rest of the chapter is organized as follows. The second section presents a literature review. The third section describes the data, the sample, and the measure of bank performance. The fourth section assesses the impact of the crisis on Islamic bank performance, and examines the main differences in the bank performance in different regions. The fifth section discusses the capacity of Islamic banks to manage crisis and risks. Finally, the summary and conclusion are provided in the sixth section.

## LITERATURE REVIEW

The focus of most research studying Islamic bank performance is on comparing the performance of Islamic banks with their conventional counterparts. Samad (1999) compares the performance of the Malaysian Islamic bank to conventional banks. Their results show that efficiency and the profit of the conventional banks was higher than that of the Islamic bank reflecting the weaker efficiency of the Islamic bank. However, Samad and Hassan (2000), evaluating intertemporal and interbank performance, found that the Islamic bank is relatively more liquid and less risky compared to conventional banks. Nevertheless, these studies were only based upon one Islamic bank in Malaysia.

Iqbal (2001) evaluated the performance of 12 Islamic banks using both trend and ratio analyses. He also compared the performance of Islamic banks with a "control group" of 12 conventional banks. He found that in general Islamic banks were fairly stable, profitable, and well capitalized during the period 1990–1998. In addition, he noted that Islamic banks outperformed in almost all areas and years than conventional banks. However, the comparative performance study showed that there are considerable variations among Islamic banks in terms of performance and growth. Brown and Skully (2005) examined the efficiency of Islamic banks on a cross country basis. Their results show that the highest bank equity ratio was in Saudi Arabia. Bahrain has the highest net interest margin (NIM) and the highest returns on adjusted assets. The UAE has the highest Islamic bank asset ratio. At the country level, Iran, which has the largest Islamic bank, was the most efficient. At the regional basis, Islamic banks from the Middle East were the most efficient, followed by Asia and Africa. Bader et al. (2008) compared the cost, revenue, and profit efficiency of Islamic and conventional banks over the period of 1990–2005. However, their results show that there are no significant differences between the overall efficiency of conventional banks versus Islamic banks.

Yudistria (2004) provides new evidence on the efficiency of 18 Islamic banks over the period of 1997–2000, where he used a frontier nonparametric approach. He found that Islamic banks suffered slight inefficiencies during the financial crisis in 1998–1999. This coincided with a period of turbulence that hit the global economy. He also noted that efficiency differences across the sample data appeared to be substantially determined by country specific factors. Sat Paul Parashar (2010) shows that Islamic banks have suffered more than conventional banks during the recent global financial crisis in terms of capital ratio, leverage, and return on average equity, while conventional banks have suffered more than Islamic banks in terms of return on average assets (ROAA) and liquidity. Over the period of 2006–2009, Islamic banks performed better than conventional banks.

Other economists have argued that Islamic and conventional banks have relied on leverage and have undertaken significant risks that make them vulnerable to the second round effect of the financial crisis. El Said and Ziemba (2009) agree that Islamic banks have avoided the subprime exposure because Islamic finance is based on a close link between financial and productive flows. But the long duration of the crisis affected Islamic financial institutions because property markets have seen a decline in a number of countries where Islamic banks have a significant presence. This has been negative for these institutions as a large number of contracts are backed by real estate and property as collateral. This is especially true in highly leveraged countries such as the UAE (Dubai) and Qatar, where a large share of financing was channeled to the real estate market. Credit risk arises from the erosion in the value of the collateral.

However, in order to have more reliable conclusions about financial stability and the resilience of the Islamic banking sector, Maher Hasan and Jemma Dridi (2010) looked at the performance of two groups of banks at the country level to control for heterogeneity across countries, with respect to regulatory frameworks, macro shocks, and policy responses. Their study suggested that Islamic banks have been affected differently than conventional banks. Factors related to the Islamic banks' business model limited the adverse impact on profitability in 2008, while weaknesses in risk management practices in some Islamic banks led to a larger decline in profitability in 2009 compared to conventional banks. Islamic banks' credit and asset growth performed better in 2008–2009 compared to conventional banks, contributing to financial and economic stability. External rating agencies' assessment of Islamic banks' risk was generally more favorable.

## METHODOLOGY

Analyzing the impact of the crisis on Islamic banks is a challenging task. In fact, a long and consistent time series for Islamic banks in countries where they represent a significant portion of the banking system are not readily available. This challenge explains why attempts to study the impact of the global financial crisis on Islamic banks have been mostly descriptive. Given the existing empirical evidence on the soundness of Islamic banks compared to conventional banks, we hypothesize in this chapter that the performance of Islamic banks was negatively and deeply affected during the global financial crisis. For this study, a sample of 43 Islamic banks in MENA region was considered. This study addresses a comparative analysis. The performance of the Islamic banking industry has been analyzed with a focus on an intertemporal comparison over the period of 2005–2010.

### *Data and Sample*

MENA covers an extensive region. It generally includes all the Arab Middle East and North Africa countries as well as Cyprus, Iran, Israel, and Turkey. In our study, data were collected for Islamic banks in Bahrain, Kuwait, Qatar, Saudi Arabia, UAE, Turkey, Egypt, Yemen, Sudan, and Jordan covering the period of 2005–2009. These countries were chosen because of the importance of Islamic banks in their banking systems and data availability. These countries could be classified in two main

***Table 1.*** Islamic and Conventional Banks in the Gulf Region, 2008.

| | Conventional Banks | Islamic Banks |
|---|---|---|
| Assets (USD billions) | 1,135,669 | 232,189 |
| Profits (USD billions) | 22,008 | 7,666 |
| Asset growth 2007–2008 | 16.3% | 38.2% |
| Profit growth 2007–2008 | −6.1% | 20.1% |
| Profits/Assets | 1.9% | 3.3% |

*Source*: El-Jarhi (2009). Islamic windows in conventional banks are not included in Islamic banks.

groups: the GCC members, Saudi Arabia, Kuwait, Qatar, the UAE, and Bahrain (Oman is excluded since it doesn't have Islamic banks) and non-GCC countries. Islamic finance has become an increasingly integral part of the global financial system especially in the gulf countries. Table 1 shows a comparison in terms of the aggregate size and the performance of conventional banks and Islamic banks in the GCC countries.

The financial sector in the GCC is generally dominated by the banking sector, which is relatively concentrated with a few domestic players dominating the market (Al-Hassan, Khamis, & Oulidi, 2010). The banking sector is mainly owned by families, the government, or government agencies. For example, the major banks in Kuwait, National Bank of Kuwait (NBK) and Gulf Bank (GB) are both owned by Kuwaiti families; the government of Qatar owns major states in the local banks; whereas the Saudi National Commercial Bank, Emirates Bank International (EBI), and Abu Dhabi Commercial Bank ADCB in the UAE are majority state owned. The GCC banks have been protected from foreign competition through restrictions imposing barriers to entry.

One important group of banking services that has experienced rapid growth over the last decade in the GCC countries (except in Oman) is Islamic financial services. Many GCC commercial banks have introduced Islamic banking services among their conventional operations. Therefore, in the GCC region, both conventional and Islamic banks are present.

In Sudan, after the Faisal Islamic Bank was established in 1977, many Islamic banks had been founded. In 1991, the decision of the government to change the hole banking system to an Islamic banking system took effect. However, unlike the experience of Iran and Pakistan, Islamic banks in Sudan have been operating in a dual system

In MENA countries there are three categories of Islamic banks: (i) historical Islamic banks such as Al Rajhi bank, Kuwait Finance house, Dubai Islamic bank, Faisal Islamic Bank Sudan, Sudanese Islamic bank; (ii) banks

***Table 2.*** Islamic Financial Institutions in MENA Countries and Ranking by Assets during 2009.

| Banks | Rank | Countries | Banks | Rank | Countries |
|---|---|---|---|---|---|
| Kuveyt Turk Katilim Bankasi A.S. – Kuwait Turkish Participation Bank Inc | 1 | Turkey | Jordan Islamic Bank | 23 | Jordan |
| Tadhamon International Islamic Bank | 2 | Yemen | Sharjah Islamic Bank 2 | 24 | UAE |
| Bank of Khartoum | 3 | Sudan | Tadamon Islamic Bank | 25 | Sudan |
| Al Rajhi Bank-Al Rajhi Banking & Investment Corporation | 4 | Saudi Arabia | Gulf Finance House BSC | 26 | Bahrain |
| Saba Islamic Bank 2 | 5 | Yemen | ABC Islamic Bank (E.C.) | 27 | Bahrain |
| Dubai Islamic Bank plc | 6 | UAE | Kuwait International Bank | 28 | Kuwait |
| Abu Dhabi Islamic Bank 2 | 7 | UAE | Islamic International Arab Bank | 29 | Jordan |
| Qatar Islamic Bank SAQ | 8 | Qatar | Boubyan Bank KSC | 30 | Kuwait |
| Shamil Bank of Yemen & Bahrain | 9 | Yemen | Bahrain Islamic Bank B.S.C. | 31 | Bahrain |
| Faisal Islamic Bank of Egypt | 10 | Egypt | Islamic Co-operative Development Bank | 32 | Sudan |
| Bank AlBilad | 11 | Saudi Arabia | Al Baraka Bank Sudan | 33 | Sudan |
| Qatar International Islamic Bank | 12 | Qatar | Sudanese Islamic Bank | 34 | Sudan |
| Islamic Bank of Yemen for Finance & Investment | 13 | Yemen | Al Shamal Islamic Bank | 35 | Sudan |
| Al Baraka Banking Group B.S.C. | 14 | Bahrain | National Bank of Sudan | 36 | Sudan |
| Tamweel PJSC | 15 | UAE | Khaleeji Commercial Bank | 37 | Bahrain |
| Kuwait Finance House | 16 | Kuwait | First Investment Company K.S.C.C. | 38 | Kuwait |
| Islamic Development Bank | 17 | Saudi Arabia | Capivest | 39 | Bahrain |
| Dubai Bank | 18 | UAE | IIB-International Investment Bank B.S.C. | 40 | Bahrain |
| Arcapita Bank B.S.C | 19 | Bahrain | International Investor Company, K.S.C. | 41 | Kuwait |
| Shamil Bank of Bahrain B.S.C. | 20 | Bahrain | Investors Bank BSC | 42 | Bahrain |
| Faisal Islamic Bank (Sudan) | 21 | Sudan | Citi Islamic Investment Bank | 43 | Bahrain |
| Emirates Islamic Bank PJSC | 22 | UAE | | | |

*Source*: BankScope database and author's classification.

recently converted to Islamic banking such as Sharjah Islamic bank, Emirates Islamic bank, Kuwait real estate bank, Dubai bank; and (iii) partial Islamic banks where conventional banks are trying to introduce Islamic windows in their attempt to attract investors who are seeking to invest their money using *Sharia*' compliant products and transactions. This category includes all Saudi banks, some of Qatar's banks and some agencies in the Emirates and Bahrain.

In this study, we will consider the two first types of Islamic banks. Islamic windows in conventional banks are not included. Our sample contains 43 Islamic financial institutions in the MENA region. Table 2 shows the ranking by assets of these institutions. The source used is BankScope database.

## *Bank's Performance*

Financial management theories provide many indexes to measure the performance of banks. The uses of various financial ratios are quite common in the literature (Sabi 1996; Samad, 2004; Samad & Hassan, 2000). In this study, we use 12 financial ratios to assess the Islamic banks' performance. These ratios are grouped under four groups: (a) profitability; (b) liquidity; (c) risk; and solvency; and (d) efficiency.

### *Profitability Ratios*

There are many ratios, which are used to measure the profitability of banks. The most often used are ROAA, return on average equity (ROAE), and NIM. ROAA and ROAE are the indicators of managerial performance. ROAA, measuring total profitability as a percentage of total average assets, shows the ability of the bank to use its assets to generate income. Similarly, ROAE, measuring total profitability as a percentage of total average equity, indicates a bank's ability to use its equity financing to generate profits. This is an adjusted version of the return on equity. The average equity is usually computed as the sum of the equity value at the beginning and end of the year, divided by two. ROAA and AOAE can give a more accurate depiction of a bank's profitability. Higher ratios of ROA and ROE indicate better performance.

NIM is a measure of a difference between the interest income generated by banks and the amount of interest paid out to their lenders relative to the average earning assets. In particular, if the non-performing assets are high for the bank, the NIM will go down as the interest earning assets are that much reduced by non-performing assets. How well a bank manages its assets and liabilities is affected by the spread between the interest earned on the bank's assets and the interest costs on its liabilities. A higher value indicates that the bank earns substantial income on its assets and has low costs on its liabilities.

*Liquidity Ratios*

Financial depository institutions share liquidity risk because transaction deposits and saving accounts can be withdrawn. The liquidity position is an important aspect that affects its ability to expand and issue loans, and expand in investment activities. Thus, liquidity ratios measure the ability of the bank to meet its short-term obligations, maintain cash position, and collect receivables. There are several measures for liquidity: Loan to deposit ratio (LDR), liquid assets to deposit and short-term funding ratio (Lqd. ADR), and Loan to asset ratio (LAR). A high LDR indicates that a bank has taken more financial stress by making excessive loans. Therefore, a low ratio shows that a bank has excessive liquidity, lower profits, and less risk. However, a high Lqd.ADR indicates that a bank has enough cash. LAR measures the percentage of total assets the bank has invested in financing. A higher LAR indicates that a bank has lower liquidity. However, it can be an indication of higher profitability and hence more risk.

*Risk and Solvency Ratios*

Risk and solvency ratios measure the bank's probability of default on its debt. A bank is conceived to be solvent when the total value of its assets exceeds its liability. A bank becomes risky when it is insolvent. To measure risk and solvency of the bank, the indicators which are usually used are: debt equity ratio (DER), debt to total assets ratio (DTAR), and equity multiplier (EM).

DER measures the ability of the bank capital to absorb financial shocks. A low DER is a good sign for a bank. DTAR determines the amount of total debt the firm used to finance its total assets. It determines the financial strength of the bank to pay its debtor. A high ratio shows that a bank is involved in risky business. EM indicates the amount of assets per dollar of equity capital. A high value of EM means that a bank has borrowed more funds to convert into assets with share capital. A low value of EM indicates a low risk for the bank.

*Efficiency Ratios*

Efficiency ratios are used to analyze how well the bank is managing and controlling its assets. Measures used to determine efficiency of the bank are asset utilization (AU), income expense ratio (IER), and non-interest expenses to net income (NIEI). AU measures how effectively the bank is utilizing all of its assets. A low AU indicates that the bank is not using its assets to their capacity and should increase its total revenues. IER measures the amount of income earned per dollar of operating expense. A higher IER indicates that a bank is better able to generate more total income. The NIEI ratio measures efficiency in generating revenues and controlling its non-interest expenses.

The performance of Islamic banks is measured in two stages. First, the performance of all Islamic financial institutions in the MENA region during three years (2005, 2006, and 2007) is compared to the performance after the financial crisis (2008, 2009, and 2010) by using the performance measures as defined above. Second, intertemporal performance is compared by region: GCC countries and non-GCC countries.

## EMPIRICAL ANALYSIS: WHAT HAS BEEN THE IMPACT OF THE CRISIS ON THE ISLAMIC BANKS' PERFORMANCE?

To assess the impact of the crisis, the focus was placed on the performance of the Islamic banks in MENA region and at sub-regional level in order to control heterogeneity effects. The four key indicators used were the profitability ratios; liquidity ratios; risk and solvency ratios; and efficiency ratios.

### *Profitability Ratios*

Table 3 compares the profitability ratios of the Islamic banks in the MENA region. In 2005–2007, Islamic banks fared better. The picture is

***Table 3.*** Profitability Ratios for Islamic Banks in MENA Countries.

| | | 2005 | 2006 | 2007 | 2008 | 2009 | 2010 |
|---|---|---|---|---|---|---|---|
| ROAA | **Mean** | **5.129** | **4.400** | **4.438** | **1.105** | **−1.819** | **−1.928** |
| | Standard deviation | 0.125 | 9.155 | 6.299 | 6.070 | 7.446 | 7.638 |
| ROAE | **Mean** | **17.762** | **15.580** | **16.212** | **9.036** | **−0.372** | **−0.451** |
| | Standard deviation | 15.565 | 20.026 | 12.47 | 14.625 | 24.743 | 22.543 |
| NIM | **Mean** | **6.632** | **4.911** | **4.273** | **3.316** | **2.637** | **2.589** |
| | Standard deviation | 10.501 | 5.083 | 5.662 | 6.533 | 3.713 | 3.824 |

*Source*: BankScope database and author's calculations.

reversed after 2007 with Islamic banks fairing clearly worse in 2008 and 2009 where the profitability ratios declined significantly.

The initial impact of the crisis on the Islamic banks' profitability in 2008 was limited. However, with the impact of the crisis moving to the real economy, Islamic banks faced larger losses in 2009. The results indicate that the ROAA of Islamic banks decreased drastically to 1,105 from 4,438 and to (−1.819) during 2008 and 2009, respectively. The total decrease was 6.217.

The profitability ratios showed a reduced trend after 2007 and till 2010. It may be observed that the negative profitability during 2010 is mainly due to the net loss suffered by some Islamic banks during 2009 and 2010. Similar to ROAA, the results show that the ROAE was consistently higher during 2005−2007. A decrease in the ROAE of Islamic banks in 2009 (9.408) was more than the decrease during 2008 (7.176). The results show that Islamic banks are experiencing difficulties in profitability. NIM decreased during the period indicating that Islamic banks had raised funds with liabilities that have high costs and/or acquire assets with low profit. The results revealed a decrease from 4.275 in 2007 to 2.589 in 2010 which was mainly due to recessionary pressures.

Table 4 presents the profitability ratios of Islamic banks in GCC and non-GCC countries separately. In GCC countries, all the profitability ratios decreased after the financial crisis indicating a drastic decrease in the Islamic banks' performance. The ROAA decreased for 5.475 between 2008 and 2007 and for 4.756 from 2008 to 2009. For the ROAE, an important decrease was noted during 2008 that is 11.855 and 14.963 in 2009. However for the non-GCC countries, the evolution of the profitability was favorable during 2008 and all variables declined during 2009. The impact of the crisis came to Islamic banks in these countries late and indirectly through a slowdown in the real economy.

From the evidence given above, it appears that the Islamic banks' performance, in terms of profitability, decreased after the global financial crisis especially in GCC countries. During the turmoil, the return on average equity and ROAA decreased more than the NIM. In the run-up to the turmoil, liquidity dried up and risks flowed back onto the balance sheets. Therefore, Islamic banks saw their average ROAE and ROAA decrease. The results also show that the Islamic banks in GCC countries spent a large amount to compensate for the negative effect caused by the crisis. A higher exposure to real estate by Islamic banks in GCC region and a decrease in global asset price during the financial crisis affect negatively the Islamic banks' performance.

***Table 4.*** Profitability Ratios for Islamic Banks in GCC Countries and Non-GCC Countries.

| | | Islamic Banks in GCC Countries | | | | | Islamic Banks in Non-GCC Countries | | | | |
|---|---|---|---|---|---|---|---|---|---|---|---|
| | | 2005 | 2006 | 2007 | 2008 | 2009 | 2005 | 2006 | 2007 | 2008 | 2009 |
| **ROAA** | **Mean** | **7.590** | **6.454** | **6.221** | **0.746** | **−4.010** | **1.365** | **1.140** | **1.605** | **1.675** | **1.659** |
| | Standard deviation | 11.020 | 11.128 | 7.468 | 7.627 | 8.768 | 1.981 | 2.370 | 1.457 | 1.982 | 1.771 |
| **ROAE** | **Mean** | **20.013** | **18.679** | **18.571** | **6.716** | **−8.247** | **14.321** | **10.660** | **12.467** | **12.720** | **12.134** |
| | Standard deviation | 15.114 | 20.042 | 12.705 | 15.462 | 27.680 | 14.068 | 19.572 | 10.487 | 12.761 | 11.381 |
| **NIM** | **Mean** | **7.855** | **5.490** | **4.620** | **2.588** | **1.869** | **4.761** | **3.992** | **3.686** | **4.829** | **4.232** |
| | Standard deviation | 12.770 | 5.920 | 6.911 | 7.646 | 3.838 | 5.337 | 3.297 | 2.527 | 2.893 | 2.967 |

*Source:* BankScope database and author's calculations.

*Liquidity Ratios*

LDR, the most important measure for the liquidity condition of the bank, shows a negative trend after 2007. This may be as result of the banking authority, which have made banks slowdown in risk assets creation. This decreasing trend could also be attributed to high cost of funds during financial crisis which have precluded many from borrowing. Lqd.ADR registered a decrease in 2007 and 2008 and an increase in 2009. LAR stayed relatively stable during the two periods before and during crisis. A decrease by 1 percent in 2009 was observed. Overall, the results indicate that Islamic banks were as liquid before as they were after the crisis.

Table 5 shows that the difference between the two periods is not statistically significant. Higher liquidity ratios mean that Islamic banks have a larger margin of safety. This result is expected since Islamic banks are not allowed to borrow money from other banks or the central bank because interest is forbidden in Islam. Therefore, Islamic financial institutions tend to keep a high level of liquidity as a first line of defense. In fact, the liquidity ratios indicate the ability of the Islamic banks to meet withdraw obligation.

The sub-regional analysis shows that the liquidity in Islamic banks as measured by LAR and LDR was less important in GCC countries. A high LDR indicates that banks in GCC region have taken more financial stress by making excessive loans before and during crisis. However, Lqd.ADR fell to 43.275 in 2008 from 80.014 in 2007. This result indicates that these financial institutions had an ample margin of current assets over current liabilities in 2007. However, after the financial crisis, Islamic banks may have difficulty meeting current obligations. Thus, the financial crisis negatively affected the liquidity position of Islamic banks in GCC countries,

***Table 5.*** Liquidity Ratios for Islamic Banks in MENA Countries (in Percent).

| | | 2005 | 2006 | 2007 | 2008 | 2009 | 2010 |
|---|---|---|---|---|---|---|---|
| **LAR** | **Mean** | **44.735** | **44.472** | **44.582** | **44.433** | **43.478** | **43.458** |
| | Standard deviation | 25.710 | 24.055 | 22.470 | 25.103 | 26.122 | 26.328 |
| **LDR** | **Mean** | **69.071** | **80.78** | **87.284** | **81.002** | **76.291** | **75.180** |
| | Standard deviation | 45.231 | 70.645 | 95.096 | 85.368 | 76.401 | 76.508 |
| **Lqd.ADR** | **Mean** | **44.552** | **73.090** | **66.332** | **43.807** | **53.355** | **54.433** |
| | Standard deviation | 38.521 | 106.616 | 110.550 | 37.128 | 82.397 | 83.215 |

*Source*: BankScope database and author's calculations.

***Table 6.*** Liquidity Ratios for Islamic Banks in GCC Countries and Non-GCC Countries.

| | | Islamic Banks in GCC Countries | | | | | Islamic Banks in Non-GCC Countries | | | | |
|---|---|---|---|---|---|---|---|---|---|---|---|
| | | 2005 | 2006 | 2007 | 2008 | 2009 | 2005 | 2006 | 2007 | 2008 | 2009 |
| **LAR** | **Mean** | **49.310** | **48.508** | **47.051** | **48.71** | **48.248** | **38.007** | **38.299** | **40.805** | **37.892** | **36.462** |
| | Standard deviation | 28.361 | 26.053 | 25.740 | 28.874 | 28.079 | 20.161 | 19.784 | 16.281 | 16.610 | 21.863 |
| **LDR** | **Mean** | **85.507** | **101.466** | **101.948** | **95.700** | **84.382** | **49.735** | **52.792** | **66.582** | **60.251** | **63.991** |
| | Standard deviation | 53.773 | 86.223 | 121.754 | 108.497 | 92.331 | 20.847 | 22.254 | 22.815 | 22.713 | 47.185 |
| **Lqd.ADR** | **Mean** | **39.264** | **92.293** | **80.014** | **43.275** | **59.125** | **50.462** | **45.980** | **47.016** | **44.527** | **45.211** |
| | Standard deviation | 48.445 | 136.353 | 142.631 | 46.034 | 106.241 | 23.139 | 18.896 | 25.145 | 21.101 | 25.052 |

*Source:* BankScope database and author's calculations.

where it reduced the confidence and trust of the depositors in these financial institutions. The same effect in non-GCC countries was been non-significant where liquidity was marginally affected by the recessionary trends since 2007 (Table 6).

### *Risk and Solvency Ratios*

The result of the DER and DTAR shows that these ratios increased in 2008 with a slight decrease in 2009. DTAR was 76.074 in 2007, which climbed to 79.041 in 2008 and then dropped to 78.016 in 2009. These solvency ratios measure the ability of the bank to pay its long debt and the interest on that debt. Moreover, these ratios help the bank keep an eye on possible bankruptcy. As the DTAR increases, the likelihood of bankruptcy also increases as the bank has more resources from debt as opposed to equity sources. The analysis of another indicator of risk, EM, notes an increase over time. It was 6.387 in 2007, which climbed to 6.390 in 2008 and then to 6.525 in 2010. It may be observed from the analysis that Islamic banks utilize more equity funds than external funds. It supports the view of many scholars that Islamic financial institutions are more equity financed. Thus, we can conclude that Islamic banks didn't become riskier and less solvent during the global crisis (Table 7).

Table 8 shows that all risk and solvency indicators for Islamic banks in non-GCC countries are higher compared to Islamic banks in GCC region, and they decreased making these financial institutions less riskier during the global crisis.

However, risk and solvency indicators had increased during the turmoil in GCC countries. This result indicates a reduction in solvency and the ability of Islamic banks to obtain additional financing for potentially attractive investment opportunities after the global financial crisis. Moreover, an increase was noted in the DER and EM in Islamic banks in GCC countries. This result indicates that Islamic banks have financed most of its assets through debt as compared to equity financing.

Two potential factors could be considered for Islamic banks in GCC countries. First, the weaker performance for Islamic banks could be a reason behind the increase in debt and excessive risks taken. In addition, these results are in line with the higher risk taking associated with the impact of the crisis on securities' values. In fact, the profitability ratio, especially in GCC countries, declined significantly during the crisis. Thus, if profitability declines in an economic downturn, depositors receive lower returns.

***Table 7.*** Risk and Solvency Ratios for Islamic Banks in MENA Countries.

| | | 2005 | 2006 | 2007 | 2008 | 2009 | 2010 |
|---|---|---|---|---|---|---|---|
| **DER** | **Mean** | **7.598** | **5.689** | **5.638** | **5.780** | **5.760** | **5.778** |
| | Standard deviation | 9.731 | 5.192 | 5.318 | 3.879 | 3.938 | 3.954 |
| **DTAR** | **Mean** | **75.648** | **73.405** | **76.074** | **79.041** | **78.016** | **78.001** |
| | Standard deviation | 22.765 | 22.046 | 18.422 | 15.067 | 17.637 | 17.549 |
| **EM** | **Mean** | **8.250** | **6.434** | **6.387** | **6.390** | **6.515** | **6.525** |
| | Standard deviation | 9.639 | 5.216 | 5.342 | 4.020 | 4.042 | 4.051 |

*Source*: BankScope database and author's calculations.

This situation increases risk for the bank and means they are more likely to become insolvent. Given the economic downturns and the fall in stock market prices globally, 2009 has been a difficult year for investors in equities screened for *Sharia'* compliance.

The results show that all risk and solvency ratios of Islamic banks in non-GCC countries are higher than those of Islamic banks in GCC countries before and during the crisis. This indicates that even with the increase in the risk and solvency ratios of Islamic banks in GCC countries, they are less risky and more solvent than those in non-GCC countries.

### *Efficiency Ratio*

The AU ratio of Islamic banks showed a downward trend and a decrease from 0.037 in 2007 to (−0.026) in 2009. A decrease in the AU ratio during the crisis proves that the performance of Islamic banks in the utilization of assets in generating total income decreased. In addition, a decrease in the income to expense ratio (IER) proves that Islamic banks are less efficient in managing their expenses. Compared with 2007, Islamic banks generated less income for every 1 USD spent in 2009. The results show that since 2007, this ratio has decreased.

Further analysis of financial statements reveals that the decreasing trend is due to an increase in expenses and a decrease in the income of some banks causing a decrease in the IER. A reduced growth from 2007 and especially till 2010 may be attributed to the effect of recessionary trend due to financial crisis that erupted worldwide. Another measure of the efficiency of the bank is a total non-interest expense to net income ratio. The results show an increase in this ratio during the financial crisis from 2.10 in 2007 to 3.078 in

***Table 8.*** Risk and Solvency Ratios for Islamic Banks in GCC Countries and Non-GCC Countries.

| | | Islamic Banks in GCC Countries | | | | | Islamic Banks in Non-GCC Countries | | | | |
|---|---|---|---|---|---|---|---|---|---|---|---|
| | | 2005 | 2006 | 2007 | 2008 | 2009 | 2005 | 2006 | 2007 | 2008 | 2009 |
| **DER** | **Mean** | **3.644** | **3.292** | **3.296** | **4.118** | **4.416** | **13.180** | **9.213** | **9.084** | **8.125** | **7.736** |
| | Standard deviation | 3.104 | 2.769 | 1.960 | 2.390 | 2.631 | 12.896 | 5.950 | 6.748 | 4.406 | 4.732 |
| **DTAR** | **Mean** | **65.907** | **64.866** | **69.216** | **74.020** | **73.142** | **89.399** | **85.961** | **86.158** | **86.131** | **85.184** |
| | Standard deviation | 25.347 | 23.084 | 19.847 | 17.036 | 20.660 | 5.367 | 12.835 | 9.860 | 7.688 | 8.071 |
| **EM** | **Mean** | **4.366** | **4.051** | **4.054** | **4.666** | **5.117** | **14.188** | **10.218** | **10.092** | **9.128** | **8.735** |
| | Standard deviation | 3.133 | 2.799 | 2.075 | 2.600 | 2.827 | 12.906 | 5.966 | 6.777 | 4.411 | 4.731 |

*Source*: BankScope database and author's calculations.

***Table 9.*** Efficiency Ratios for Islamic Banks in MENA Countries.

| | | 2005 | 2006 | 2007 | 2008 | 2009 | 2010 |
|---|---|---|---|---|---|---|---|
| **AU** | **Mean** | **0.040** | **0.040** | **0.037** | **0.006** | **−0.026** | **0.002** |
| | Standard deviation | 0.070 | 0.062 | 0.053 | 0.070 | 0.095 | 0.083 |
| **IER** | **Mean** | **1.361** | **1.521** | **1.444** | **0.600** | **−0.065** | **−0.050** |
| | Standard deviation | 1.790 | 2.602 | 2.105 | 2.296 | 1.905 | 2.205 |
| **NIEI** | **Mean** | **1.960** | **2.790** | **2.106** | **3.078** | **3.126** | **3.139** |
| | Standard deviation | 2.671 | 6.091 | 4.048 | 5.735 | 17.703 | 17.221 |

*Source*: BankScope database and author's calculations.

2008 and to 3.139 in 2010. This increase means that Islamic banks in MENA countries are losing a larger percentage of their income to expenses.

An overall analysis of all efficiency measures reveals that Islamic banks were less efficient in AU, income generation and in reducing expenses during the global financial crisis (Table 9).

Analysis by region shows that in GCC countries the financial crisis changed the capacity of Islamic banks to operate their expenses. Total non-interest expenses to net income increased drastically after financial crisis. It was 1.368 in 2007, which climbed to 2.467 in 2008 and then to 5.061 in 2009. The analysis of IER proves that Islamic banks in GCC countries generated less income during the crisis. Thus, the efficiency of Islamic banks was negatively affected with lower revenue to higher expenses. This decrease in IER was caused by the loss occurred during the crisis (Table 10).

Results drawn from this study indicate that Islamic banks in non-GCC countries were more efficient during the turmoil. Total non-interest expenses to net income decreased in 2009 indicating that Islamic banks were more efficient compared to those in GCC region. In non-GCC countries, a growth in AU ratio reflects the availability of financial and non-financial resources to support the organization's growth. However, performance measured by AU and IER are quite stable during all five years. We can conclude that financial crisis didn't affect significantly the efficiency of Islamic banks in this region.

## HOW TO STRENGTHEN THE CAPACITY OF ISLAMIC BANKS TO MANAGE CRISIS AND RISKS?

Islamic banks avoided direct exposure to toxic financial derivative such as CDOs and CDSs, but when the global financial crisis become a global

***Table 10.*** Efficiency Ratios for Islamic Banks in GCC Countries and Non-GCC Countries.

| | | Islamic Banks in GCC Countries | | | | | Islamic Banks in Non-GCC Countries | | | | |
|---|---|---|---|---|---|---|---|---|---|---|---|
| | | 2005 | 2006 | 2007 | 2008 | 2009 | 2005 | 2006 | 2007 | 2008 | 2009 |
| **AU** | **Mean** | **0.062** | **0.058** | **0.050** | **0.001** | **−0.052** | **0.012** | **0.009** | **0.015** | **0.014** | **0.016** |
| | Standard deviation | 0.082 | 0.071 | 0.063 | 0.088 | 0.112 | 0.018 | 0.021 | 0.012 | 0.018 | 0.016 |
| **IER** | **Mean** | **1.992** | **2.230** | **2.041** | **0.667** | **−0.419** | **0.416** | **0.412** | **0.512** | **0.492** | **0.509** |
| | Standard deviation | 2.071 | 3.128 | 2.507 | 2.906 | 2.319 | 0.412 | 0.499 | 0.493 | 0.559 | 0.618 |
| **NIEI** | **Mean** | **1.211** | **1.586** | **1.368** | **2.467** | **5.061** | **3.062** | **4.747** | **3.477** | **4.048** | **−0.138** |
| | Standard deviation | 1.765 | 3.481 | 3.962 | 5.945 | 17.021 | 3.382 | 8.638 | 3.980 | 5.417 | 18.901 |

*Source*: BankScope database and author's calculations.

economic crisis, Islamic banks were been affected in an indirect manner. The business model of many Islamic financial institutions that depend on Murabaha and Ijjara financing and mainly invested in real estate sector and in the growing equity market, faced higher risks. Islamic banks in the GCC region were more exposed to risks related to real estate market and international equity market. The results show that their performance was reduced during the global crisis. Therefore, lessons have to be learned and measures to improve the soundness of the Islamic financial institutions have to be designed.

Some organizations have a key role in promoting and enhancing the soundness and stability of Islamic financial industry. Due to the fragility of Islamic banks observed during the global crisis, Islamic Financial Services Board (IFSB), Islamic Development Bank (IDB), and Islamic Research and Training Institute (IRTI) in 2010 have identified together some building block to strengthen the stability of the Islamic financial system. Volker Nienhaus (2010) suggests and discuss some strategies to strengthen Islamic banks. In particular, he focuses on participatory modes of finance that limit or eliminate the risk of losing the provided capital as a financial innovation supporting Islamic banks.

Islamic banks should make all efforts to develop adequate instruments and techniques for profit business. They can gain a competitive advantage by offering lower financing costs and by providing better services to entrepreneurial customers. However, participatory modes of finance are not enough applied in practice due to severe information asymmetries. Innovative mode of financing, especially in partnership contracts and participatory finance, may increase Islamic banks market share. In fact, partnership financing, the true alternative to riba-based financing, offers some specific benefits. First, it is suitable for real economic activity and not appropriate for financing consumption. Second, it is enterprise based which provide liquidity by calculating profits and losses on a regular basis. Third, partnership contracts are a suitable instruments providing medium to long term liquidity to entrepreneurial customer.

Innovation in participatory mode of finance can establish a new link between finance and enterprise, and create new avenues for the profitable employment of funds in the real investment. Islamic financial institutions can only exploit the potential benefits of this mode of finance if they strengthen and enhance their capacities in the assessment of business prospects in real economic activity. This includes competencies in evaluating strengths and weaknesses of individuals firms, as well as capacities for industry forecasts. In fact, Islamic banks can provide support especially to small- and medium-sized enterprises. The approach of German Banks to mobilize and invest saving locally, creating self-sustaining resources is a successful example to strengthen the local economy. A successful in this field will expand the entrepreneurial class, create employment and therefore reduce the poverty which is an individual and social obligation. The Islamic banking industry can exploit the opportunities in these areas. Moreover, with the effects of global crisis in Islamic banks, it becomes important to encourage research to strengthen and elaborate a suitable system of supervision and regulation that takes into consideration the specificities of the country and the Islamic financing mode.

## SUMMARY AND CONCLUSION

Modern Islamic finance has existed since the 1970s, geographically concentrated in Muslim-majority countries. The Middle East continues to be the primary geographic center for *Sharia'* compliant financing where major Islamic finance industry is primarily located in Bahrain, Kuwait, Qatar, Saudi Arabia, and the UAE. Internationally, Islamic banks appear to have been more resilient to the primary effects of the global financial crisis than conventional banks. However, the global economic turndown differently affects various Islamic banks in MENA countries.

Examination of the empirical analysis allows us to shed some light on our findings and draw some conclusions. Our results suggest that Islamic banks fared differently from region to region during the global financial crisis. Factors related to the Islamic finance model helped to contain the adverse effect on performance in 2008. However, weaknesses in risk management practices in some Islamic banks led to larger decline in performance in 2009. The performance of Islamic banks in GCC countries declined more than that in the other MENA countries.

The weak performance was associated with the regulatory framework for Islamic banks and strengthening risk management in some banks. Despite higher liquidity and profitability during the pre-global crisis period (2005–2007), Islamic banks' profitability declined during the global crisis. Zarrouk (2012) indicates that the initial impact in 2008 was limited; however, with the impact of the crisis moving to the real economy, Islamic banks faced larger losses in 2009 concluding that the pre-crisis profitability was not driven by a strategy of greater risk taking. This result didn't appear in our study. Islamic banks' profitability fell drastically in 2008. This difference could be explained by the fact that we consider average equity and average assets to measure profitability instead of equity and assets at the end of the year.

The important decrease in profitability of Islamic banks, especially in GCC countries, could be explained by two potential factors. First, during the crisis, property markets have seen a decline in a number of countries in GCC region. These affected negatively Islamic banks as a large number of contracts are backed by real estate and property as collateral. In UAE and Qatar, a large share of financing was channeled to the real estate market. Second, the fall in oil prices might adversely affect the progress of Gulf Islamic banks. However, there was no case of failure of Islamic bank in the region.

Islamic banks' loan growth was higher during the crisis suggesting a growing market share. Higher resources, as indicated by liquidity ratios, has facilitated the relatively higher demand for Islamic financial services and contributed to the macroeconomic stability. The relative soundness of Islamic banks can be explained by the fact that finance in non-GCC countries derived from deposits rather than being funded by borrowings from wholesale markets. Consequently, when the credit crunch came, the effect on these Islamic banks was limited. Findings show that LDR of Islamic banks especially in GCC countries is decreasing during the global crisis (2007–2009). This decreasing trend is due to increase in its deposits base which can be considered a positive sign indicating that level of trust and confidence of the people is increasing in Islamic banks. A positive attitude of people makes Islamic finance an alternative source of finance.

Islamic financial institutions are not immune from the effects of the global recession. In fact, the global crisis highlighted the need to address important challenges. The financial crisis has led to a greater recognition of the importance of liquidity risks, and the requirement for efficient bank resolution structure. Therefore, setting up a strong liquidity management framework is a key priority. In addition, regulators and standard-setters for Islamic institutions should make certain that the supervisory and legal framework appropriate for the fast progressing Islamic financial prospect and global economic development. Reinforcing regulations and developing products are needed to improve the industry to meet market demands and requirements to keep sustainable growth.

Moreover, to keep up the above challenges, Islamic financial institutions and regulators have jointly required to built-up of necessary educational programs and to generate the needed human capital.

# REFERENCES


Al-Hassan, A., Khamis, M., & Oulidi, N. (2010). *The GCC banking sector: Topography and analysis*. IMF Working Paper, WP/10/87.

Bader, M. K., Mohamad, S., Ariff, M. & Hassan, T. (2008). Cost, revenue, and profit efficiency of Islamic versus conventional banks: International evidence using data envelopment analysis. *Islamic Economic Studies*, *15*(2), 23–76.

Beck, T., Demirgue-Kent, A., & Merrouche, O. (2013). Islamic vs. conventional banking – Business model, efficiency and stability. *Journal of Banking and Finance*, *37*, 433–447.

Brown, K., & Skully, M. (2005). Islamic banks: A cross-country study of cost efficiency performance, accounting, commerce & finance. *The Islamic Perspective Journal*, *8*(1–2), 43–79.

El Qorchi, M. (2005). Islamic finance gears up. *Finance and Development, IMF*, *42*(4), 46–49.

El Said, A., & Ziemba R. (2009). Stress-testing Islamic Finance, *Roubini Global Economics*, May 10.

Ernst & Young. (2012). The world Islamic banking competitiveness report 2011/2012. Presented at the 18th Annual World Islamic Banking Conference.

Ernst & Young. (2013). The world Islamic banking competitiveness report 2012/2013. Presented at the 19th Annual World Islamic Banking Conference.

Grais, W., & Pelligrini, M. (2006). *Corporate governance in institutions offering Islamic financial services: Issues and options*. World Bank Policy Research Working Paper No. 4052, November.

Hasan, M., & Dridi, J. (2010). *The effects of the global crisis on Islamic and conventional banks: A comparative study*. IMF Working Paper, WP/10/201.

Hassan, M. K., & Bashir, A.-H. M. (2003). Determinants of Islamic banking profitability. *Proceedings of the ERF 10th annual conference*, Marrakesh, Morocco, December 16–18, 2003.

IFSB-IDB-IRTI. (2010). *Islamic finance and global financial stability*. Kuala Lumpur and Jeddah.

Imam, P., & Kpodar, K. (2010). *Islamic banking: How has it diffused?* IMF, WP/10/195.

Iqbal, M. (2001). Islamic and conventional banking in the nineties – A comparative study. *Islamic Economic Studies*, *8*(2) 1–28.

Parashar, S. P., & Venkatesh, J. (2010). How did Islamic banks do during global financial crisis? *Banks and Bank Systems*, *5*(4).

Report of the Meeting of the Central Banks and Monetary Authorities of the Member Countries of the Organization of the Islamic Conference (OIC). (2009). *Impacts of the current crisis on OIC member countries*. Istanbul: Republic of Turkey, October 3.

Sabi, M. (1996). Comparative analysis of foreign and domestic bank operation in Hungary. *Journal of Comparative Economics*, *22*, 179–188.

Salman, S. A. (2012). Islamic banking in the MENA region. *Islamic Economic Studies*, *20*(1), 1–44.

Samad, A. (1999). Comparative efficiency of the Islamic Bank Malaysia vis-à-vis conventional banks. *Journal of Economics and Management*, *7*(1), 1–25.

Samad, A. (2004). Performance of interest-free Islamic banks vis-à-vis interest-based conventional banks of Bahrain. *Journal of Economics and Management*, *12*(2), 1–15.

Samad, A., & Hassan, K. (2000). The performance of Malaysian Islamic bank during 1984–1997: An exploratory study. *International Journal of Islamic Financial Services*, *1*(3), 3–11.

Shehzad, M. (2013). Financial performance of Islamic banking and conventional banking in Pakistan: A comparative study. *International Journal of Innovative and Applied Finance, 1*(1), 1–22.

Siraj, K. K., & Sudarsanan, P. (2012). Comparative study on performance of Islamic banks and conventional banks in GCC region. *Journal of Applied Finance & Banking, 2*(3), 123–161.

Volker, N., & IFSB. (2010). *Capacity building in the financial sector: Strategies for strengthening financial institutions*. Inaugurable Islamic Financial Stability Forum, Khartoum, Sudan.

Yudistira, D. (2004). Efficiency in Islamic banking: An empirical analysis of eighteen banks. *Islamic Economic Studies, 12*(1), 1–19.

Zaher, T. S., & Hassan, M. K. (2001). A comparative literature survey of Islamic finance and banking. *Financial Markets, Institutions and Instruments, 10*(4), 155–199.

Zarrouk, H. (2012). Does financial crisis reduce Islamic banks' performance? Evidence from GCC countries. *Journal of Islamic Finance and Business Research, 1*(1), 1–16.

# PART II
# THE DEVELOPING ROLE OF NON-ISLAMIC BANKING FINANCE

# APPROACH TO THE INTEGRATION OF TAKAFUL INSURANCE IN THE ALGERIAN MARKET

Nesrine Bouzaher, Okba Necira and Sabrina Kerdoudi

## ABSTRACT

Objective – *The purpose of this chapter is to provide a description of the integration of Takaful in the domestic market, based on experiences in regional markets, focusing on the explanation of factors that could enhance the position of Takaful in certain areas.*

Methodology – *The chapter describes the evolution of Takaful insurance in international and regional markets, and explains the articulation of this product in these markets. The chapter also provides an analysis of the Algerian market characteristics related to the Takaful product.*

Value – *This work will be based on an analytical research of emerging markets and their success factors; then it will be necessary to provide an overview of the product containing Takaful; and finally we will try to follow the experience of the national insurance market with the new product, supplied by the Salama Company, and determine the potential of Algeria in this area.*

**The Developing Role of Islamic Banking and Finance: From Local to Global Perspectives**
**Contemporary Studies in Economic and Financial Analysis, Volume 95, 73–87**

**ISSN: 1569-3759/doi:10.1108/S1569-3759(2014)0000095012**

Findings/prospects – *This work offers an opportunity to understand the mechanisms needed to activate the local market and opens the prospects for effective integration of Islamic financial products gradually, in order to prepare for changes that would provide more financial products suited to the requirements of social development in the Algerian economy.*

**Keywords:** Market insurance structure; Algerian insurance sector; Takaful product; Salama company

# INTRODUCTION

The financial crisis in industrialised countries has clouded the near-term economic outlook, commodity prices in many sectors have already fallen significantly, and are expected to continue their slide, leading to lower inflation; at the same time we observe an important growth in the emerging markets of insurance, as various Islamic insurance models that comply with *shariah* are being adopted in many Muslim countries. This contradiction in growth levels requires thinking and analysis.

It turns out that the new Islamic financial products have economic and social characteristics that can bring new techniques for good financial management of sectors. Globally, the Takaful industry has been growing rapidly, appealing to both Muslims and non-Muslims alike.

We need to understand the function and the dynamics of such new products, in order to predict change process in the right way, focusing on the shifts that must take place in the Algerian area, by analysing the case of the Salama Company.

# STUDY OBJECTIVES

The first objective in this chapter is to demonstrate the benefits of Takaful as a *shariah*-compliant financial instrument, economically and socially, and also to promote the implantation of such product. The second objective is to define the managerial approach to ensure a successful implantation of Takaful in the Algerian market.

This research will focus on three critical questions:

To what extent can the market structure be a pillar of Takaful?
What is the contribution of Takaful in insurance literature?
What are the initial results of Takaful in the Algerian Salama Company?

# METHOD

The chapter describes the evolution of Takaful insurance in international and regional markets, and explains the articulation of this product in these markets. The chapter provides also an analysis of the Algerian market characteristics related to the Takaful product.

### *Market of Takaful*

Abstract 1

*The objective of the first part is to study the relationship between the market insurance structure and the conditions for a successful implantation of Takaful; to achieve this aim, it is essential at first to follow the emergence of specialised Takaful markets, applying Takaful product in such areas as Malaysia and Saudi Arabia. Afterwards, there is an overview of market data of Algerian insurance, and demonstration of the characteristics of the domestic market as well as the favourable environment for the introduction of new products. Then, the analysis of the correlation between insurance market structure and the potential Takaful growth rates, applying the correlation coefficient that links up the percentage of compulsory insurance (X) with Takaful growth averages (Y) using the available data which ranges from 2005 to 2009 in Saudi Arabia (KSA).*

The Islamic finance sector is a growing global phenomenon, contributing positively and substantially to the world economy.

The increase in Islamic finance assets was about 11% annual average over the past decade and reached 500 billion American dollars (US$) in 2008 (PricewaterhouseCoopers, 2008).

Its contribution was US$ 6.8 billion in 2009, and reached US$ 12 billion in gross contribution in 2010 (Essen, 2011).

In 2008, there were 179 companies specialising in Takaful; in 2010, the number reached 200; this data is clearly represented in (Fig. 1) where

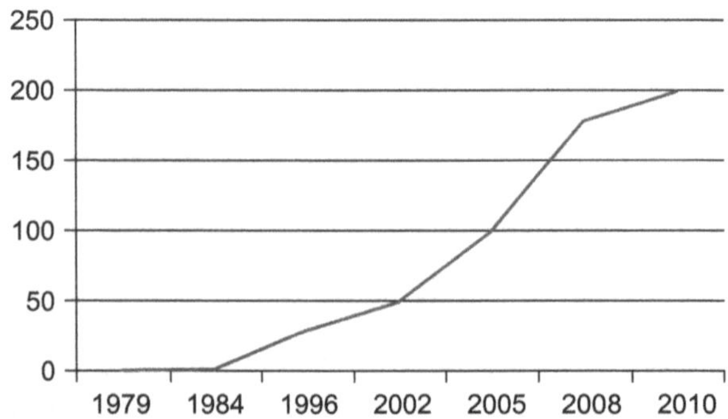


*Fig. 1.* The International Evolution of Takaful Companies. *Source*: Authors.

the international annual growth rate of this product is about 39% (Zaatar, 2008).

In order to develop Takaful in the Algerian markets, we will analyse the correlation between the characteristics of emergent markets and the application of Takaful.

*Emergence of Specialised Takaful Markets*

We observe the emergence of an important number of markets applying the Takaful product that achieved remarkable level of growth compared with traditional insurance.

- Malaysia is now leading the Takaful insurance industry; it has raised 59.9% and 44% in assets and net contribution respectively, from 1986 until 2010. This industry has proven its resilience during the period of the Asian financial crisis, maintaining a stable average annual growth rate of 61.9% in terms of assets from 1997 to 2000 (Ansari, 2011).
- The Middle East and North Africa (MENA) region is a new emerging market that has to achieve a considerable level of development, if we compare between North Africa and Indonesia; in 2009, the contribution of Takaful in the insurance market was 29% in the first and 67% in the second (Buck, 2011).
- Saudi Arabia emerged as the largest market for Takaful insurance following Malaysia. The protection: savings and health insurance lines show the most growth in Saudi Arabia. Health insurance has counted toward approximately 50% of the overall insurance market at the end of 2009 (Ansari, 2011).

*Algerian Insurance Market Data*

Algeria continues to develop its insurance sector, which currently enjoys the highest penetration rate, at over 5%, among Maghreb countries. According to Algeria's Insurance Industry Association, Algeria witnessed an 8.5% growth from 2005 to 2010; while 80% of insurance revenues were generated from automobile insurance, followed by fire and miscellaneous risk coverage with 19% of total revenues. With a plethora of foreign exchange earnings from increased prices in their primary export of hydrocarbons, Algeria's government has increased public spending in sectors vital to the insurance industry, including a recently initiated program aimed at investing $60 billion to help property owners acquire insurance plans, boosting penetration levels in the process (Annual report of insurance business – Insurance Board – Algerian Ministry of Finance, 2010).

The 'auto insurance' branch which achieved a turnover of 35.1 billion dinars takes the first position with a market share of 46% and a growth rate of 18.3% due to optional coverage expansion that continues to drive growth in the branch with 24% compared to 2008 (Annual report of insurance business – Insurance Board – Algerian Ministry of Finance, 2010).

The Algerian insurance market has many advantages that may make it a fertile area to implant the Takaful product:

- The emergence of a new middle – educated class, more aware of their insurance needs, created an effective demand for *shariah*-compliant alternatives.
- In 2010, the level of premium made by the Algerian market was about one billion dollars; Algeria is ranked fifth in Africa in terms of total premium value (http://executive-magazine.com/getissue.php?issue=153, 4 October 2012).
- The auto insurance industry represents about 50% of the total insurance sales in Algeria, but the individual insurance represents only 8% of the global market; this structure shows the domination of compulsory insurance (Annual report of insurance business – Insurance Board – Algerian Ministry of Finance, 2010).
- The absence of a natural demand for insurance product requires the course of time and the use of smart tools to market and win new business.
- The demographic data may represent a new source of prosperity: about 5% of the population is over 65 years old, 30% is younger than 14 years; these indicators show the large human capitalisation that Algeria has (Cheddad, 2011).

- The increase in oil prices has generated an important amount of investment opportunities in the Middle East and North Africa.
- The new investment projects planned between 2010 and 2014 expect that the Algerian insurance market will grow by at least 10% by the end of 2012 (http://www.made-in-algeria.com/data_5/even_detail.php?id=6526, 25 February 2012).

*Analysis of the Correlation between Insurance Market Structure and Takaful Growth Rates*

In this chapter, we will analyse the relationship between the insurance market structure and the potential growth of Takaful, applying the correlation coefficient that links up the percentage of compulsory insurance with Takaful growth averages using the available data of the Saudi market, which is considered favourable economic space for two important reasons:

- The similarity in some aspects between Saudi Arabia and Algeria: both have an oil-based economy with strong government control, encouraging the growth of private sector.
- The greater experience of Saudi Arabia regarding the product of Takaful.

The variable $X$ represents the growth rate of health insurance (compulsory insurance) that forms 50% of total insurance in Saudi Arabia (Saudi Arabian Monetary Agency, 2008). The variable $Y$ represents the growth rate of Takaful premiums. The study ranged from 2005 to 2009 (Fig. 2).

| | 2005 | 2006 | 2007 | 2008 | 2009 |
|---|---|---|---|---|---|
| X<br>Growth rate of health insurance* | 26% | 32% | 36% | 44% | 49.9% |
| Y<br>Growth rate of tactful premiums ** | 24.72% | 27.2% | 29.5% | 30.8% | 35% |

*Fig. 2.* The Calculation of the Correlation Coefficient between the Growth Rates of Takaful and the Growing Importance of Health Insurance in KSA. *Source*: *www.sama.gov.sa/insurance/insuranceLib/4600_R_InsualMarketSurvey2007_En_1429_06_01_V1. **www.takaful-re.ae.

$r = 0.98$. The correlation coefficient is positive, so we have a positive relationship. This means when the rate of health insurance increases (or decreases), the values of the Takaful rate premium tend to go in the same direction. If one decreases, so does the other in a predictable manner.

The correlation coefficient is equal to 0.98, so there is a strong relationship between the variables. We are able to predict what will happen to the values of the Takaful rate premium based on the knowledge we have about the values of the health insurance rates.

The Coefficient of Determination $r^2 = 96.04\%$ signifies that 96.04% of variations scored on Takaful premiums is directly related to variations of health insurance rates.

We need to determine whether we can infer that the relationship we found in our sample is true; in other words, is 'generalisable' in the larger population. So we have to compare '*r*' with the critical values of the correlation coefficient in a special table.

Our correlation coefficient was based on 5 successive years ($n = 5$); therefore, our degree of freedom ($n - 2$) is 3.

Under the heading 'Type 1 Error Rate' we find that '*r*' is bigger than the critical values of correlation coefficient in degree of freedom = 3 (5% and 1%); the evidence shows that there is a relationship between the two variables.

In other words, in our research we ensure that there is in fact a relationship between the two variables we have been studying with a chance of 1% of being wrong.

After this analysis, we gather that there is a considerable relationship between the growing rates of compulsory insurance (health insurance in KSA) and the growth rates of Takaful premiums. So the growing importance of compulsory insurance in the market insurance structure can make favourable conditions for a successful implantation of Takaful in the market.

## *The Contribution of Takaful in Insurance Literature*

Abstract 2

*The second part of the chapter describes the understanding of the product containing Takaful. First, it is technically proven that Islamic finance products are an important part of the solution of the applied international systems because it does not allow Riba; second, there are solid alternative contracts that can be used as Takaful models, where any profit is shared according to ratio or percentage agreed by the parties. However, it is greatly proven that: Takaful has economic efficiency; the international experiences confirm that; the fair distribution of risks is a way to minimise the economic damages in times of economic crises; the Takaful is a tool that protects the financial and economic resources.*

Takaful is an Arabic word that means 'guaranteeing each other's'. It is imperative and of perennial concern to Takaful practitioners to understand this definition. It must be entrenched in all participants' minds who take up Takaful protection that the contribution into the Takaful system must be performed with utmost sincerity in order to help those who may face difficulties (Ma'sum Billah, 2001).

*The Comparison between Takaful and Conventional Insurance*

Compared to conventional insurance, Takaful does not allow what is called *Gharar* (uncertainty or speculation) and *Maisir* (gambling). In investment or fund management, *Riba* (Usury) is also not allowed.

These three, *Gharar*, *Maisir* and *Riba*, must be totally avoided by the Takaful operation. In order to avoid *Ghara* (speculation), there must be a complete clarity or full disclosure of any Takaful contract. Full disclosure is applicable on the contract subject matter terms and scope of cover, etc. It is not allowable to enter into a Takaful contract if there is any unknown element on the subject matter and/or unknown exposure to the extent of the contract itself. As this ideal situation hardly exists, the Takaful contract then needs to be made in a way where there is no exchange of *Gharar*.

*Maisir* (gambling) is regarded as the excessive side of *Gharar*: the participants (insured) may have an insurable interest in the subject matter, if the risks transfer (risk sharing in Takaful) contains any speculative element, then it will be prohibited under the Takaful.

*Riba* (usury) is totally prohibited under the *shariah* law and under a Takaful arrangement. In order to avoid *Riba*, Takaful treats participants' contribution to the risk-sharing scheme not as a premium in the way conventional insurance does, but as being a contribution (*Musahamah*) in the form of donation with a condition of compensation (*Tabarru*). Furthermore, the pool of funds secured from those participants' contributions or donations must be managed and invested in accordance with the *Shariah*. In the same way, *Gharar* and *Maisir* represent a continuous challenge for Takaful operators to ensure that pure Takaful arrangements are free of them (Wang-Fuppy, Katsias, & Kwan, 2011).

*Takaful Contract Criteria*
Inside the contract, the following Takaful best-practice tasks must be carried out:

- Proper risk identification and risk analysis.
- Proper underwriting practice to ensure an adequacy of funds to pay losses, but at the same time this should not be of an excessive level that would in turn become a burden to the participants.
- Proper risk sharing and the risk spreading: Operators must ensure proper and healthy risk sharing between participants; furthermore, by anticipating potential losses above their capacity, operators could further spread the risk to other operators in the Takaful or Retakaful market (Lezoul, 2011).

*Models of Takaful*
There are solid alternative contracts that can be used as Takaful models: (Wang-Fuppy et al., 2011).

- *Mudharabah Contract* (Profit and Loss Sharing). This is a contract between capital providers with management, where any profit is shared according to ratio or percentage agreed to by both parties., In Takaful practice, participants provide capital to the Takaful operator, and any loss is borne entirely by the capital provider.
- *Musharakah Contract* (Joint-Venture). Both parties provide capital and/or management. Profit is split either based on capital or on negotiation, and any loss is distributed in proportion to capital contributions. Establishment of a mutual insurance company such as Oil Insurance Limited (OIL) can use this type of contract.
- *Kafalah Contract* (surety-ship). In the event the debtor fails to honour the obligation toward the creditor, a guarantor becomes the surety.
- *Wakalah Contract* (contract of agency). The principal appoints and authorises someone to act on his behalf. The authorisation could be either specific or general. The *Wakeel* (Agent) could then charge a fee to the principal. This model is suitable for most of Takaful products, including products for corporate risks.
- *Ju'alah Contract* (Contract of Commission). Basically similar to the *Wakalah* contract except that the payment to the agent is measured on the output and performance. This contract could be used to develop distribution channels for Takaful.

*Specificity of Takaful*

Takaful is a real and indubitable economic contribution that has proven the specificities of Islamic finance:

Resorting to Takaful was not done because of its compliance with *shariah*, but because it has greatly proven its economic efficiency. The international experiences confirm that; the fair distribution of risks is a way to minimise the economic damages in times of economic crises, so Takaful is a tool that protects financial and economic resources.

Solidarity is the crucial background of a Takaful contract, it is found that the benefit of this contract is of general economic utility, and it is totally opposite to the economy of debt where the benefit of one party is the loss of the other, which leads to enlarging the gap between economic stakeholders.

It is technically proven that Islamic finance products and especially Takaful is an important part of the solution of the applied international systems, and as Muslims we have to use our scientific knowledge and religious know-how to develop, implement and manage these products economically.

### *Introduction of Takaful in Algeria, the 'Salama Company'*

Abstract 3

*Finally, the study of the initial experience of the national insurance market with the new product, supplied by the Salama Company, can prove that the success factors of Takaful technically exist and determine the potential of Algeria in this area. So the postponement on the national extent can be caught up by the use of appropriate marketing tools, to introduce the product gradually to the middle class in the Algerian market.*

Until now, the company Salama Insurance was the only one to offer Takaful products in Algeria. Salama Islamic Arab Insurance Company is one of the principal *Shariah*-based insurers and reinsurers in the world (Saud, 2011). It was adopted in Algeria under Resolution No. 46 issued on 02 July 2006 by the Minister of Finance and it has absorbed Al-Baraka and Amane Company for Insurance and Reinsurance, which was established in 2000, to become today the Salama Algeria Insurance Company (Saud, 2011).

Currently, Salama Company provides a variety of services in the Algerian market with over 150 sale points across all the national territory and 4 regional directorates. The private insurance companies share, in the

Algerian market, amounts to 20%, and Salama Company has not less than 3%. Compensation volume to customers in 2010 was 54% of the total turnover for the year 2009, a large bill to maintain the reputation that the company enjoys in the Algerian market (http://ribh.wordpress.com/).

The company has considerable competitive advantages, which are (Saud, 2011):

- Salama Company is the only Takaful insurance company operating in the Algerian market.
- It is only insurance company that has a legitimate oversight commission (headed by Sheikh Al Qasimi).
- It has a balanced and diversified portfolio divided 76% for personal insurance and 24% for small and medium business insurance.
- The company offers a fast car insurance compensation in service and payment centres.
- The company has the ability to innovate by creating new products adapted to customers, including: assistance for automotive insurance, ensuring judicial protection, and other products under study.

*The Evolution of Takaful in Algeria*

To follow the Takaful development in Algeria, we have to consider a study of the Salama Company activity in the national territory (Figs. 3 and 4).

There is a continuous increase in the turnover made by the company; the average growth carried out in 2008 and in 2009 was very important and was consistent with averages achieved in the emergent markets (e.g. KSA: Fig. 2), and this indicates the important opportunities about the national market.

The data presented shows a steady increase in deferent risks insured by the company from 2005 to 2011. The car insurance premiums have a large share in the total sales realised by the company. In 2005, the share of car insurance reached 71% of total insured risks, the same percentage achieved during the next five years.

| Years | Premiums | Growth% |
|---|---|---|
| **2008** | 1876 | 32% |
| **2009** | 2489 | 39% |
| **2010** | 2659 | 7% |

*Fig. 3.* The Evolution of Turnover of SALAMA Company in Algeria. *Source*: www.iefpedia.com/arab/wp.content/upload/2011/04/.pptx (Saud, 2011).

| Risks insured | 2005 | 2006 | 2007 | 2008 | 2009 | 2010 | 2011 |
|---|---|---|---|---|---|---|---|
| Cars risks | 472 | 717 | 900 | 1346 | 1826 | 1865 | 1970 |
| Simple risks | 56 | 75 | 150 | 184 | 194 | 185 | 386 |
| Business risks | 92 | 159 | 214 | 162 | 307 | 353 | 486 |
| Transport risks | 32 | 75 | 161 | 91 | 96 | 41 | 158 |
| Personnel risks | 2 | 28 | 79 | 92 | 123 | 213 | 267 |
| Total | 654 | 1.054 | 1.500 | 1.876 | 2548 | 2659 | 3267 |

*Fig. 4.* The Development of the Company's Growth from 2005 to 2010 with the Expectations of 2011 (Million Dinars). *Source*: www.iefpedia.com/arab/wp.content/upload/2011/04/.pptx (Saud, 2011).

There is a considerable and constant increase in insurance of persons realised by the company, whereas in 2005, it was 2 million Algerian dinars, reaching 213 million Algerian dinars in 2010.

*The Analysis*

So the compulsory insurance shows a significant capacity to achieve a considerable rate of sales for insurance companies, and the correlation coefficient previously calculated confirmed that. The investment opportunities in the Algerian market are as important as in the Saudi one; we can assume that the success factors of Takaful technically exist, and any obstacle is strictly organisational.

In an analytical opinion, the development of the Takaful Algerian market is a matter of time and the next step will be to carry out a detailed study about the nature and the specificities of the product in the intellectuals' circles to create a real demand and activate the market mechanism. Consequently, Takaful in Algeria will know a prosperous future; it can build up one of the favourable alternatives for the development of private insurance and insurance of persons. Its expansion relies on the following conditions: (Lezoul, 2011)

- The existence of the first Islamic banks, as far as these will be convenient partners in bank insurance, and in the financial investments complying with the *Shariah*
- The institution of a Takaful regulation
- The creation of an offer of Takaful in compliance with the purchasing power and with the religious mentalities of the population
- Encouraging the competition between the Takaful traders
- The emergence of Islamic finance investment funds
- The development of competencies in Islamic finance.

## CONCLUSION

The emergence of specialised markets in Takaful reveals that there is an important know-how in Islamic finance that can be exploited by using the key success factors.

The share of compulsory insurance is an important field for investment in new insurance products; for the Takaful, we used the correlation coefficient to prove the existence of a considerable relationship between the growth rates of compulsory insurance and the growth rates of Takaful premiums.

So the domination of compulsory insurance in the market as a whole is an important support to boost Takaful in Algerian markets.

The theoretic treatment of the subject shows that the Takaful specificities could make major changes in insurance industry. Now the economy system has a better alternative which will bring about community well-being through Islamic finance instruments.

In Algeria, the Takaful may have an opportunity to build up a new line in the insurance sector; the postponement on the national extent can be caught up with the participation of the stakeholders that would contribute in order to benefit from the development of Islamic financial products, and through this research, we try to prove the feasibility of the development of the local Takaful insurance market. It is important to determine the parties that play a direct role for the development of the Takaful market at the national level; the national policies appear as a key measure of development of monetary policy within the central bank under the adjustment factors with the Islamic financial market, in order to set up an initial and appropriate framework to develop financial products in the national market.

This would encourage investors and expert creative institutions at the international level to exploit market shares untapped and from there, develop an environment with potential in terms of supply and demand for the adoption of Islamic finance in Algeria. These tools are appropriate socially, and may help to open channels of financing small and medium-sized investments, which is a strategic goal for the national economy.

## REVIEWS

Ansari, Z. A. (2011). Analysis of the impact of reforms on insurance industry of Saudi Arabia. *Interdisciplinary Journal of Research in Business*, *1*(8), 31.

Buck, G. (2011). Corporate financial management, Islamic finance. *The Middle East Treasurer Reviews*.

Cheddad, T. (2011). L'assurance islamique ou Takaful: A-t-elle un avenir en Algérie? Colloque international: Les sociétés d'Assurances Takaful et les sociétés d'assurances Traditionnelles Entre laThéorie et l'Expérience Pratique. Université Ferhat Abbas, Avril, p. 6.

Essen, Y. (2011). Takaful poised for growth, but greater focus is required. *Market Review*. http://www.ambest.com/press/TAKAFULMARKETREVIEW.pdf.

Lezoul, M. (2011). La situation Actuelle du Secteur Des Assurances en Algérie, Quelles Sont Les Alternatives? Colloque international: les sociétés d'assurances takaful entre la théorie et l'expérience pratique. Université Sétif, Algérie, Avril, pp. 16–19.

Ma'sum Billah, M. (2001). Modern re-discovery of Takaful (Islamic insurance): Principles and practices. International Cooperative and Mutual Insurance Federation (ICMIF), London.

Saud, W. (2011). A regional commercial inspector Salama company for Algeria insurance. *Salama experience of Algeria in the marketing of insurance Takaful insurance in the Algerian market*. Ferhat Abbas University, Algeria, April. www.iefpedia.com/arab/wp.content/upload/2011/04/.pptx.

Wang-Fuppy, C., Katsias, V., & Kwan, B. (2011). *Rating methodologie for takaful (shari'a compliant) insurance company*. AM Best's Takaful Review, p. 5.

Zaatar, R. (2008). Le takaful, une alternative à l'assurance traditionnelle. chea. Retrieved from http://www.enass.fr/PDF/seminaires/supports_du_seminaire/seminaire_innovation_takaful.pdf

## REPORTS

5th Annual Report. (2010). www.takaful-re.ae.p17.

Annual report of insurance business – Insurance Board – Algerian Ministry of Finance. (2010).

Saudi Arabian Monetary Agency. (2008).

# ELECTRONIC SOURCES (WEBSITES)

http://english.nuqudy.com/North_Africa/Small_Algerian_Insu-789. Accessed on 20 February 2012.

PricewaterhouseCoopers. (2008). Takaful: Growth opportunities in a dynamic market. Insurance Review, p. 9. Retrieved from pwc.com. Accessed on 4 April 2012.

http://executive-magazine.com/getissue.php?issue = 153. Accessed on 10 April 2012.

http://www.bi-me.com/inden.php. Accessed on March 2012.

# CHALLENGES AND OPPORTUNITIES FOR DEVELOPMENT OF ISLAMIC STOCKBROKING IN MALAYSIA

Mohammad Mahbubi Ali


## ABSTRACT

Purpose – *The chapter aims to examine the challenges and the opportunities for the development of Islamic stockbroking in Malaysia.*

Methodology – *The chapter adopts library research to discuss the concept of Islamic stockbroking. It also employs a semi-structured interview with industry players to prognosticate the future development of Islamic stockbroking in Malaysia.*

Research Findings – *The study concludes that the future of Islamic stockbroking in Malaysia is very promising, triggered by drivers on both the supply side and the demand side. The large Muslim population, wealth and economic growth are among the key factors for the development of Islamic stockbroking from the demand side. On the other hand, the* Shari'ah *compliance of 89% of Malaysian stocks, Malaysia's position as an Islamic finance hub and the natural progression of Islamic*


**The Developing Role of Islamic Banking and Finance: From Local to Global Perspectives**
**Contemporary Studies in Economic and Financial Analysis, Volume 95, 89–102**

**ISSN: 1569-3759/doi:10.1108/S1569-3759(2014)0000095013**

*finance are all factors underpinning the future of Islamic stockbroking from the supply side. However, lack of qualified human resources, political inconsistency, information technology infrastructure, product innovation as well as public perception are obstacles to its development.*

Value – *This chapter will add new literature in contemporary Islamic finance, as not many studies have been done on the subject.*

**Keywords:** Islamic stockbroking; Malaysia; *Shari'ah*; challenges; opportunities

## INTRODUCTION

Islamic finance has marked a significant development in Malaysia over the last three decades, representing an enormous demand for *Shari'ah*-compliant schemes. It has involved not only the Malay Muslims but also non-Muslim clients. Historically, Islamic finance in Malaysia began to develop with the institutionalisation of the Pilgrimage Fund (Tabung Haji) in 1963, followed by the establishment of the first full-fledged Islamic bank, Bank Islam Malaysia Berhad in 1983 (Laldin, 2008). Thirty years later, Islamic banking in Malaysia has witnessed dramatic growth, as represented in total assets. According to the Ministry of Finance's Economic Report (2011–2012), Malaysia's Islamic banking assets up to July 2011 had reached a total of 389.3 billion ringgit ($123 billion), 21% of Malaysia's total banking system. The Islamic capital market was missing in the early stages, and its introduction marks another significant milestone in the development of Malaysia's Islamic financial system (Laldin, 2008). The International Organisation of Securities Commissions (IOSCO) (2004) identified two main factors driving the development of the Malaysian Islamic Capital Market: the 1997 Asian financial crisis, and excess liquidity in the Islamic finance industry. Growing awareness of and increasing demand for *Shari'ah*-compliant investment at the global level have also served as a driving factor in the development of the Islamic capital market in Malaysia.

Islamic stockbroking, by serving as a pseudo-gatekeeper for entrance to the stock markets (Tellner, n.d.), plays a critical role in stimulating the development of the Islamic stock market. It has not yet, however, fully developed in Malaysia. Currently, there are only four Islamic stockbroking firms operating in Malaysia: one full-fledged Islamic stockbroking firm, namely Bank Islam Malaysia Berhad, and three Islamic stockbroking 'windows' services, AmInvestment Bank, CIMB Bank and Maybank Investment Bank. In addition, the research and literature on Islamic stockbroking are very limited. This chapter, therefore, undertakes to discuss the challenges and opportunities for the development of Islamic stockbroking in Malaysia.

## CONCEPT OF ISLAMIC STOCKBROKING IN ISLAM

Islam is a universal and comprehensive religion guiding every sphere of human life and preserving all issues of public interest (Osmani & Abdullah, 2009). It places emphasis on the principles of flexibility and simplicity and avoids difficulty and complexity. While the basic principle with regard to worship is that it is fixed, the fundamental principle in *mu'amalah* (financial matters) is flexibility and simplicity: everything is permissible so far, with no clear evidence indicating otherwise (Imrani, 2006). As a financial service, Islamic stockbroking falls under the purview of *mu'amalah.* Ibn al-Qayyim mentioned that the default ruling for any *mu'amalah* matter is its validity, unless a clear prohibition in the Qur'an or *hadith* indicates otherwise (Jauzi, 1991). The Securities Commission (2007) of Malaysia defined Islamic stockbroking service as 'a business in securities carried out by an Islamic participating organisation on the stock market of Bursa Securities, whether on a fully fledged basis or via an Islamic window service'.

The basic principle of an Islamic stockbroking firm in regard to its relation with its clients is commonly a *wakalah* (agency) contract. According to AAOIFI *Shari'ah* Standard, Standard No. 23 Clause 2/1, *wakalah* is 'the act of one party delegating the other to act on its behalf in what can be subject matter of delegation'. However, the concept of brokerage is also found in classical Islamic jurisprudence literature. Islamic jurists use the term '*samsarah*' to reflect the meaning of brokerage in their writings. The majority of the scholars from *Maliki, Shafi'i* and *Hanbali* schools believe that the contract of *samsarah* is permissible. Meanwhile, some scholars from the Hanafi School viewed otherwise.

## ISLAMIC STOCKBROKING IN MALAYSIA

In Malaysia, Islamic stockbroking is categorised as a participating organisation which provides beginning-to-end *Shari'ah*-compliant stock. It serves as an agent on behalf of clients to buy or sell *Shari'ah*-compliant equities based on a *wakalah* contract. In practice, the *wakalah* contract is applied in the form of two-tier agency contracts: the first layer of *wakalah* is between the client and the Islamic stockbroking firm, while the second layer is between the Islamic stockbroking firm and Bursa Malaysia. *Shari'ah* scholars have laid down some guidelines to ensure that Islamic stockbroking activities in Malaysia are in accordance with *Shari'ah* principles. These are summarised as follows (Aziz, 2009):

1. The accounting and reporting treatment should be segregated between the Islamic stockbroking sheet and the conventional sheet.
2. All terms and conditions reflected in legal documents or agreement should always comply with *Shari'ah* principles and prescriptions.
3. The standard practice of conventional stockbroking for late payment penalty charges shall be superseded by the concept of *ta'wid* which reflects the actual loss. It is because, unlike penalty, *ta'wid* is used to compensate for actual loss of late payment not as a penalty to discourage late payment. The current recommendation of the securities commission (SC) *Shari'ah* Advisory Council (SAC) for Islamic Capital Market instruments is 1% p.a. on the profit portion overdue, and the rate for Islamic Interbank Money Market for the cost (or principal) portion overdue. Neither can be compounded.
4. Any margin product or other financing offered to a *Shari'ah* broking client should be established on the concept of appropriate and suitable *Shari'ah* nominate Islamic contracts, i.e., *murabahah* share financing.
5. Contra trading has been approved by *Shari'ah* scholars. However, standard conventional practices such as charging interest for the contra days have to be eliminated.

As *Shari'ah*-compliant business entities, Islamic stockbroking in Malaysia applies different operating methods from their conventional counterparts. For example, in conventional stockbroking, the charge for purchase outstanding is based on interest on losses – BLR + X%, while the charge imposed in Islamic stockbroking is based on *ta'wid* (compensation) allowed by the *Shari'ah*. However, they also share many similar features with their conventional counterparts, e.g., evaluation criteria to determine approval limits, selling limits, multiplier for cash and shares, fees, stamp duty and settlement (Maybank IB, 2009). Besides the variations between conventional and Islamic stockbroking, Islamic stockbrokers may also differ from one another in certain practices. This is because they are in competition with one another for investors, whom they seek to attract by offering various advantages. For example, regarding *ta'wid* (compensation) for purchase outstanding on T + 5, Maybank IB requires investors to pay a composition on purchase position (COPP) at 6.64% p.a. based on Islamic Interbank Money Market (IIMM), while CIMB Investment Bank charges 8% p.a. and Ambank Investment Bank imposes 6.15%. Another example, Maybank IB will force the sale of collateral to recover losses on the 15th day onward, while Ambank Investment Bank will request the sale of collateral on the 17th day onward (Maybank IB, 2009).

## CHALLENGES IN DEVELOPING ISLAMIC STOCKBROKING IN MALAYSIA

The introduction of Islamic stockbroking as a financial service designed to facilitate investing clients' funds in *Shari'ah*-compliant equities has no doubt attracted a number of challenges, which can be categorised into internal and external challenges. The internal challenges among others are products and services, human resources and information technology infrastructure, while the external challenges are political inconsistency and public awareness.

### *Internal Challenges*

#### *Product and Services*

The product and services offered by Islamic stockbroking firms in Malaysia seem to be merely replicating the conventional products and features with few modifications to be *Shari'ah* compliant. Many view that as the product is only 'a twin conventional' product, it is therefore not much different than investing either in conventional and Islamic avenue, as the end results are the same. As a case in point, the imposition of *ta'wid* (compensation) for Outstanding Purchase Position or Unpaid Losses, although derived from the different concept and different formula, will end with the same economic result. Furthermore, many argue that investing in *Shari'ah*-compliant stocks will make the investment avenue limited and narrow, as the investment is restricted for only *Shari'ah*-compliant listed stocks. All these facts will be challenges in developing Islamic stockbroking in Malaysia.

#### *Human Resources*

Highly dedicated and qualified personnel undoubtedly play a paramount role in the success of any initiatives and business in all fields. The highly dedicated and qualified manpower will determine the end result of every planning and action. As a *Sharia'h*-based entity, Islamic stockbroking should be ideally managed by highly dedicated people with hybrid qualifications: *Shari'ah* understanding and market knowledge. They should be operated by people having at least basic understanding on *Shari'ah* matters and principles while at the same time having adequate insights and experiences on the technical and fundamental aspects as well as managerial skill. In practice, however, Malaysian Islamic stockbroking firms are mostly managed by well-trained staffs in managerial and financial terrain, yet with very minimum understanding and capability in *Shari'ah*.

*Information Technology Infrastructure*

Technology plays a very important role in every business activities. Over the years, businesses have become very dependent on technology. Technology has played a key role in the growth of trade and business in the world. The quality of a company's technology also determines the efficiency of the company's performance. What the company does is solely to meet the customer's needs. Creating and keeping the customer are very important in business. The parameters are a certain level of satisfaction. One of the factors that affects customer satisfaction is the quality of services. In order to improve the quality of service, the company should be focused on technology development services. Technology allows a company to improve service quality for a customer's satisfaction. Companies with significant technology will help customers get information about the products or services of a company.

The rapid development of information technology infrastructure is a pivotal challenge facing Islamic stockbroking in Malaysia, particularly in regard to the separation of systems between Islamic and conventional operations, as well as compatibility with the need and requirements of *Shari'ah*. In practice, in fact, the operational systems of Islamic stockbroking are largely leveraged to the conventional counterpart which may create some difficulties in terms of segregation of funds and accounting treatments.

## *External Challenges*

*Political Inconsistency*

The development of Islamic stockbroking is also hindered by the 'unequal' political treatment in the agenda of fostering Islamic finance in Malaysia. It is particularly true given the fact that the Malaysian government shows its full support of the development of Islamic commercial banks and *sukuk* issuances, which positively affects the considerable size of the industry. However, it does not happen to Islamic stockbroking. The incentive for Islamic stockbroking is only given to income tax or deduction on expenditures for establishing an Islamic stockbroking Business, Rules 2007 (Securities Commission, 2007). In the *sukuk* issuance case for example, the Malaysian government provides various tax incentives and exemptions in various layers and processes, for both investors and issuers.

*Public Awareness*

The research conducted by Bursa Malaysia, 2009 on Rethink Retail, Market Research & Insight concluded that the main obstacles in developing the stock market in Malaysia are the lack of awareness of potential investors. The research found that almost 50% of potential investors reject investing in shares. In their perception, investing in shares is riskier than that in other investment instruments, including option/futures (Fig. 1).

Moreover, the research found that 48% of potential investors are of the view that investing in shares is high risk. Twenty-seven per cent of potential investors said that they do not have enough money to invest. Others argued that they do not know how to invest in shares, do not have time to monitor and do not have time to research about the shares. As compared to shares,

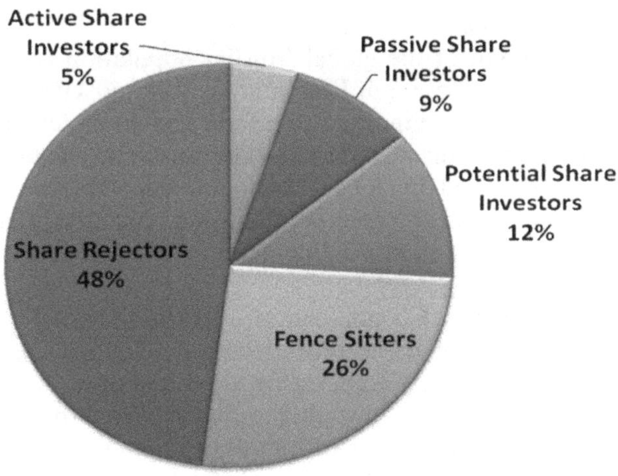


*Fig. 1.* Investors' Perception on Shares. *Source*: Bursa Malaysia, Market Research and Insight (2009).

there is a greater awareness in savings and fixed deposits. Furthermore, there is a perception that investing in stock requires brokerage fees which are relatively expensive compared to investments in other financial sectors. Many of Malay Muslims are not even aware of Islamic stockbroking.

## OPPORTUNITIES FOR ISLAMIC STOCKBROKING IN MALAYSIA

Despite a number of challenges facing Islamic stockbroking in Malaysia, its future development is undoubtedly very promising, and is determined by two main driving catalysts, namely the demand side and the supply side. The large Muslim population, wealth and economic growth are among the key factors for the development of Islamic stockbroking from the demand side. On the other hand, the *Shari'ah* compliance of 89% of Malaysian stocks, Malaysia's position as an Islamic finance hub and the natural progression of Islamic finance are all factors underpinning the future of Islamic stockbroking from the supply side.

### *Demand Side*

#### *Large Muslim Population*

The exponential growth of the global Muslim population is undeniably a positive indicator for the future of Islamic stockbroking. There is increasing evidence in the behavioural literature that faith and ethnicity may influence financial literacy and financial decisions (Gerrans et al., 2009 and Khan, 2010). A study conducted by Khan (2010) on the influence of religious beliefs on individual financial choices in Pakistan concluded that the 'faith premium' may explain the increasing demand for Islamic accounts and the Islamic banking industry.

In 2009, the global Muslim population was approximately 21% of the global population, making it the second largest religious segment in the world. Moreover, the numbers are growing at a rapid pace. Although many Muslims are poor, there are a substantial number of wealthy Muslims, and the size of the Muslim middle class continues to expand, which represents a relatively untapped market for *Shari'ah*-compliant stocks and stockbrokers. According to research conducted by the Pew Forum on Religion & Public Life (2011), titled 'The Future of the Global Muslim Population', it is projected that the number of Muslims in the world will double from 1.1 billion in 1990 to 2.2 billion in 2030 (Jones, 2011).

Of the top ten most populous nations, Indonesia continues to be the largest Muslim population in the world, followed by Pakistan and Bangladesh. This presents good possibilities for Islamic stockbrokers in Malaysia, as they are poised to capture the Indonesian market by establishing branches or subsidiaries in Indonesia. In addition, Malaysia shares a similar culture with Indonesia, which will ease Malaysian penetration of the Indonesian market.

In Malaysia, Muslims are a majority of the population at 61.3% (Department of Statistics, 2010), and could potentially make up a core target group for Islamic stockbrokers. It is also important to note that Islamic finance in general progressively penetrates the non-Muslim sector as well. Thus, it can be concluded that the growth of Islamic finance in Malaysia has been supported by both the Muslim and non-Muslim populations. However, the potential for targeting the Malaysian Muslim segment continues to be a priority. The growing need of the Muslim population in Malaysia for *Shari'ah*-compliant products as an alternative to conventional banking and capital market instruments serves as a catalyst for the development of Islamic stockbroking in Malaysia.

*Wealth Growth*

The number of high net worth individuals (HNWIs) over the world is projected to be dramatically climb, supported by economic expansion in Asia Pacific and the MENA (Middle-East-North-Africa) region. Some USD 1.5 trillion of Gulf Cooperation Council (GCC) countries' funds are held in assets worldwide, vested in treasuries, corporate bonds, equities and funds. The GCC region accounts for 3.2% of the global high net worth population (Lim, 2008).

In Malaysia, the number of HNWIs has been increasing dramatically. The report released by *Asia Wealth Report* stated that the number of HNWIs in Malaysia is expected to significantly increase from 32,000 in 2011 to 68,000 in 2015. The net worth is projected to increase from USD 140 billion (RM 433 billion) to USD 330 billion by the same year (Nayagam, 2011).

The research conducted by Gallery et al. (2011a, 2011b) found that wealthier persons had higher financial literacy. It is also concluded that the wealth factor has a positive correlation with investment literacy. Atkinson (1956) revealed that there is a cause-and-effect positive relationship between income level and investment choice. The income level will determine the attitude towards risk, liquidity and broad outlines of investment decision. Therefore, a growing class of HNWIs and the growing income level will be positive indicators for the development of Islamic stockbroking due to the need for investment avenues in portfolio management.

*Economic Growth*

The positive economic outlook for the country also bodes well for the development of Islamic stockbroking in the future. The Malaysian economy in 2011 was very impressive, especially during the first three quarters of 2011, witnessing an average growth of 5.1% (1Q11: 5.2%, 2Q11: 4.3%, 3Q11: 5.8%) (Malaysian Institute of Economic Research, 2012).

Malaysia's economic growth is supported by the government commitment to realise the New Economic Model (NEM), the Government Transformation Programme (GTP) and the Economic Transformation Programme (ETP). The NEM, GTP and ETP have witnessed constructive output reflected by the different indices where the total investment commitment stands at RM95 billion, which should create almost 225,000 jobs over the next 10 years. Moreover, the ETP has found a total of 131 Entry Point Projects (EPP) with a total investment value of RM 794.5 billion as part of a main initiative to boost the country's Gross National Income to RM 1.1 trillion and generate 3.3 million jobs. To date, a total of 72 projects have been launched, and 41.2% of them are at various stages of implementation, reflecting private sector confidence in the government (Bernama, 2011).

A study by Ericsson and Irandoust (2000) found that there is a causal relationship between Foreign Direct Investment (FDI) and total factor productivity growth in Norway and Sweden over the long run. Chen and Zhu (2008) concluded that there is bidirectional Granger causality between housing investment and Gross Domestic Product (GDP) in both the short term and long term in China. Therefore, it can be concluded that the economic performance of Malaysia represented by GDP growth, wealth income growth, business environment as well as government initiatives will be a positive indicator for the future of Islamic stockbroking in Malaysia.

## *Supply Side*

While economic growth, income growth and a large number of Muslims are among key factors driving Islamic stockbroking in Malaysia from the demand side, it is also important to investigate the catalytic factors from the supply side.

*Malaysia as an Islamic Finance Hub*

In August 2006, the Malaysia International Islamic Financial Centre (MIFC) initiative was launched to promote Malaysia as a major hub for international Islamic finance with the following key initiatives (MIFC, 2011):

- Adoption of global legal and regulatory best practices;
- A well-developed *Shari'ah* governance framework;
  Bank Negara Malaysia has established a centralised *Shari'ah* Advisory Council (SAC).
- Comprehensive human capital development:
  A large and diverse pool of Islamic finance talent;
  Established higher education in Islamic finance;
- Tax Incentives (10-year tax exemption, 10-year exemption on stamp duty);
- Liberal foreign exchange administration (FEA) rules;
- Establishing an International Currency Business Unit (ICBU).

In 2007, the Malaysian government has legislated substantial tax incentives for the benefit of Islamic finance, as decided in the 2007 budget announced on the first of September, 2006. This incentive will provide a chance for Malaysia to benefit from an influx of liquidity, particularly from the Middle East (Chang, 2006).

The vision to become a viable Islamic finance hub has come true as Malaysia is proving itself capable of continuing lead Islamic finance in the world. In 2009, Malaysian *sukuk* are placed in the first rank in the *sukuk* market, equity market and fund management, the second position of the *takaful* market after Iran, and the third ranking in the banking market, after Iran and Saudi Arabia (MIFC & PWTC, 2010). These will be the determinant factors for the development of Islamic stockbroking, as Malaysia will continue to endeavour to lead in each and every aspect of Islamic finance.

*89% Shari'ah-Compliant Stock*

Another key factor driving the development of Islamic stockbroking in Malaysia is the wide range of the *Shari'ah*-compliant listed stocks approved by the *Shari'ah* Advisory Council. As at 25 November, 2011, 89% of the securities listed on Bursa Malaysia are *Shari'ah*-compliant, tapping 839 *Shari'ah*-compliant equities (Securities Commission, 2011), and representing more than two-thirds of Malaysia's market capitalisation. In other words, only 11% of the stocks of listed companies are not *Shari'ah*-compliant. This fact answers the perception of some that the Islamic market is narrow and not sufficient to cater to investor needs. The 89% *Shari'ah*-compliant stocks listed on Bursa Malaysia will allow the investors to diversify their choice in ethical investment schemes and end-to-end Shari'ah portfolio management.

*Natural Progression*

While the early stage of Islamic finance was dominated by deposits and saving products, IFI products and services over the last decade have become much more sophisticated structures, comprising a wide variety of *sukuk* models, derivative products, Islamic structured products, and Islamic exchange traded funds (i-ETF). The need for diversified *Shari'ah*-compliant securities with various features and instruments is indeed immense. It is perhaps, an opportune moment for Islamic stockbroking to capture the need, bridge the gap and fill in the missing link. It is the turn of Islamic stockbroking to flourish and boom in the market as it represents a natural progression and evolution of Islamic finance.

## CONCLUSION

Islamic stockbroking is a gate to the Islamic stock market. It has a pivotal role to play in providing an avenue for investment in *Shari'ah*-compliant equities. However, its existence has not yet been well developed in Malaysia. Various emerging challenges are hindering its development. These challenges are classified into two aspects, notably internal and external challenges. The internal challenges include the products and services, human resources, and information technology infrastructure, while the external challenges include political inconsistency and public awareness. Despite a number of challenges that impede the growth of Islamic stockbroking in the country, there are some promising factors that are catalysts to its development, determined by both supply and demand sides. The large number of Muslims, economic growth and increasing wealth are among the key factors on the demand side. On the other hand, the *Shari'ah* compliance of 89% of Malaysian stocks, Malaysia's position as an Islamic finance hub and the natural progression of Islamic finance are all factors driving the development of Islamic stockbroking from the supply side.

Moving forward, some following recommendations might be useful for future development of Islamic stockbroking in Malaysia:

1. There is a need for innovative marketing and continuous campaigns to create awareness and to capture untapped potential markets, primarily Malay Muslim investors.
2. Tax incentives across various layers and processes are paramount for acceptance of Islamic stockbroking products in the market. These have proven very effective in promoting the *sukuk* market and Islamic banking.
3. The products offered should place emphasis more on the differentiation factors which clearly reflect the Islamic values and the objectives of *Shari'ah*. This is important to create acceptance of particularly Malay Muslim investors to Islamic stockbroking products.
4. There is a need to widen market coverage and penetration rate for Islamic stockbroking in Malaysia. It can be done through the establishment of subsidiaries in neighbouring countries, such as Indonesia, Singapore or Thailand.
5. As lack of skilled personnel is one of the most critical challenges in developing Islamic stockbroking in Malaysia, it is crucial to provide continuous and systematic training, education and learning for staffs to enhance understanding on *Shari'ah* matters as well as operational aspects in equity trading.

## REFERENCES

Al-'Imrani, A. (2006). *Al-'Uqud Al-Maaliyah Al-Murakkabah, Dirasah Fiqhiyyah Ta'shiliyyah wa Tathbiqiyyah*. Riyadh: Daar Kunuuz Isybiliya li Nashr wa al.

Atkinson, T. R. (1956). *The pattern of financial asset ownership: Wisconsin individuals*: Princeton, NJ: Princeton University Press.

Aziz, M. Z. A. (2009). *Islamic stockbroking for Maybank Investment Bank*. Kuala Lumpur: Muamalah Financial Consulting.

Bernama. (2011). Malaysia ranked no.7 in economic performance. *Economic Performance*. Retrieved from http://dinmerican.wordpress.com/2011/05/20/malaysia-ranked-no-7-in-economic-performance. Accessed on August 4.

Bursa Malaysia. (2009). *Rethink retail market research and insight*. Kuala Lumpur: Bursa Malaysia Bhd.

Chang, J. (2006). *Positioning Malaysia as an Islamic financial center*. Malaysian Islamic Finance Report.

Chen, J., & Zhu, A. (2008). The relationship between housing investment and economic growth in China: A panel analysis using quarterly provincial data. Working Paper 2008:17. Department of Economics, Uppsala University.

Department of Statistics, Malaysia. (2010). *Population and housing census Malaysia 2010 (2010 census)*. Retrieved from www.statistics.gov.my

Ericsson, J., & Irandoust, M. (2000). On the causality between foreign direct investment and output: A comparative study. *International Trade Journal*, *15*, 1–26.

Gallery, N., Gallery, G., Brown, K., Furneaux, C., & Palm, C. (2011a). Financial literacy and pension investment decisions. *Financial Accountability and Management*, *27*(3), 286–307.

Gallery, N., Gallery, G., Brown, K., Furneaux, C., & Palm, C. (2011b). Framework for assessing financial literacy and superannuation investment choice decisions. *Australasian Accounting Business and Finance*, *5*(2), 3–22.

Gerrans, P., Clark-Murphy, M., & Truscott, K. (2009). Financial literacy and superannuation awareness of indigenous Australians: Pilot study results. *Journal of Social Issues*, *44*(4), 417–439.

IOSCO. (2004). *Islamic capital market fact finding report*. Report on the Islamic Capital Market Task Force Report of the International Organization of Securities Commission, July.

Jauzy, I. Q. (1991). *I'lam al-Muqi'in 'an Rabb al-'Alamin*. Beirut: Dar al-Jil.

Jones, H. (2011). *2.2 Billion: World's Muslim population doubles*. Retrieved from http://newsfeed.time.com/2011/01/27/2-2-billion-worlds-Muslim-population. Accessed on April 9, 2012.

Khan, A. K. (2010). *Is faith a luxury for the rich? Examining the influence of religious beliefs on individual financial choices*. Boston, MA: Harvard University.

Laldin, M. A. (2008). Islamic financial system: The Malaysian experience and the way forward. *Humanomics*, *24*(3), 217–238.

Lim, M. W., (2008). Malaysia as a Hub for Islamic wealth management. *The international financial planning advisors conference*. Sunway Pyramid Convention Center, Malaysia February 22–24.

Malaysian Institute of Economic Research. (2012). *Malaysian economic outlook*. Retrieved from http://www.mier.org.my/outlook/

Maybank, I. B. (2009). *H.O.T broking board paper 2009*. Kuala Lumpur: Maybank IB.

MIFC. (2011) *Malaysia's value propositions – Islamic fund and wealth management*. http://www.mifc.com/index.php?ch = menu_foc_ifm&pg = menu_foc_ifm_prop

MIFC & PWTC. (2010). *Gateway to Asia, Malaysia an International Islamic Finance Hub*. Kuala Lumpur: MIFC & PWTC.

Ministry of Finance. (2011). *Monetary and financial development*. Economic report 2011/2012. Retrieved from http://www.treasury.gov.my/pdf/economy/er/1112/chap5.pdf

Nayagam, J. (2011). *Number of wealthy Malaysians to double by 2015*. Retrieved from http://www.theedgemalaysia.com/in-the-financial-daily/192998-number-of-wealthy-malaysians-to-double-by-2015.html. Accessed on April 10, 2012.

Osmani, N. M., & Abdullah, M. F. (2009). Towards an Islamic stock market: A review of classical and modern literatures. *International Review of Business Research Papers*, *5*(5), 121–130, World Business Institute, Australia.

Securities Commission. (2007). *Best practices in Islamic stockbroking services undertaken by participating organisations*. Kuala Lumpur: Securities Commission.

Securities Commission. (2011). *List of Shariah-compliant securities by the Shariah advisory council of the securities commission Malaysia*. Kuala Lumpur: Securities Commission.

Tellner, T. D. (n.d.). *A model of an Islamic stockbrokerage firm*. Retrieved from http://www.kantakji.com/fiqh/Files/Finance.

# THE OPPORTUNITY FOR IMPLEMENTING ISLAMIC PROJECT FINANCING TO THE INDONESIAN INFRASTRUCTURE DEVELOPMENT

Ayomi Dita Rarasati, Bambang Trigunarsyah and Eric Too

## ABSTRACT

Purpose – *This chapter discusses the opportunity of Islamic project financing implementation for public infrastructure development in Indonesia.*

Design/methodology/approach – *This chapter, firstly, reviewed existing literature on Islamic finance to explore the applicability of Islamic financing in infrastructure development. Interviews were conducted as the first stage of Delphi method approach. This was then followed by reviewing Indonesia's government policies and regulations in infrastructure industry and Islamic financing.*

**The Developing Role of Islamic Banking and Finance: From Local to Global Perspectives**
**Contemporary Studies in Economic and Financial Analysis, Volume 95, 103–116**

**ISSN: 1569-3759/doi:10.1108/S1569-3759(2014)0000095015**

Findings – *This chapter enlightens the implementation of Islamic financing on infrastructure project financing in Indonesia. The findings indicate that the government policies and regulations on both infrastructure investment and Islamic financing support the implementation of Islamic project financing, whereas, an improvement is still needed in order to overarch infrastructure business and Islamic financing investment.*

Research – *Financing framework development for Indonesia infrastructure projects.*

Limitations/implications – *The result reported comprises the preliminary study of Islamic project paper written based on published research papers and interviews. Furthermore, the data collected for the study are limited to the case of Indonesian infrastructure projects.*

Practical implication – *Islamic financing in Indonesia infrastructure projects development has not been optimally implemented. Therefore, this chapter serves as a catalyst to explore alternative financial scheme such as Islamic financing for infrastructure development.*

Originality/value – *This chapter highlights possibilities and obstacles in applying Islamic scheme to infrastructure project financing. This provides a framework to analyse the steps to implement Islamic financing successfully in infrastructure development.*

**Keywords:** Islamic project financing; Indonesia; public infrastructure; investment

## INTRODUCTION

Accelerating infrastructure provision is one of the main priorities in Indonesia's national development. In 2011, the government announced the establishment of six economic corridors with different development themes for Sumatra, Java, Kalimantan, Sulawesi, Bali-Nusa Tenggara and Papua-Maluku Islands to accelerate and expand Indonesia economic development. To support these economic corridors, it is projected that the total investment cost is about USD 401.2 billion. The Government of Indonesia (GOI) plans to contribute approximately 10% of that total investment with the rest come from state owned enterprises, private sector and public private partnership (PPP). For the infrastructure development projects, such as road, port, power and energy, airport, railway, water utility and information communication technology, it requires an estimated USD 178.6 billion (CMEA, 2011).

Project financing in public infrastructure has been implemented extensively in many countries. However, in Indonesia it is still developing and slowly gaining momentum. Private sector involvement, through project financing, provides an avenue for the use of Islamic project financing for infrastructure development. It is, therefore, expected that Islamic project financing can play an active part in supporting Indonesia infrastructure development.

This chapter explores factors that influence the implementation of Islamic project financing for infrastructures development in Indonesia. It begins with the discussion on project financing in infrastructure development. Next, it examines how Islamic financing can be incorporated into project financing. Finally, it illustrates the barrier of Islamic project financing implementation of infrastructure projects in Indonesia.

## PROJECT FINANCING IN INDONESIA INFRASTRUCTURE DEVELOPMENT

In 2005, the GOI embarked on a comprehensive programme of infrastructure reforms and issued an Infrastructure Policy Packages. In the same year, the Indonesian Government also established the Policy Committee for Accelerating the Provision of Infrastructure (KKPPI) through Presidential Regulation No. 42 of 2005. It is an inter-ministerial committee chaired by the Coordinating Minister of Economic Affairs (CMEA), who is responsible to endorse requests for government guarantee as a basis for the Ministry of Finance (MOF) consideration and approval.

In order to support economic growth and to bridge infrastructure investment gap, the GOI has encouraged private sector participation in infrastructure projects in the form of PPP. The PPP programme can be used for a wide range of infrastructure sector such as transportation (airports, ports, railways, roads and bridges), water supply, solid waste and sanitation, and power.

The PPP scheme is developed based on project financing concept. To support the use of PPP, the GOI has established various government contracting agencies (GCA) for the various infrastructure sectors. For example, the Toll Road Authority (BPJT) was established for the governing of road infrastructure sector. The contracting agencies then invite investors, in the form of special purpose vehicle (SPV), through bidding process. Once granted, an SPV will develop the particular infrastructure asset and generate its revenue from the asset operation for certain period as stated in the contract. By the end of the contract the SPV will return the asset to the GOI.

In attracting the development of private sector participations in infrastructure provision, the GOI issued Presidential Regulation No. 67 of 2005, which was later amended by Presidential Regulation No. 13 of 2010, on cooperation between the government and business entities in infrastructure provision. Institutional issues also form important aspect in developing an effective PPP framework. Therefore, the GOI established public private partnership central unit (PPPCU or P3CU). P3CU is currently managed by the Directorate for PPP Development within the National Planning Agency (BAPPENAS). It has several functions including supporting KKPPI for policy formulation and government guarantee assessment, preparing the Government's PPP book, supporting GCA for project preparation, and developing capacity for PPP implementation within government agencies. The key stakeholders that participate in a PPP infrastructure project in Indonesia and the relationship amongst them are shown in Table 1.

In Indonesia infrastructure projects, the principle risks that typically occur include land acquisition, tariffs, demand, country and political risks,

***Table 1.*** Indonesia PPP Stakeholders.

| Institution Category | Stakeholders |
|---|---|
| Providers of capital and guarantees | State infrastructure guarantee company<br>Multilateral development banks<br>Foreign and domestic commercial banks<br>State infrastructure fund<br>Project sponsors |
| Government policy makers, regulators and counterparties | Ministry of Finance (Risk Management Unit)<br>KKPPI<br>PPP Central Unit<br>Advisors<br>Government contracting agency<br>Licensing and permitting agencies |
| Third party service providers | EPC Contractors<br>Operational and maintenance operators |
| Service off taker | Users |

*Source*: CMEA (2010).

and off-taker creditworthiness. It is the P3CU and GCAs responsibility to ensure that project risks are clearly identified and allocated among the stakeholders. Therefore, the GOI established support mechanisms for PPP infrastructure project risks through several regulations such as MOF Regulation No. 38 of 2006 on guidance for controlling and management of risks in infrastructure provision, CMEA Regulation No. 4 of 2006 on evaluation methodology for PPP infrastructure projects that require government support and Government Regulation No. 35 of 2009 on state participation for a limited liability company establishment for infrastructure guarantees.

The forms of support in PPP projects consist of (1) direct support, for project which is economically justified but not financially feasible; (2) land acquisition, by reimbursing the land acquisition cost to government contracting agency (GCA) through project revenues; (3) contingent support, for guarantees covering political risk, project performance risk and demand risk; (4) tax incentives; and (5) special economic zones (CMEA, 2010). The government support will be analysed based on the minimum support required for financial viability and bankability under the selected form of cooperation.

## ISLAMIC FINANCING IN INFRASTRUCTURE PROJECT

Infrastructure investment is suitable to be financed with Islamic financing scheme, because infrastructure is considered an asset and it does not contain any activities that are prohibited in *shariah* law. Although there are various types of Islamic finance, only several types of Islamic financial instrument might be suitable in infrastructure investment, such as *mudaraba* (trusty financing or investment), *musharaka* (partnership or joint venture), *ijara* (leasing), *istisna* (production or manufacture sale), *sukuk* (Islamic bond), *murabaha* (mark-up sale) and *kafalah* (*guarantee*).

Islamic finance has several advantages compared to conventional finance. First, Islamic finance is now considered as one of the fastest growing financial segments in the world. Second, Islamic finance business area has been broadening in many aspects such as private equity, project financing or *sukuk*. Currently, Islamic finance is internationally recognised and contributes to global financial assimilation. It is therefore close to real economic sector. Within the foundation of profit and loss sharing, Islamic finance is capable to minimise the severity and frequency of financial crises (Ahmed, 2010; Chazi & Syed, 2010; Hasan & Dridi, 2010).

Several previous printed works describing Islamic project financing were started in the late 1990s. For example, Khan (1997) proposed an alternative Islamic structure for project finance deals in power plant project. The structure combined Islamic and Western financiers to participate in infrastructure projects without dealing with the religious principle and financial interest. Wilson (1998) agreed that *istisna* has the same character with build own operate transfer (BOOT) scheme, although different in terms of ownership and control of the project. Ebrahim (1999) proposed an integrated model of Islamic and western project finance, which more focuses in synthesising *mudaraba* security as a combination of *murabaha* facility and call option to derive profit sharing ratio endogenously.

In the Equate Petrochemical project located in Kuwait, co-financed structures, combination of Islamic and Western sponsors financing, were successfully implemented (Esty, 2000). This project used *ijara*, *istisna* and *murabaha* structures. Since the successful introduction of Islamic finance, several other co-financed deals in infrastructure projects were noted. These projects include the Kuala Lumpur Light Rail Transit 2 project, Thuraya Space Telecommunications project, Shuaiba power plant project, the TAG and Mersin Motorways project and the Kuala Lumpur International Airport. However, the number of projects which used co-financed structures is still not plentiful.

Based on several infrastructure projects that incorporate Islamic project finance innovation, Camacho (2005) concluded that some innovative way to earn capital in infrastructure projects are combining Islamic and Western financing, creating new structures of financing or finding other methods to mitigate risks. Camacho also stated that there were institutional problems which can increase financial cost. Therefore, the scheme of using *adl*/trustee, a uniform Islamic finance body and accounting practices should be well-established.

Although there is no concept of trustee in Islamic law or civil jurisdictions law, the use of trustee is a crucial component of project financing, especially projects under New York or English law. On the contrary, Islamic law allows the use of *adl*. *Adl* is a trusted and honourable person selected by both borrower and lender. The use of *adl* can improve stability, certainty and fairness of a transaction (Camacho, 2005; Stoakes, 1998).

Principally, government guarantee is less needed when profit sharing is high. However, it can increase creditworthiness and raise debt capacity of the project (Hassan & Soumaré, 2006). Therefore, government guarantee is still needed in infrastructure projects.

Alexander (2011) explicates potential sources of problem when projects with Islamic financing scheme attempt to accommodate Western financing. First, the lack of cohesive regulatory body, in this context is the *shariah* boards. *Shariah* boards' decision can somehow be unpredictable and subjective. Although the board will consider similar transactions, there is no guarantee the decision will be the same. This happens because a *fatwa* is only valid for one specific circumstance. Therefore, *shariah* boards also take the most significant decision in project endorsement. Second, the requirement in *shariah* compliant that lender should accept the project risk which may enhance risk from the perspective of Western lenders.

*Shariah* board examines investment structure and documentation to ensure that every transaction acknowledge the cultural, moral, ethical and religious principles (McMillen, 2001). *Shariah* board will make decision whether the project can be implemented based on the *fiqh*, *shariah* principle and the financing period. The *shariah* principle is also determined based on *fiqh*. Usually, Islamic financing is utilised in short term or medium term of finance. Therefore *shariah* board should also understand and analyse infrastructure project condition in term of financial length.

In principle, Islamic financing can be implemented for infrastructure projects. However, the implementation can encounter some obstacles such as Islamic finance knowledge and understanding amongst infrastructure project stakeholders. Additionally, stakeholders should also have understood the concept of project financing. In the Indonesian context, a framework to implement Islamic project financing in infrastructure is needed.

## RESEARCH METHODOLOGY

To achieve the implementation of Islamic project financing in Indonesia infrastructure projects, this research uses qualitative approach that explores, emphasises meanings and experiences, and describes social and human problem (Creswell, 2009; Naoum, 2007). It is also considered as descriptive research because reasonable knowledge has been achieved; however, more detailed information is still needed to be addressed (Cavana, Sekaran, & Delahaye, 2001). Therefore, structured interviews, focus groups and questionnaires are more likely to be used in this research.

In this research, Delphi method is used instead of focus group. Delphi is chosen because participant can make contribution from anywhere and anytime even via electronic communication (Steurer, 2011). In addition to that, Delphi was used to maintain anonymity and limited contact amongst research participants. As such, they can freely give their opinions, beliefs and judgements without other participant influences (Rowe & Wright, 1999; Skulmoski, Hartman, & Krahn, 2007; Steurer, 2011), and avoid direct confrontation (Okoli & Pawlowski, 2004). Anonymity can protect participants from disgrace if they have opposite opinions (Steurer, 2011).

Delphi is used to combine expert knowledge and opinion (Singh & Schmidgall, 2000) to achieve consensus when dealing with uncertainty in an area of inadequate knowledge (Paliwoda, 1983). Delphi method in this research aims to develop an implementation framework for Islamic project financing in infrastructure projects. Delphi methodology is appropriate for this research because firstly, the problem is complex and has no adequate communication history. Secondly, the panels are from various stakeholders to keep validity assurance in the results. Thirdly, focus group meetings are not feasible to conduct due to time and cost limitation (Linstone & Turoff, 1975; Singh & Schmidgall, 2000). It is also suitable because the problem has multiple dimensions (Paliwoda, 1983). The research problems arise from infrastructure investment framework, project financing issue and Islamic financing concept.

There are three rounds of Delphi method in this research. The first round started with in-depth interview to gather and to explore panel members' knowledge and experience. Members of the panel were selected from infrastructure stakeholders and Islamic financing practitioners who are considered as expert in view of their knowledge in infrastructure project financing and/or Islamic financing. The panel members include both academics and practitioners to ensure a wide spectrum of viewpoints is included (Baldwin & Trinkle, 2011). The infrastructure project stakeholders consist of people who work for guarantee fund company, risk management unit at the Ministry of Finance (MOF), *shariah* debt management office at MOF, Coordinating Ministry of Economic Affair (CMEA) as part of KKPPI institution, Islamic bank, government contracting agency, infrastructure special purpose company and PPP consultant. The panels were recruited by invitation and snowball technique.

The interview questions were developed based on information gathered from literature review. Data from first round interview are analysed and used to generate questions for the following round. The iterative round stops when consensus is reached on factors related to the topic (Azadeh, Keramati, & Songhori, 2009). However, instead of reaching a convergence of opinion, Delphi in this research stops at the third round because the panels have begun to exhaust their interest and not willing to do so (Azadeh et al., 2009; Baldwin-Morgan, 1993). Additional rounds also tend to yield redundancy and cause a significant withdrawing of returns for substantial additional effort (Azadeh et al., 2009). At the final round, the opinion may reflect agreement, disagreement or some of each (Pivo, 2008).

This chapter, however, only focuses on Delphi first round, which involved in-depth interview process. It drew an interpretative theoretical framework of infrastructure projects' key stakeholder point of view.

## ISLAMIC PROJECT FINANCING IN INDONESIA INFRASTRUCTURE PROJECT

The results from the first round Delphi interview suggest that there are some barriers to the successful implementation of Islamic project financing. These barriers relate to: cost of fund; Islamic finance institution capability; government policy and regulation; government support and commitment; infrastructure and Islamic finance business conflicts; profit-oriented mindset; understanding of Islamic project financing knowledge in infrastructure; and project readiness (Rarasati, Too, Trigunarsyah, & Cheung, 2012). However, this chapter focuses more on government policy and regulation discussion. The result from interview then is compared with the current regulation and government policies in Islamic financing and infrastructure investment.

There are seven panel members mentioned about government policy and regulation. All contexts are referring to Islamic financing, *sukuk*, Islamic banking and infrastructure financing. Three panel members referred to the existence and regulatory readiness. Two panel members stated that regulations in Islamic financing are limited or not solid enough. Two panel members mentioned that all regulations regarding Islamic financing have to be harmonised with *fatwa*. One member suggested that mismatch fund maturity between Islamic finance and infrastructure need should be protected by regulation. Details on panels' expressions of regulation are presented in Table 2.

In general, government is responsible for public infrastructures provision. However, infrastructure project development can be initially triggered by private sector. Indonesian government has broadened public infrastructure delivery to include private sector involvement by the provision of supporting policies and regulations. In the case of Islamic project financing,

***Table 2.*** Summary of Interview Result on Government Policy and Regulation.

| Phrase | Context | Panel Members Category |
|---|---|---|
| Regulatory readiness | Islamic financing | Guarantee company |
| Regulations are not solid enough | Project-based *sukuk* for PPP project | Debt Management Office |
| Harmonisation in regulation | Project-based *sukuk* | |
| Minimum/limited regulation | Islamic financing | CMEA |
| Regulation in Islamic finance only State *sukuk* | State *sukuk* | |
| Harmonisation in fatwa and government regulation | Islamic financing | *Shariah* National Board |
| Existence and readiness of regulation in *shariah* financing for infrastructure | Islamic financing in infrastructure | Government Contracting Agency |
| Existence of legal and regulations | Islamic banking | Special Purpose Company |
| Regulation should protect mismatch fund maturity | Infrastructure financing | Academic |

several laws, government regulations and ministry regulations have been issued to support Islamic financing and infrastructure investment as summarised on Table 3.

Although infrastructure regulations do not specifically mention *shariah* investment, Indonesian law through *sukuk* and Islamic banking can reinforce investment with *shariah* principle. Additionally, Government Regulation No. 56, 2011, allows infrastructure projects to be funded with *sukuk*, which complements the possibility of Islamic finance to penetrate the market. However, the government regulation is not yet applicable for infrastructure investment with project financing scheme, it is applicable to infrastructure projects within government budget only.

The Head of Regulatory Body of Capital Market and Financial Institution (Bapepam LK) regulations support infrastructure investment in *shariah* scheme within permissible activities. Through those regulations, infrastructure financial enterprise can legally have *shariah* investment transactions, such as *mudaraba mutlaqah* (unrestricted investment), *mudarabah muqayyadah* (restricted investment), *mudaraba mushtaraka* (combination of *mudaraba* and *musharaka*), *musharaka* or any other financing investment. Those regulations also mention the objects of each type of *shariah* transactions, the right and obligations of each stakeholder.

***Table 3.*** Law, Regulation and Policy on Islamic Financing and Infrastructure Investment.

| Islamic Financing | Infrastructure Investment | |
|---|---|---|
| Law | • Law No. 19/2008 on Islamic state securities/state *sukuk*<br>• Law No. 21/2008 on Islamic banking | • Law No. 7/2004 on water resources<br>• Law No. 38/2004 on road<br>• Law No. 23/2007 on railway<br>• Law No. 17/2008 on sea transportation<br>• Law No. 1/2009 on air transportation<br>• Law No. 30/2009 on electricity |
| Government regulation (GR) | • GR No. 56/2011 on Project budgeting with state sukuk | • GR No. 8/2007 on government investment<br>• Presidential Regulation (PR) No. 13/2010 on amendments of PR no. 67/2005 on public private partnership for infrastructure provision |
| Ministry regulation | Ministry of Finance (MOF) regulation:<br>• No. 129/PMK.08/2011 on Project utilisation for state *sukuk* | MOF regulation:<br>• No. 38/PMK.01/2006 on Risk control and management guideline for infrastructure<br>• No. 100/PMK.010/2009 on Infrastructure finance enterprise |
| Other supportive regulation or policy | Head of regulatory body of capital market and financial institution (Bapepam LK) Regulation:<br>• No. PER-03/BL/2007 on Financial enterprise activities based on Islamic principles<br>• No. PER-04/BL/2007 on financial enterprise *aqd* transactions based on Islamic principles | |

In the water infrastructure sector, although private involvement is considered new, the investment opportunity is huge. The government opens the water sector financial source of fund as mention in the Law No. 7 Year 2004 about Water Resources. The infrastructure investment can be sourced from private sectors, non-bank institution, even from community participation.

Therefore, Islamic financing is applicable in water infrastructure development projects. The water sector contracting agency does not have an obligation to buy the clean water. However, there is an assurance that the communities or industries surrounded by the water services will obtain their water supply from the water supply company. Regarding the capital expenditures, water supply infrastructure does not require a very massive amount of fund, contrasting with other sectors such as power plant or toll road. Hence, it is at ease for *shariah* financing mode to step in to the water supply sector.

Other aspect that can support Islamic finance scheme in infrastructure is the settlement of regulations in Islamic banking or Islamic finance instruments. It was started by enacting Law No. 19 Year 2008 in Islamic state securities (*Sukuk*) and Law No. 21 Year 2008 in Islamic banking, followed with other supportive regulations such as government regulation, ministry decree and regulation and general director decree. The establishment of regulations in Islamic finance shows government support and seriousness in Islamic investment opportunity. The Indonesian Government also open investment in infrastructure projects through project-based *sukuk*, although the project is based on government budget funding (APBN). Therefore, it provides another opportunity for Islamic scheme in financing infrastructure within private investment.

## SUMMARY

Several public infrastructure sectors, such as water, energy and road, concern to assort Islamic financing scheme. This chapter shows the possibilities of Islamic project financing implementation for infrastructure development projects through the issuance of government policies and regulations. Although there are already some regulations relating to the *shariah* finance, none of them relate to infrastructure project financing. The regulations in infrastructure provision itself also not correlated to Islamic financing. For example, Law No. 19 Year 2008 only covers Islamic financing within obligation instrument, while other Islamic financial instruments such as *murabaha*, *mudaraba*, *musharaka* or *ijara* are not concealed with the law. Meanwhile Law No. 21 Year 2008 only regulates banking sector activities which compliant with *shariah* law, while in Islamic project financing, banking is not the only institution of financing. There are other financial institutions in infrastructure project financing such as multilateral agencies and guarantee agency that might use Islamic financing transactions. Islamic pension funds and insurance are most likely applicable to invest on infrastructure projects. The same circumstance also happens in infrastructure regulation. It never converges with project financing nor Islamic financing. Most of infrastructure regulations focus in sectors development or institutional role. Therefore, it is needed to improve policies and regulations regarding infrastructure project financing. These policies and regulations will bridge the gap and overarching infrastructure business and Islamic finance investment.

# REFERENCES

Ahmed, A. (2010). Global financial crisis: An Islamic finance perspective. *International Journal of Islamic and Middle Eastern Finance and Management*, *3*(4), 306–320. doi:10.1108/17538391011093252

Alexander, A. J. (2011). Shifting title and risk: Islamic project finance with western partners. *Michigan Journal of International Law*, *32*(3), 571–612.

Azadeh, A., Keramati, A., & Songhori, M. J. (2009). An integrated Delphi/VAHP/DEA framework for evaluation of information technology/information system (IT/IS) investments. *International Journal of Advanced Manufacturing Technology*, *45*(11/12), 1233–1251. doi:10.1007/s00170-009-2047-2

Baldwin, A. A., & Trinkle, B. S. (2011). The impact of XBRL: A Delphi investigation. *International Journal of Digital Accounting Research*, *11*, 1–24.

Baldwin-Morgan, A. A. (1993). The impact of expert system audit tools on auditing firms in the year 2001: A Delphi investigation. *Journal of Information Systems*, *7*(1), 16–34.

Camacho, J. (2005). Islamic financing for large infrastructure projects. Retrieved from http://people.hbs.edu/mdesai/IFM05/Camacho.pdf.

Cavana, R. Y., Sekaran, U., & Delahaye, B. L. (2001). *Applied business research: Qualitative and quantitative methods*. Milton, Queensland: Wiley & Sons.

Chazi, A., & Syed, L. A. M. (2010). Risk exposure during the global financial crisis: The case of Islamic banks. *International Journal of Islamic and Middle Eastern Finance and Management*, *3*(4), 321–333.

CMEA. (2010). *Public private partnership (PPP): Investor's guide*. Jakarta: Coordinating Ministry of Economic Affairs.

CMEA. (2011). *Masterplan: Acceleration and expansion of Indonesia economic development 2011–2025*. Jakarta: Coordinating Ministry for Economic Affairs.

Creswell, J. W. (2009). *Research design: Qualitative, quantitative, and mixed methods approaches*. Thousand Oaks, CA: Sage.

Ebrahim, M. S. (1999). Integrating Islamic and conventional project finance. *Thunderbird International Business Review*, *41*(4–5), 583–609. doi:10.1002/tie.4270410416

Esty, B. C. (2000). The equate project: An introduction to Islamic project finance. *Journal of Project Finance*, *5*(4), 7.

Hasan, M., & Dridi, J. (2010). *The effects of the global crisis on Islamic and conventional banks: A comparative study*. Washington, DC: International Monetary Fund.

Hassan, M. K., & Soumaré, I. (2006, December 16–18). Financial guarantee as an innovation tool in Islamic project finance. Paper presented at the ERF 13th Annual Conference, Kuwait.

Khan, M. H. (1997). Designing an Islamic model for project finance. *International Financial Law Review*, *16*(6), 13.

Linstone, H. A., & Turoff, M. (1975). *The Delphi method: Techniques and applications*. Reading, MA: Addison-Wesley, Advanced Book Program.

McMillen, M. J. T. (2001). Islamic shari'ah-compliant project finance: Collateral security and financing structure case studies. *Fordham International Law Journal*, *24*(4), 1184–1264.

Naoum, S. G. (2007). *Dissertation research and writing for construction students*. Oxford: Butterworth-Heinemann.

Okoli, C., & Pawlowski, S. D. (2004). The Delphi method as a research tool: An example, design considerations and applications. *Information & Management*, *42*(1), 15–29. doi:10.1016/j.im.2003.11.002

Paliwoda, S. J. (1983). Predicting the future using Delphi. *Management Decision*, *21*(1), 31–38. doi:10.1108/eb001309

Pivo, G. (2008). Responsible property investment criteria developed using the Delphi method. *Building Research & Information*, *36*(1), 20–36.

Rarasati, A. D., Too, E., Trigunarsyah, B., & Cheung, F. (2012, October 31). Islamic project financing implementation for sustainable infrastructure development in Indonesia. Paper presented at the 2nd International Conference on Sustainable Technology Development, Bali.

Rowe, G., & Wright, G. (1999). The Delphi technique as a forecasting tool: Issues and analysis. *International Journal of Forecasting*, *15*(4), 353–375. doi:10.1016/s0169-2070(99)00018-7

Singh, A. J., & Schmidgall, R. S. (2000). Financing lodging properties. *Cornell Hotel and Restaurant Administration Quarterly*, *41*(4), 39–47.

Skulmoski, G. J., Hartman, F. T., & Krahn, J. (2007). The Delphi method for graduate research. *Journal of Information Technology Education*, *6*, 1–21.

Steurer, J. (2011). The Delphi method: An efficient procedure to generate knowledge. *Skeletal Radiology*, *40*(8), 959–961.

Stoakes, C. (1998). Unlocking Islamic project finance. *Euromoney*, (352), 22.

Wilson, R. (1998). Islamic project finance and private funding schemes. *IIUM Journal of Economics and Management*, *5*(1), 41–60.

# PART III
# DETERMINANTS OF EFFECTIVE ISLAMIC FINANCE CONTRIBUTION – COUNTRY CASE STUDIES

# ISLAMIC BANKS' MERGERS AND ACQUISITIONS – IMPACTS ON PERFORMANCE AND FINANCIAL CRISIS IN THE UNITED KINGDOM

Tarek Kandil and Dababrata Chowdhury


## ABSTRACT

Purpose – *The purpose of this chapter is to reflect the impact of mergers and acquisitions processes on performance of Islamic banking industry in the United Kingdom through studying within.*

Design/methodology/approach – *The present research uses explanatory approach in order to examine the research problems, methodology used in the research is quantitative methods through calculating the long-term share prices performance of the UK Islamic banks' sample. First, the researchers use the control Islamic bank in the event-time approach. The researchers calculate annual abnormal returns using the buy-and-hold abnormal return (BHAR) method over a period of five years, counting from the quarter of a year when the transaction is said to be effective.*


**The Developing Role of Islamic Banking and Finance: From Local to Global Perspectives**
**Contemporary Studies in Economic and Financial Analysis, Volume 95, 119–140**

**ISSN: 1569-3759/doi:10.1108/S1569-3759(2014)0000095016**

Research findings – *The research findings found that there are significant differences in the Islamic mergers and acquisitions post-long-run performance of the UK Islamic banks to the control the crises that face the United Kingdom from 2007 to 2010. However, the acquiring Islamic bank in high-tech industries had a negative effect on their long-term performance.*

Limitations/implications – *The present research has been applied for the Islamic banking industry in the United Kingdom after the Western Europe industry from 2007 to 2010.*

Practical implication – *The main implementations of the present research is valuing UK banks carried out the Islamic mergers and acquisitions of a broad range of management disciplines encompassing the financial, strategic, behavioral, operational, and cross-cultural aspects of this challenging and high-risk activity.*

Originality/value – *The Islamic mergers and acquisitions have placed a significant amount of value added on the motivation of large banks for engaging in banking mergers and acquisitions' transactions.*

**Keywords:** Islamic finance; mergers and acquisitions; banking sector; ROI; ROE

## INTRODUCTION

Our data set consists of the British Islamic banks of England carried out Islamic mergers and acquisitions as a strategic decision of their extension in 2000. We use yearly share returns from the London share price database to calculate long-horizon returns.

Mergers and acquisitions have long been represented an important alternative for organic expansion. However, acquisitions appear to provide at best a mixed performance to the broad range of stakeholders involved. While target Islamic bank shareholders generally enjoy positive short-term returns, investors in bidding Islamic banks frequently experience share price underperformance in the months following acquisition, with negligible overall wealth gains for portfolio holders (Cartwright & Schoenberg, 2006).

The complex phenomenon that mergers and acquisitions represent has attracted the interest and research attention of a broad range of management disciplines encompassing the financial, strategic, behavioral, operational, and cross-cultural aspects of this challenging and high-risk activity. The mergers and acquisitions literature continues to be dominated by financial and market studies, with a high concentration of interest in the United States and United Kingdom (Cartwright & Schoenberg, 2006).

Our initial aim is to reflect the impact of the mergers and acquisitions processes on performance of UK Islamic banks within 14 different types of industries and services (Table 1).

The impacts Theoretical and empirical contributions of Merger and Acquisition on banking performance.

The literature on mergers and acquisitions have placed a significant amount of value added on the motivation of large banks for engaging in banking mergers and acquisitions' transactions. Mergers and acquisitions dealers' banks frequently cite synergy and valuation (the banking mergers and acquisitions' deal having a high return on investment and return on equities in the post financial performance) objectives to justify their financial deals (Hoang & Lapumnuaypon, 2008).

Mahmood et al. (2012) also note additional contribution for Islamic banks in their researches carried on the Islamic banks in Pakistan that there is significant evidence in both practice and research on the motives implied

***Table 1.*** Numbers and Values of UK Islamic Banks Involving in Domestic Mergers and Acquisitions in 1996–2007.

| Industries | Numbers | Values in £bill |
|---|---|---|
| Chemicals and pharmaceuticals | 12 | 8.977 |
| Computers and electronics | 106 | 7.895 |
| Construction | 42 | 16.325 |
| Energy | 28 | 8.89 |
| Engineering | 73 | 11.812 |
| Financial services | 89 | 10.987 |
| Food and drink | 52 | 5.756 |
| Health care | 21 | 8.976 |
| Leisure | 28 | 4.874 |
| Media | 21 | 3.898 |
| Motor | 9 | 1.865 |
| Packaging | 39 | 3.734 |
| Retailing | 51 | 3.956 |
| Transport | 16 | 8.971 |
| *Total* | *587* | *106.916* |

*Source*: National Statistics-Mergers and Acquisitions in the UK 2008 (www.nationalstatisticsuk.co.uk).

by the Islamic banking behaviors for enlarging their synergy among Islamic banks for more mergers (Mahmood et al., 2012). Mahmood et al. (2012) also asserted that banking mergers and acquisitions of Islamic banks is then considered at the macroeconomic level rather than the microeconomic.

Moreover, Natt et al. (2007) take a more pragmatic point of view to identify Islamic motives by referring back to theories but heavily supporting with multiple empirical case studies (Natt et al., 2007). They consider Islamic mergers and acquisitions as a means for Islamic banks to grow quickly and gain because of economies of scale or scope, as they will have a better access to capital market, which later leads to a lower cost of capital, that is, financial benefits. Therefore, the ROI and ROE in mergers Islamic banks will be higher than other types of banks (Natt et al., 2007).

The dominant rationale used to explain Islamic mergers and acquisitions activity is that acquiring Islamic banks seek improved financial performance. It has been widely accepted that the release of important corporate information such as mergers and acquisitions announcements may trigger significant reactions of share prices of the Islamic banks. When the market learns about these kinds of events, the involved share price may immediately climb or fall.

Hence, it appears that the market connects a merger between two Islamic banks with the prospect of future increases or decreases of cash flow. Another way of putting this is that the share price will immediately reflect "the good news" or "the bad news" (Rieck & Doan, 2009). Previous researchers explained why Islamic banks are undertaking mergers and acquisitions. There are two main reasons: efficiency gains and the strategic rationale (Lommerud et al., 2006). The first reason arises through economies of scale or scope, which is due to the increased synergy between the involved Islamic banks. The second reason follows the idea that mergers and acquisitions can change the structure of the market, which in turn affects the Islamic banks' profits. Other reasons could be summarized in reduction of risk and change in Islamic bank focus (Rieck & Doan, 2009).

The following motives are considered to add shareholder value (i) Synergy: This refers to the fact that the combined company can often reduce duplicate departments or operations, lowering the costs of the company relative to the same revenue stream, thus increasing profit (Barney et al., 2001); (ii) Cross-selling: For example, a bank buying a share broker could then sell its banking products to the share broker's customers; (iii) Economies of scale: For example, managerial economies such as the increased opportunity of managerial specialization; (iv) Taxes: A profitable company can buy a losing maker to use the target's loss as their advantage by reducing their tax liability. In the United States and other countries in the Western Europe, the rules are in place to limit the ability of profitable companies to "shop" for loss making companies, limiting the tax motive of an acquiring company. In such a way, they can reduce the taxation in case that the target company achieves losses. The losing companies would, then, be more attractive targets for those acquires in order to reduce tax rate. (v) Geographical or other diversification.

There is a degree of differences and similarity between the UK mergers and acquisitions activities and corporate cycles and the previous researchers that have a typical agreement of a general activity in terms of mergers and acquisitions waves (see Table 2). Theoretically, the global macroeconomic context has an impact on the general level of mergers and acquisitions of any corporation. For instance, the general macroeconomic level determines the corporate profitability and expectation the anticipating period driven by the country stock markets.

The period of time between 1895 to 1903, considers as the monopoly of mergers, and acquisitions, such a stage were explained by a single motivation to merge. Hence, mergers and acquisitions start to structure oligopolistic market formalization from 1920 to 1929. The conglomerate mergers and acquisitions waves have been established as a peak in the mergers activities in the 1960s similar to the mergers of Islamic banks took place in the 1980's. In the 1990s, globalization and competition have raised new waves of mergers and acquisitions as associated with the outcomes of such waves.

In the present work, the researcher attempts to divide this chapter into five sections: the first section discusses the conceptual framework to mergers and acquisitions' waves. The second section is mergers and acquisition theories in terms of the manufacturing and services economics. The third section attempts to discuss mergers and acquisitions theories in the financial economy. The fourth section is concerned with the efficient market hypotheses. The final section discusses the research gap and the conceptual framework of the present study and finally conclusion is presented.

## THE CONCEPTUAL FRAMEWORK TO MERGERS AND ACQUISITIONS' WAVES

The literature review of the previous research has discussed mergers and acquisitions as restructure strategies of corporations as an investment decisions like the other corporate decisions (Budros, 1999). They focus on

***Table 2.*** Mergers and Acquisitions Waves.

| Merger Waves | Main Objectives | Underlying Factors | Characteristics | Reasons for Ending |
|---|---|---|---|---|
| First 1897–1904 | Merging for monopoly | Technological developments like:<br>Transcontinental Railroads<br>Electricity<br>Rapid economic expansion<br>Lax antitrust enforcement | Horizontal mergers<br>Heavy manufacturing industry | Majority of mergers failed – didn't achieve increase in efficiency<br>Economic recession in 1903<br>Stock market crash in 1904 |
| Second 1916–1929 | Merging for oligopoly | Post-World War I economic boom<br>Lax margin requirements<br>Technological developments<br>Government encouraged Islamic banks to work together during WWI, maintained this policy in 1920s | Produced fewer monopolies, rather oligopolies, vertical mergers, and conglomerates (usually related) | October 29, 1929 stock market crash<br>Great depression 1940s |
| Third 1965–1969 | Conglomerate mergers | Booming economy<br>Rising stock prices<br>High interest rates<br>Tough antitrust enforcement<br>Management science developments<br>Financial manipulations | Primarily conglomerate mergers<br>Some bidders smaller than targets<br>Primarily equity-financed – investment banks did not play central role | Attorney General announced plans to crack down on conglomerates in 1968 |
| Fifth 1992–2000 | Strategic restructuring | Expanding economy, rising stock prices<br>Technological developments<br>Globalization<br>Deregulation | Emphasized longer term strategy rather than immediate financial gains<br>More often financed with equity than debt | Bursting of stock market bubble<br>Economic slowdown<br>Loyalty challenges |

*Source*: National Statistics-Mergers and Acquisitions in the UK 2008 (Nogueira & Porteous, 2003).

the expected role of the mergers and acquisitions decisions to be similar to those influencing other forms of expenses such as fixed cost of capital structure (Gertsen et al., 1998). In the UK mergers and acquisitions structure, expenditure forms capital investment as fixed and stable proportion. In the UK corporations, it is clear that their investment appraisal takes into account the internal and the external expansion of the Islamic banks (Auster & Sirower, 2002).

## ISLAMIC MERGERS AND ACQUISITION THEORIES AND THE MANUFACTURING AND SERVICES ECONOMICS

The official and formal analyses of corporate mergers and acquisitions have been rising up by highlighting the theories of mergers and acquisitions between control and ownership of the modern corporation. If corporate managers act positively in the interest issues of shareholders, mergers and acquisitions no longer will act against managerial interests of the Islamic banks' shareholders by engaging in merger activity. Corporate managers might direct the competition in product markets and accrue benefits to their sides and benefits by engaging in nonprofit maximizing behavior (Vennet, 1996). That happened during the *Far East* financial crises in the early 2000s (Conyon et al. (2002)). The corporate general managers act solely against the corporate shareholders' interests of which the way they, on purpose, can achieve up normal returns during the financial crises.

Therefore, the rules and regulations of corporate governance were established in such area (Piloff & Santomero, 1998).

## WHAT DO SHAREHOLDERS NEED FROM ISLAMIC MERGERS AND ACQUISITIONS?

In general, shareholders want any type of growth in their shares' profits. Their main point should be highlighted in the issue of shareholders' needs (Goyal & Joshi, 2011): (1) The growth in cash and earnings in which the shareholders are looking for from mergers and acquisitions? Close revisions of mergers and acquisitions literature state that most of the previous researches have concentrated on impacts of post-mergers and acquisitions, especially, in relation to increased shareholder wealth (Goyal & Joshi, 2011). (2) The shareholders' expected time of their cash flow returns. (3) The risk rate that the shareholders are willing to accept of those cash flows? (4) The measuring tools that used in tracking and accurately reporting the progress of the post mergers and acquisitions' performance?

The empirical evidences indicate that Islamic banks that merge and then divest often perform well in the interim period. Kaplan and Weisbach (1992) argue that many acquisitions are not failures from an ex post perspective and suggest that an acquirer may sell a business it has improved or a business that it once had synergies with but no longer does (Kaplan & Weisbach, 1992). In addition, recent evidence from the 1960s conglomerate merger wave shows that Islamic banks involved in conglomerate mergers over that period were more likely to be financially distressed than Islamic banks involved in related mergers (Otero-Serrano, 2011).

An Islamic merger can be viewed as a technology that allows marginally profitable projects, which investors would otherwise reject, to obtain financing. As a result, some Islamic banks operate below their potential and consequently have low efficiency. Such Islamic banks are likely to be acquired by other, more efficient Islamic banks in the same industry. This is because Islamic banks with greater efficiency would be able to identify Islamic banks with good potential operating at lower efficiency. They would also have the managerial ability to improve the latter's performance (Otero-Serrano, 2011).

## FINANCIAL LEVERAGE CHANGES AROUND ISLAMIC MERGERS AND ACQUISITIONS

The previous studies empirically examine whether Islamic banks increase financial leverage following mergers. The results are an increase in financial leverage could arise due to two potential reasons, which are not mutually exclusive, an increase in debt capacity, and unused debt capacity of target and acquiring Islamic banks from pre-merger years. An increase in financial leverage benefits shareholders of merging Islamic banks through the tax deductibility of interest payments on corporate debt (Ghosh & Jain, 2000).

Moreover, they found that if Islamic bank's size and industry are surrogates for Islamic banks' debt capacity, then the optimal financial leverage of the target and acquiring Islamic bank will be given by a "typical" Islamic bank that represents the industries of the two merging Islamic banks and is close to their combined Islamic bank size. It is possible that the increase in financial leverage is the result of exhausting unused debt capacity from pre-merger years, rather than an increase in debt capacity (Majumder et al., 2000). Moreover, unused debt capacity is not correlated with wealth gains around merger announcements (Ghosh & Jain, 2000)

The announcement period's market-adjusted returns, in the cross-sectional analysis, are positively related to the increases in financial leverage following mergers. The results support the argument that the share market incorporates future benefits from anticipated financial leverage increases around the announcement date (Majumder et al., 2000).

An increase in leverage following mergers might also enhance shareholder wealth through an expropriation of wealth from bondholders. An immediate consequence of a higher debt capacity following mergers is the co-insurance effect – existing bondholders are better off because debt becomes relatively safer evidence of tax benefits from mergers (Ghosh & Jain, 2000).

## HYPOTHESIS DEVELOPMENT

According to the resource-based theory of the Islamic bank synergy, two directions can be distinguished. The first is based on finance theory and investigates the degree of market segmentation or market integration. The second takes into account the financial development and looks into the maturity of the markets and their institutions.

One may expect that the news of the merger announcement (i.e., new information) will have the highest impact in the markets that are most developed. This results from the fact that in these markets new information will have a larger impact on share prices than in less developed markets (Fama, 1991). Bert and Wit (2004) reveal that corporate mergers have had different effect in different markets.

The literature evaluates a merger based on the initial market reaction to the merger announcement (Jensen & Ruback, 1983) and on the long-run returns to the merger (Loughran & Vijh, 1997). The empirical studies have not always documented positive wealth effects for acquiring Islamic banks' shareholders. Merger activity comes in waves and returns to acquiring Islamic banks depend, among others, on the method of payment (Travlos, 1987), on the acquirer's book-to-market ratio (Rau & Vermaelen, 1998) and size (Moeller et al., 2004), and type of target (Fuller et al., 2002). A more recent strand of the literature attempts to link takeover activity with share market performance (high merger activity is correlated with high share market valuations as shown by Jovanovic & Rousseau, 2001).

Empirically, there are attempts to expose some differences among types of corporate industries in every single market in the long-term performance. For example, the Islamic bank's operating performance in the long term, traded on the Tokyo stock exchange during 1969 to 1999, was significantly greater following mergers of Islamic banks operating in different industries (Timothy et al., 2007). However, the acquiring Islamic bank in high-tech industries had a negative effect on their long-term performance (Myriam, 2006). Hence, the first hypothesis is as follows:

**H1:** The Islamic mergers and acquisitions post-long-run performance differs from sample Islamic banks to the control Islamic banks according to the industry that sample Islamic banks operate in.

Ghosh and Jain (2000) use the financial leverage of industry and size matched Islamic banks as a second measure of debt capacity. It is possible that either the acquirer, or the target, or both have unused debt capacity from pre-merger years. The increase in financial leverage could result from utilization of past unused debt capacity rather than an increase in debt capacity.

Galai and Masulis (1976) argue that although merging Islamic banks are able to reduce risk because of the co-insurance effect, the total value of the merged Islamic bank remains unchanged. A reduction in risk increases the value of existing debt, but it also reduces equity value. Since equity is an option on the face value of outstanding debt, its value decreases with a decrease in variability. The increase in the value of debt is offset by the decrease in the value of equity. Based on the above argument, our second hypothesis is as follows:

**H2:** The post-long-run performance of mergers and acquisitions is affected by financial leverage of the sample Islamic banks according to the size of the Islamic banks.

## METHODOLOGY AND DATA

### *Post-Merger and Acquisition Performance*

It is widely accepted that, in measuring the long-run performance of Islamic banks after significant events, such as mergers and acquisitions, the use of operating cash flows was accepted by other previous studies (Barber & Lyon, 1996) while other measures, such as earnings (Erickson & Wang, 1999), provide some evidences, which suggest earnings manipulation is practiced by managers of acquiring Islamic banks in share for share mergers. Others use short-term event studies (Fama et al., 1969). The same is not true for long-term studies aimed at evaluating the extent to which gains reported by financial markets at the time of mergers and acquisitions announcement are later maintained. Kothari and Warner (1997), Barber and Lyon (1996, 1997), Lyon, Barber, and Tsai (1999), and Mitchell and Stafford (2000) specifically question the validity of the usual parametric tests for detecting abnormal long-term returns. According to Barber and Lyon (1997), the results obtained through these methods are very sensitive to financial performance calculation and benchmark methods.

We use two methodologies to calculate the long-term share prices performance of our sample Islamic banks. First, we use the control Islamic bank in the event-time approach proposed by Barber and Lyon (1997a) and Lyon, Barber, and Tsai (1999). We calculate annual abnormal returns using the *Buy-and-hold abnormal return (BHAR)* method over a period of five years, counting from the quarter of a year when the transaction is said to be effective.

## CONTROL VARIABLES

### *The Industry Effect*

This variable captures the similarities between the merged and nonmerged Islamic banks and the similarities between the acquirer and the target. Islamic banks are said to be similar when the target Islamic bank operates in the same industry as the acquiring Islamic bank.

### *Islamic Bank Size*

We measure the size by the magnitude of revenues, using the natural logarithm of total revenues. We use the median as the cut-off point between small and large Islamic banks. Following Markides and Ittner (1994), we use this variable to identify the impact of the acquiring Islamic bank's size on the abnormal returns generated. Eckbo and Thorburn (2000) suggest that the gains obtained highly diluted when the size of the merged Islamic banks are relatively large compared to nonmerged Islamic banks.

## FINANCIAL LEVERAGE

Financial leverage of combined Islamic banks increases significantly following mergers. A cross-sectional analysis shows that the change in financial leverage around mergers is significantly positively correlated with the announcement period market-adjusted returns (Ghosh & Jain, 2000).

Islamic financial leverages measured as the fiscal year-end ratio of debt to total Islamic bank value. Debt is defined as the book of long-term debt and debt included in current liabilities as reported in the Compustat tapes. Total Islamic bank value is computed as the book value of debt plus the market value of equity (Ghosh & Jain, 2000).

Previous researchers argue that Islamic finance, among other factors, is an important determinant of debt capacity (Titman & Wessels, 1988). We will follow Ghosh and Jain (2000) who use the financial leverage of industry and size matched Islamic banks as a second measure of debt capacity. Islamic banks are matched on the combined size of the target and acquiring Islamic banks one year prior to the merger from their industries using market value of the Islamic bank as a proxy for size. If size is positively related to debt capacity, financial leverage of nonmerging Islamic banks will be higher than the pro-forma leverage of merging Islamic banks. This is because Islamic banks matched on the combined size of target and acquiring Islamic banks will be able to borrow more than the amount nonmerged Islamic banks can borrow.

## DATA

Our empirical tests are based on a sample of mergers and acquisitions involving of UK banks which have Islamic financial services occurred in the period from 1999 to 2009 before and after the financial crisis of Europe using the year 2000 as a cut-of-point year.

Our data set consists of UK Islamic banks carried out mergers and acquisition as a strategic decision of their extension in 2000. We use yearly share returns from the London Share Price Database to calculate long-horizon returns. Data on market capitalization and the book-to-market (BTM) ratio are from the London Stock Prices Database and the World scope database, respectively.

We apply several criteria to choose the sample recommended by (Ericson et al., 2004). We include transactions which are (1) completed,

(2) over £100 million in value, (3) where the acquirer and target partially have shares after the transaction, and (4) acquirer is publicly traded (Ericson et al., 2004).

We use the announcement date of the acquisition in constructing the sample. The acquirer Islamic banks are then matched with available share market returns data from DataStream.

## SAMPLE

This chapter provides evidence on the importance of strategic corporate extension that comes from mergers and acquisitions value of by documenting the long-run share price performance of mergers and acquisitions Islamic banks in the United Kingdom. The analysis is based *on a sample of 87* UK banks dealt with Islamic financial services, which have involved in mergers and acquisitions in 2000. We measure share price performance of mergers and acquisitions' Islamic banks relative to benchmarks consisting of a set of control Islamic banks that have not carried out mergers and acquisitions in 2006. Table 2 shows merged Islamic banks from 1999 to 2009.

## FINDINGS

One of most well-established modeling techniques is a multiple regression. It is appropriate when the dependent variable is continuous. Independent variables can be continuous or categorical (Tarling, 2009). A multiple regression model is a model that has two or more independent variables (Kahane et al., 2001). A multiple regression model has two main uses: prediction and casual analysis. In prediction it aims to develop a formula to predict the dependent variable based on independent variable observed values. For casual analysis, a multiple regression model is used to determine whether particular independent variables really affect the dependent one and how significant is that effect (Mostashari et al., 2001). Where multiple regression is a logical extension of simple regression with several predictors. It is calculated by the equation (Field, 2009; Mostashari et al., 2001):

$$y_i = \alpha + \beta_1 x_1 + \beta_2 x_2 + \beta_3 x_3 + \beta_4 x_4 + \varepsilon_i$$

where:

$y$ is the dependent variable (outcome variable)
$x_1$, $x_2$, $x_3$, and $x_4$ are the independent variables (predictors)
$\alpha$ is a constant called the intercept
$\beta_1$, $\beta_2$, $\beta_3$, and $\beta_4$ are the regression coefficients
$\varepsilon$ is the error term (the difference the difference between the score predicted by the participant i and the actual obtained score of that participant).

The first step in conducting multiple regression is to check the linear relationship among variables. The variables in this study are ROE, ROI, merger–nonmerger, and industry. The first two variables are interval data while the last two are dichotomous. ROE and ROI data are calculated as the average values calculated from the data of years 1996 to 2008. The study seeks to measure the impact of the Islamic banks merged or not ($x_1$) and sector of industry ($x_2$) on their ROE ($y_1$) and ROI ($y_2$).

## LINEAR ASSOCIATION

The first assumption of linear regression is there is a linear association among $x$ and $y$ variables. Running bivariate correlation, the correlation matrix in Table 3 shows that there is a linear relationship among variables.

From Table 3, it is shown that there is a positive linear association between meger–nonmerger Islamic banks and ROE and ROI where $R=0.260$ and $P<0.01$ and $R=0.261$ and $P<0.01$, respectively. While a positive relationship was found between industry sector and ROE and ROI where $R=0.239$, $P<0.05$ and $R=0.235$ and $P<0.05$, respectively. $N$ is 101

***Table 3.*** A Linear Relationship among Variables.

| | | Merger and Nonmerger Islamic Banks | Industry Sector |
|---|---|---|---|
| ROE | Pearson correlation | 0.260** | 0.239* |
| | Significance (2-tailed) | 0.009 | 0.016 |
| | *N* | 101 | 101 |
| ROI | Pearson correlation | 0.261** | 0.235* |
| | Significance (2-tailed) | 0.008 | 0.018 |
| | *N* | 101 | 101 |

*significancy in level 0.001, **significancy in level 0.05.

cases for correlation statistics. The first assumption supposing that there is a linear association between variables is valid.

## REGRESSION MODEL

To calculate the above mentioned equation of multiple regression model, the hypotheses of $\beta$ should be made:

$H_0$: $\beta_1 = 0$ and alternative hypothesis $H_A$: $\beta_1 \neq 0$
$H_0$: $\beta_2 = 0$ and alternative hypothesis $H_A$: $\beta_2 \neq 0$

Regression model: ROE
The first regression model relates with measuring the relationship among merger–nonmerger ($x_1$), industry sector ($x_2$), and ROE ($y_1$).

$$\text{ROE} = \alpha + \beta_1 \text{ merger} - \text{nonmerger} + \beta_2 \text{ industry sector} + \varepsilon_i$$

From Table 4 it is clear that all $\beta$ coefficients are not equal to zero which means rejecting the null hypothesis, where $t$ for $x_1 = 2.325$, $x_2 = 2.065$, and $P < 0.05$ for all $x$ variables. Checking collinearity, from Table 4, it is clear that VIF for all variables < 4 which means no need for further investigation.
Building upon Table 4:

$$\text{ROE} = -105.623 + 69.296 \text{ merger} - \text{non merger} + 63.547 \text{ industry sector} + \varepsilon_i$$

Furthermore, to check condition index, Table 5 shows that all indices <3 which means no serious problems.
To know exactly how much independent variables affect or change the ROE (as a dependent variable), $R^2$ value should be calculated as shown in

***Table 4.*** Regression Output.

| Model | Unstandardized Coefficients | | Standardized Coefficients | *T* | Significance | 95.0% Confidence Interval for *B* | | Collinearity Statistics | |
|---|---|---|---|---|---|---|---|---|---|
| | *B* | Standard error | Beta | | | Lower bound | Upper bound | Tolerance | VIF |
| Constant | −105.623 | 26.676 | | −3.96 | 0.00 | −158.560 | −52.686 | | |
| Merger/nonmerger | 69.296 | 29.810 | 0.225 | 2.32 | 0.02 | 10.139 | 128.454 | 0.971 | 1.03 |
| Industry | 63.547 | 30.766 | 0.200 | 2.06 | 0.04 | 2.493 | 124.602 | 0.971 | 1.03 |

Dependent variable: ROE.

**Table 5.** Collinearity Diagnostics.

| Model | Dimension | Eigenvalue | Condition Index | Variance Proportions | | |
|---|---|---|---|---|---|---|
| | | | | Constant | Merger and nonmerger | Industry |
| 1 | 1 | 2.426 | 1.000 | 0.04 | 0.06 | 0.05 |
| | 2 | 0.376 | 2.538 | 0.03 | 0.82 | 0.31 |
| | 3 | 0.198 | 3.500 | 0.92 | 0.12 | 0.64 |

Dependent variable: ROE.

**Table 6.** Model Summary.

| Model | $R$ | $R^2$ | Adjusted $R^2$ | Standard Error of the Estimate | Durbin-Watson |
|---|---|---|---|---|---|
| 1 | 0.326[a] | 0.106 | 0.088 | 147.57616 | 2.077 |

Predictors: Constant, industry, merger and nonmerger Islamic banks. Dependent variable: ROE.

**Table 7.** $F$-Test for the Significance of Regression Model.

| Model | | Sum of Squares | Df | Mean Square | $F$ | Significance |
|---|---|---|---|---|---|---|
| 1 | Regression | 253,841.575 | 2 | 126,920.788 | 5.828 | 0.004[a] |
| | Residual | 2,134,314.830 | 98 | 21,778.723 | | |
| | Total | 2,388,156.406 | 100 | | | |

[a]Predictors: Constant, industry, merger and nonmerger Islamic banks. Dependent variable: ROE.

Table 6. $R^2$ is "Co-efficient of Determination" or in other words the proportion of variance that is explained by the regression model. It is shown that $R^2$ value is (0.106) and that means that the regression model of $x$ variables explains 10.6% of the variation in ROE. That leads to validate the second assumption where ROE is changed/affected by level of changes in $x$ variables. Furthermore, this leads to reject the null hypothesis says that $H_0$: $R^2 = 0$.

To test the significance of linear relationship between $x$ variables and $y$, $F$-test is used as shown in Table 7.

From Table 7, it is clear that $F_{2,98} = 5.828$ and $P < 0.01$ and this means that there is a significant relationship between $x$ variables and ROE; therefore, null hypothesis can be rejected.

Looking at Figs. 1 and 2, it appears that residuals appear to be normally distributed from the Histogram of the Residuals and the P-P plot and this validates the assumption of normality.

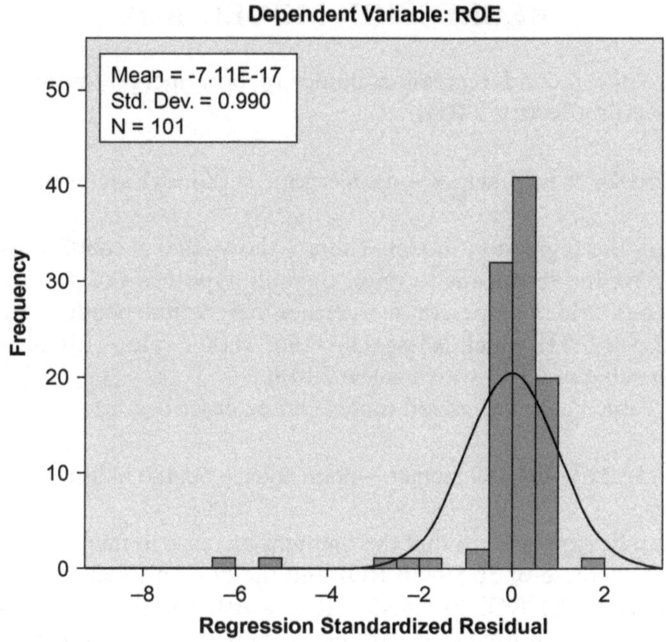


*Fig. 1.* Histogram of Regression Residual.

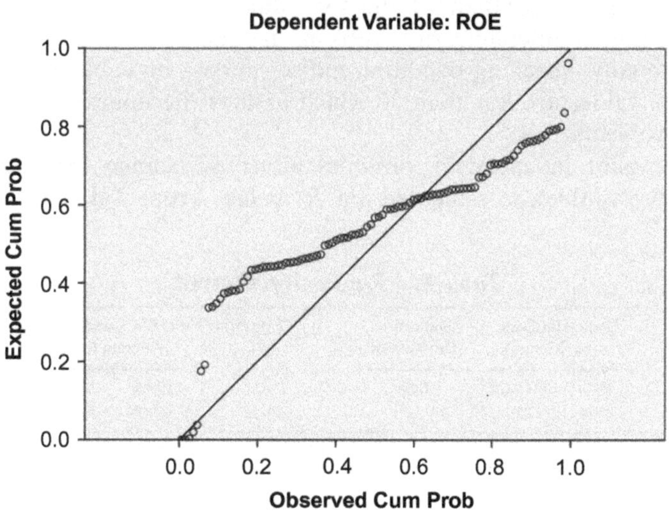


*Fig. 2.* Plot of Regression Residual.

## REGRESSION MODEL: ROI

Moving to the second regression model of how merger–nonmerger and industry sector affects the ROI:

$$\text{ROI} = \alpha + \beta_1 \text{ merger} - \text{nonmerger} + \beta_2 \text{ industry sector} + \varepsilon_i$$

Running the regression model, Table 7 shows that $\beta$ coefficients are not equal to zero and that leads to reject the null hypothesis of $\beta_1$ and $\beta_2 = 0.0$. It is obvious that $t$ value for merger/nonmerger independent variable is 2.347 and $p$ of 0.021 which is less than 0.05, while $t$ value of industry sector is 2.018, $p$ value of 0.046 which is less 2.018.

Using Table 8, the regression model can be described as:

$$\text{ROI} = -52.212 + 56.899 \text{ merger} - \text{nonmerger} + 50.480 \text{ industry sector} + \varepsilon_i$$

That can be expressed in that the one-unit increase in merger–nonmerger leads to an increase of 56.899 in ROI and the one-unit increase in industry sector increases the ROI by 50.480. It is worth mentioning here that the one-unit increases in predictor variables means that Islamic banks become merger and manufacturing sector. To ensure that there is no association between independent variables, collinearity investigation shows that tolerance values are greater than 0.1 and VIF values are less than 4 which means that there is no multicollinearity problems in data.

Additionally, checking condition indices appear in Table 9 depicts that all indices values are less than 30 which assures the nonexistence of collinearity problems.

The amount independent variables affect or change the ROE (as a dependent variable), is estimated via $R^2$ value. From Table 10, $R^2$ value

***Table 8.*** Regression Output.

| Model | Unstandardized Coefficients | | Standardized Coefficients | $t$ | Significance | 95.0% Confidence Interval for $B$ | | Collinearity Statistics | |
|---|---|---|---|---|---|---|---|---|---|
| | $B$ | Standard error | Beta | | | Lower bound | Upper bound | Tolerance | VIF |
| Constant | −52.212 | 21.689 | | −2.40 | 0.018 | −95.254 | −9.170 | | |
| Merger/nonmerger | 56.899 | 24.23 | 0.228 | 2.34 | 0.021 | 8.799 | 104.99 | 0.971 | 1.03 |
| Industry | 50.480 | 25.01 | 0.196 | 2.01 | 0.046 | 0.837 | 100.12 | 0.971 | 1.03 |

Dependent variable: ROI.

***Table 9.*** Collinearity Diagnostics.

| Model | Dimension | Eigenvalue | Condition Index | Variance Proportions | | |
|---|---|---|---|---|---|---|
| | | | | Constant | Merger and nonmerger | Industry |
| 1 | 1 | 2.426 | 1.000 | 0.04 | 0.06 | 0.05 |
| | 2 | 0.376 | 2.538 | 0.03 | 0.82 | 0.31 |
| | 3 | 0.198 | 3.500 | 0.92 | 0.12 | 0.64 |

Dependent variable: ROI.

***Table 10.*** Model Summary.

| Model | $R$ | $R^2$ | Adjusted $R^2$ | Standard Error of the Estimate | Durbin-Watson |
|---|---|---|---|---|---|
| 1 | 0.325[a] | 0.105 | 0.087 | 119.99103 | 1.926 |

[a]Predictors: Constant, industry, merger and nonmerger Islamic banks. Dependent variable: ROI.

***Table 11.*** *F*-Test for the Significance of Regression Model.

| Model | | Sum of Squares | Df | Mean Square | $F$ | Significance |
|---|---|---|---|---|---|---|
| 1 | Regression | 166,196.174 | 2 | 83,098.087 | 5.772 | 0.004[a] |
| | Residual | 1,410,988.947 | 98 | 14,397.846 | | |
| | Total | 1,577,185.121 | 100 | | | |

[a]Predictors: Constant, industry, merger and nonmerger Islamic banks. Dependent variable: ROI.

(the proportion of variance that is explained by the regression model) is (0.105). This means that the regression model of $x$ variables explains 10.5% of the variation in ROI. That validates the assumption of ROI is changed/affected by level of changes in $x$ variables. Furthermore, this leads to reject the null hypothesis says that $H_0$: $R^2 = 0$.

To test the significance of linear relationship between merger–nonmerger Islamic banks and industry sectors as independent variables and ROI as dependent variable, *F*-test is used as shown in Table 11. It is clear that $F_{2,98} = 5.772$ and $P < 0.01$ and this means that there is a significant relationship between merger–nonmerger and industry sector variables and ROI; therefore, null hypothesis can be rejected where there is no significant relationship between independent and dependent variables.

To check the assumption of normality, Figs. 3 and 4 show that appear to be normally distributed from the Histogram of the Residuals and the P-P plot and this validates the assumption of normality.

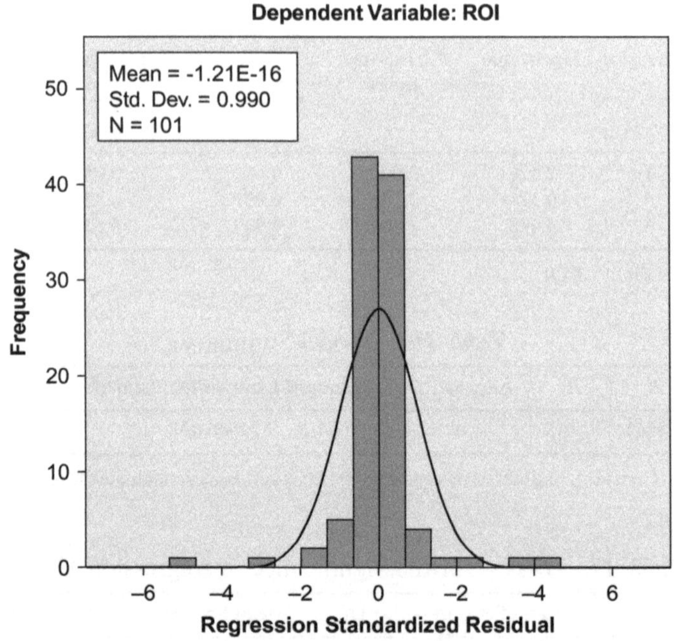


*Fig. 3.* Histogram of Regression Residual.

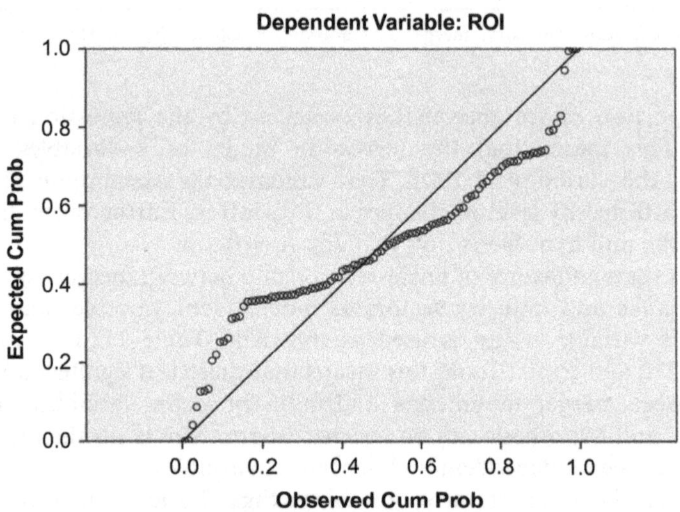


*Fig. 4.* Plot of Regression Residual.

## CONCLUSION

The overall relationship between ROE and the two predictor variables of merger–nonmerger and industry sector is significant ($F_{2,98} = 5.828$ and $P < 0.01$ and $R^2 = 10.6\%$). The regression model is: ROE = −105.623 + 69.296 merger–nonmerger + 63.547 industry sector. All the predictor variables in the model were significant; merger–nonmerger ($t = 2.325$, and $P < 0.05$), industry sector ($t = 2.065$, and $P < 0.05$). With variables held constant, ROE increased by 69.296 for every one-unit increase in merger–nonmerger; 63.547 for every one-unit increase in industry sector. Assumption of normality was explored and no serious violations were detected (Mostashari et al., 2001).

For the second regression model of ROI (outcome variable) and merger–nonmerger Islamic banks and industry sector (predictor variables), it is found that there is a significant relationship where $F_{2,98} = 5.772$ and $P < 0.01$ and $R^2 = 10.5\%$. The regression model is ROI = −52.212 + 56.899 merger–nonmerger + 50.480 industry sector. The predictors in the model were significant; merger–nonmerger ($t = 2.347$, and $P < 0.05$), industry sector ($t = 2.018$ and $P < 0.05$). With variables held constant, ROI increased by 56.899 for every one-unit increase in merger–nonmerger; 50.480 for every one-unit increase in Islamic banking sector (Mostashari et al., 2001); assumption of normality was explored and no serious violations were detected.

## REFERENCES


Auster, E. R., & Sirower, M. L. (2002). The dynamics of merger and acquisition waves a three-stage conceptual framework with implications for practice. *The Journal of Applied Behavioral Science*, *38*(2), 216–244.

Barney, J., et al. (2001). The resource-based view of the firm: Ten years after 1991. *Journal of management*, *27*(6), 625–641.

Budros, A. (1999). A conceptual framework for analyzing why organizations downsize. *Organization Science*, *10*(1), 69–82.

Cartwright, S., & Schoenberg, R. (2006). Thirty years of mergers and acquisitions research: Recent advances and future opportunities. *British Journal of Management*, *17*(S1), S1–S5.

Conyon, M. J., et al. (2002). The impact of mergers and acquisitions on company employment in the United Kingdom. *European Economic Review*, *46*(1), 31–49.

Ericson, L. M., et al. (2004). Macroscopic, neat, single-walled carbon nanotube fibers. *Science*, *305*(5689), 1447–1450.

Field, A. (2009). *Discovering statistics using SPSS*. London: Sage.

Gertsen, M. C., et al. (1998). Different approaches to the understanding of culture in mergers and acquisitions. *De Gruyter Studies in Organization*, 17–38.

Ghosh, A., & Jain, P. C. (2000). Financial leverage changes associated with corporate mergers. *Journal of Corporate Finance*, *6*(4), 377–402.

Goyal, K., & Joshi, V. (2011). Mergers in banking industry of India: Some emerging issues. *Asian Journal of Business and Management Sciences*, *1*(2), 157–165.

Hoang, T. V. N. & Lapumnuaypon, K. (2008). *Critical success factors in merger & acquisition projects: A study from the perspectives of advisory firms*. Warren Gorham & Lamont of RIA, USA: Umeå University.

Jensen, M. C., & Ruback, R. S. (1983). The market for corporate control: The scientific evidence. *Journal of Financial Economics*, *11*(1), 5–50.

Kahane, N., et al. (2001). The third wave of myotome colonization by mitotically competent progenitors: Regulating the balance between differentiation and proliferation during muscle development. *Development*, *128*(12), 2187–2198.

Kaplan, S. N., & Weisbach, M. S. (1992). The success of acquisitions: Evidence from divestitures. *The Journal of Finance*, *47*(1), 107–138.

Lommerud, K. E., et al. (2006). *Cross border mergers and strategic trade policy with two-part taxation: Is international policy coordination beneficial?* Discussion Papers, WZB, Wissenschaftszentrum Berlin für Sozialforschung, Schwerpunkt Märkte und Politik, Abteilung Marktprozesse und Steuerung.

Loughran, T., & Vijh, A. M. (1997). Do long-term shareholders benefit from corporate acquisitions? *The Journal of Finance*, *52*(5), 1765–1790.

Mahmood, I., et al. (2012). Impact of merger/acquisition on share price-a case study of Pakistan. *European Journal of Scientific Research*, *67*(4), 617–624.

Majumder, S., et al. (2000). A pilot study on the use of autofluorescence spectroscopy for diagnosis of the cancer of human oral cavity. *Current Science*, *79*(8), 1089–1094.

Markides, C., & Ittner, C. D. (1994). Shareholder benefits from corporate international diversification: Evidence from US international acquisitions. *Journal of International Business Studies*, *2*, 343–367.

Mostashari, F., et al. (2001). Epidemic west nile encephalitis, New York, 1999: Results of a household-based seroepidemiological survey. *The Lancet*, *358*(9278), 261–264.

Natt, A., et al. (2007). *A proposed framework for human capital development in the Islamic financial services industry*. Knowledge Economy and Management Congress, Istanbul, Turkey.

Nogueira, M. J. M. & Porteous, D. (2003). The socio-cultural characteristics and needs of a Portuguese community in south London. In G. Abreu, T. Cline, & H. Lambert (Eds.), *Tlie Education of Portuguese Children in Britain: Insights from Research and Practice in England and Overseas* (pp. 51–74). London: Department of Basic Education and Calouste Gulbenkian Foundation, 2003.

Otero-Serrano, J. (2011). Does firm diversification represent a value added for stockholders? *International Journal of Business and Finance Research*, *5*(4), 99–113.

Piloff, S. J. & Santomero, A. M. (1998). The value effects of bank mergers and acquisitions. In Y. Amihud & G. Miller (Eds.), *Bank mergers and acquisitions* (pp. 59–78). Boston, MA: Kluwer Academic Publishers.

Rieck, O., & Doan, C. T. (2009). Shareholder wealth effects of mergers and acquisitions in the telecommunications industry. *Telecommunication markets* (pp. 363–394). Warren Gorham & Lamont of RIA, USA: Springer.

Tarling, R. (2009). *Statistical modelling for social researchers: Principles and practice*. USA: Taylor & Francis.

Vennet, R. V. (1996). The effect of mergers and acquisitions on the efficiency and profitability of EC credit institutions. *Journal of Banking & Finance*, *20*(9), 1531–1558.

# ATTITUDE OF MUSLIMS AND NON-MUSLIMS TOWARDS ISLAMIC BANKING – AN EXPLORATORY STUDY IN INDIA

Mohammad Faisal, Asif Akhtar and Asad Rehman

## ABSTRACT

Purpose – *India is a home to the second largest Muslim population in the world. It is equally crucial to understand the attitude of non-Muslim population towards the interest-free banking in India. The firms desirous of entering into this nascent field in India are required to know the aspirations and motivations of both Muslims and non-Muslims with respect to interest-free banking. For a large number of Muslims interest-free banking may be a matter of adhering to their faith, but for the non-Muslim customers it has to address real issues like security, risk minimisation, profitability, etc.*

Design/methodology/approach – *The present study is an attempt to understand the perceptions of Indian customers towards Islamic banking. For this purpose, a representative sample of 259 respondents is surveyed with the help of a structured questionnaire developed for this purpose.*

**The Developing Role of Islamic Banking and Finance: From Local to Global Perspectives**
**Contemporary Studies in Economic and Financial Analysis, Volume 95, 141–162**

**ISSN: 1569-3759/doi:10.1108/S1569-3759(2014)0000095017**

Findings – *It has been found that there are differences in the attitude of Muslims and non-Muslims towards Islamic banking. Surprisingly both groups have a similar perception about the institutions of Islamic banking. Findings of the study reveal that the attitude of Indian customers can be classified into factors like awareness, ideology, implementation, features and institutions. Therefore, such factors should be considered seriously by the Islamic banks in designing their marketing strategies.*

Research limitations/implication – *This is a survey-based study. Hence a representative sample is mandatory. Due care has been taken to arrive at a sample size which is representative of the population; however, a large sample size shall lead to better results.*

Practical implications – *This study can help decision makers to identify the major factors that may shape the attitude of Indian customers towards Islamic banks. This should also be of some help to the management of commercial banks in devising appropriate marketing strategies for reaching and attracting young customers.*

Originality/value – *The originality of this study lies in the fact that it is a pioneering study in the Indian context which brings out the attitudinal differences between Muslims and non-Muslims with respect to Islamic banking. Further, the classification of attitude of Indian customers into factors like awareness, ideology, implementation, features and institutions adds to the originality of the study. Both these aspects of this study add value to the existing literature in the field of Islamic banking.*

**Keywords:** Islamic banking; Sharia'h; attitude

## INTRODUCTION

Islamic banking is fast emerging as an alternative financial system in the world. This phenomenon has registered exponential growth in last two decades (1990–2000 and 2000–2010). The recent global financial crisis and its impact on the conventional banking have further given impetus to the concept of Islamic banking as an alternative system of banking. The concept of interest-free financing was practised by Arabs prior to the advent of Islam, and was later adopted by Muslims as an acceptable form of trade financing. Though the system of interest-free financing has been used on a small scale for centuries, its commercial application began in the 1970s (Naser & Moutinho, 1997).

Islamic banking refers to a system of banking or banking activity that is consistent with the principles of Islamic law (Sharia'h) referred to as fiqh muamalat (Islamic rules on transactions), and guided by Islamic economics. Islamic banking is often thought to be financing the needs of the Muslim community alone, but this notion as it will be seen, is far from the reality. With the rapid growth of the global economy along with the economic expansion in the Islamic countries, interest-free banking is evolving to play a vital role in today's global village. Islamic banking in the Middle Eastern countries has witnessed exponential growth in the past few years. Despite the global economic slowdown, the Islamic banking industry has been continuously growing in double digits. The Islamic banking sector is gradually building momentum and popularity around the world, and is expected to lead the re-emergence of the overall global financial industry over the next five years.

Some of the features of Islamic investments have always held an appeal for the non-Muslim investors. This may be attributable to the fact that Islamic funds and investors screen out those companies which take part in activities that are considered unethical by the Sharia'h. According to the Islamic law the companies that are overleveraged or rely too heavily on accounts receivable are screened out which may appeal to a large number of non-Muslim investors who are concerned with issues of accountability and social responsibility. In the words of Steven Amos, head of marketing the Islamic Bank of Britain, 'Our core business will always be Muslims, but the numbers of non-Muslims are really picking up. We've had massive interest – and that's down to a number of reasons, all of which have kept us insulated from the credit crunch'.[1]

India is reported by the World Bank as the second largest growing economy of the world. The Indian economy entered a new growth phase since 2003 with an average growth rate of 8.6 per cent compared to an average growth rate of 5.7 per cent in the decade between 1993–1994 and 2002–2003. Since the second quarter of 2008–2009, however, there has been a deceleration in growth reflecting the effects of global economic slowdown. The GDP growth in 2010–2011 was 8.5 per cent (*The Economic Times*, 22 March 2011). India with the largest Muslim population in the world is one of the biggest and untouched markets for Islamic banking and Sharia'h compliant financial services. Islamic finance has debuted in the Indian republic in the form of Sharia'h compliant equities, commodities and mutual funds. There are some Sharia'h friendly insurance products also available in the Indian financial market.

In India, Jamaat-E-Islami Hind[2] started the practice of interest-free loans in 1968 (Erol & El-Bdour, 1989). In the year 2008 Kerala became the first Indian state to permit the NBFCs (Non-Banking Financial Companies) to operate according to Islamic principles. TASIS (Taqwaa Advisory and Sharia'h Investment Solutions Pvt. Ltd.) launched the first Sharia'h index in BSE (Bombay Stock Exchange) in December 2010. BSE has the largest number of Sharia'h Compliant companies in the world, in fact more than the whole of Middle East and Pakistan. There are many Sharia'h compliant brokerage houses in India like Parsoli and Idafa investments. There are many other Sharia'h compliant products like Taurus, Secura, NSE e-commodities, etc. Sharia'h friendly products are also being offered by Reliance Capital[3] and Bajaj Allianz.[4]

The Reserve Bank of India is also seeking approval from the government so as to allow the establishment of the first Islamic bank in the country. Turkey's Bank Asya has also offered to start its Sharia'h compliant banking facilities in India (*The Economic Times*, 22 March 2011). Many more national and international banks are in the process of studying the Indian market for launching their Islamic Banking products and services but the issue regarding the attitude of the Indian customer towards Islamic banking remains a puzzle.

## ISLAMIC BANKING AND INDIVIDUAL CONSUMER'S ATTITUDE

One of the concepts often discussed by economists these days is Islamic banking. This concept applies Islamic teachings in banking system, particularly related to interest-free financial transactions (Caragata, 2000). There are several excellences in Islamic banking, which can make the banking industry survive even in very difficult situations (Khoirunissa, 2003).

Erol and El-Bdour (1989) is considered to be the pioneering study of individual consumers' attitude towards Islamic banking. Later, Omer (1992), in the survey of 300 Muslims in the United Kingdom, reported that a high level of ignorance prevailed among Muslims in the United Kingdom concerning Islamic finance principles. Metwally (1996) in a study of attitudes of Muslims in three Arabic dual-banking systems (Kuwait, Saudi Arabia and Egypt) towards Islamic banking reported differences in the patronage of Islamic and conventional banks. Haron, Ahmad, and Planisek (1994) likewise highlighted the differences in the patronage of

Islamic and conventional banks in their study of Muslims and non-Muslims in Malaysia. Hamid and Azmin (2001) focused on the awareness of Malaysian customers towards Islamic banking within the context of the wider promotion of Islamic education. Surprisingly it was found that most Malaysians did not differentiate between Islamic and conventional banking products and services.

Subsequently, Zainuddin, Jahyd, and Ramayah (2004) surveyed Malaysian customers to illustrate the different perceptions of users and non-users of Islamic banking services. Two recent studies on the perceptions and understanding of Islamic finance deserve a special mention. Bley and Kuehn (2004) in a survey of business students' knowledge of financial aspects of Islamic and conventional banks in Sharjah have found that Muslim students preferred Islamic banking mainly because of religious motivations. Another study on customer satisfaction with interest-free banking and banks election criteria in Turkey by Okumkus (2005) has reported a moderate degree of customer satisfaction with respect to interest-free banking. The analysis itself focused on the degree of satisfaction and awareness of customers dealing with Special Finance Houses offering Islamic banking products services. It is of strategic relevance to know the factors which motivate the consumer to choose Islamic banking (Khoirunissa, 2003). The co-existence of the relationship between economic and religious preferences proves that, in making decision, consumers wish to attain two satisfaction levels, that is satisfaction in the world and in the hereafter (Khoirunissa, 2003).

Fundamentally, Muslims' objection on conventional banking system comes from the understanding that interest is equal to forbidden 'riba', besides the operational activities of the banking system, within which un-Islamic business activities exist. These activities include the channelling of fund to businesses concerning unlawful goods and services, the speculative activities (maysir), the unjust profit sharing for lenders and borrowers (jahala) and the uncertain contracts (gharar) (Iqbal, 1997).

In Islam the act of consumption should take place within boundaries of Islamic law. In modern economics, the problem of choice is much dependent on individual behaviour and possibly taking no account to the norms prevalent in the society. In Islamic economics, there is a serious ethical boundary imposed by the Quran and Sunnah (Traditions of Prophet Muhammad, peace be upon him) on the consumer behaviour (Mannan, 1993).

Metawa and Almossawi (1998) have shown that consumers' decision in choosing an Islamic bank is motivated by religious factors, where consumers emphasise their adherence to Islamic principles. Further, this decision is also motivated by the factors of profit, families and friends and a bank's location. Consumers choose an Islamic bank because of its quick and efficient services, its reputation and its banking practices. It may be concluded that profit motive (economic factor) does exist in choosing Islamic banking (Erol, Kaynak, & El-Bdour, 1990). Thus, if every consumer is also considered to have economic motive and expecting more profit, then Islamic banking will have to compete with the conventional bank by offering higher returns to their customers (Khoirunissa, 2003).

A substantial literature on individual consumers' attitudes towards Islamic financial products and services is already in place, especially concerning selection criteria (or patronage) and customer satisfaction. However most of them are confined to limited geographical locations like Malaysia, the United Kingdom and the Middle Eastern region. Relatively little work has been undertaken in the Indian perspective. Information on customers' characteristics and behaviours is very important for developing commercially viable products by the Islamic banks. This is pioneering research in the Indian context which seeks to study the customer attitude towards Islamic banking. It also aims at identifying attitudinal differences among Indian customers primarily on the basis of religion.

## METHODOLOGY

The main objective of this study is to explore the differences in the attitude of Indian Muslims and non-Muslims towards Islamic Banking. For this purpose, a questionnaire consists for the measurement of attitude of respondents regarding Islamic banking has been developed. In the present study, relationship between consumer attitude towards Islamic banking and specific demographic characteristics such as religion, education, age and income are examined.

### *Questionnaire and Sampling*

Attitude of the respondents is assessed using a structured questionnaire consists of 30 statements classified under five broad dimensions. A five-point Likert scale was used to gauge the response of the respondents, where 5 represented strongly agree and 1 represented strongly disagree.

1) Awareness
2) Ideology

3) Implementation
4) Features
5) Institutions

Questionnaire pre-testing was considered in a sample of 30 respondents. All comments and suggestions were incorporated in the final version of the questionnaire to adequately capture the concept of Islamic banking in the Indian context. For 23 questions scales were scored in such a way so that higher values represented positive attitude about Islamic banking and for the remaining 7 questions higher values represented negative attitude about Islamic banking. Therefore, reverse scoring method was used to analyse these questions. An online version of questionnaire was also created to collect responses online. Approximately 493 survey questionnaires were distributed among bank customers in different cities of North India selected on the basis of convenience, out of which a total of 259 usable questionnaires were returned. Using SPSS 17, results in the form of frequency and percentage data were obtained. *T*-test and ANOVA was used to determine the differences in the variables of customer's attitude towards Islamic banking along with the demographic variables.

## RELIABILITY AND VALIDITY OF THE RESEARCH INSTRUMENT

Reliability of a scale refers to how consistent or stable the ratings generated by the scale are likely to be (Malhotra, 2007). The most commonly used approach to measure internal consistency of a scale is Cronbach's alpha (Cronbach, 1971; Warner, 2008). Cronbach's alpha tends to be high if the scale items are highly correlated (Hair, Anderson, Tatham, & Black, 1998). According to Schuessler (1971), a scale is considered to have good reliability if it has an alpha value greater than 0.60. The overall reliability of the scale used in the present study has been found to be quite high with a Cronbach's alpha value of 0.906, while individual dimension-wise Cronbach's alpha has been found to be more than 0.6.

The content validity of the measurement instrument was assessed by requesting subject experts to provide feedback. The expert panel included faculty members and experts from the disciplines of banking, marketing, consumer behaviour and finance. After they reviewed the questionnaire, based on their feedback changes were made to clarify and eliminate ambiguous statements.

## EXPLORATORY FACTOR ANALYSIS

The results of factor analysis were confirmed by Bartlett test, and the suitability of variables for the factor analysis was ratified by Kaiser-Meyer-Olkin (KMO). Testing of correlation scale for factor analysis, showed, that KMO coefficient is 0.753; therefore it is suitable for factor analysis. Value of Bartlett spherical criteria $p$ is less than 0.05. That shows that between selected variables exists statistically correlating ones. So, both metrics confirm that data are suitable for factor analysis (see Appendix). Variance table (see Appendix) shows the percentage of variance explained by the extracted factors. The analysis extracted five factors having a percentage cumulative variance of 79.43%. This indicates that the five factor framework explained nearly 80% variations in this study. The results of the factor loading are calculated and all statements having a factor loading of more than 0.4 have clubbed together. The high factor loading gives us an idea that no statement is dropped and hence considered. Factor loading is 0.886 for awareness, 0.695 for ideology, 0.615 for implementation, 0.879 for features and 0.696 for institutions (see Appendix).

## HYPOTHESES FOR THE STUDY

Hypotheses were formulated to explore whether significant differences existed across age group, education, religion and occupation of the respondents with respect to awareness, ideology, implementation, features and institutions of Islamic banking.

## RESULTS

### *Sample Description*

Table 1 shows the break-up of the sample on the basis of religion, educational qualification, occupation and age group. About 73% of the respondents are Muslims and remaining 27% are Non-Muslims. Among these consumers, 26.6% are university graduates, 39% are private sector employees. Moreover, 55.2% belong to the age group of 25–35 years.

***Table 1.*** Sample Profile.

| Demographic Variables | | Frequency | Per cent |
|---|---|---|---|
| Religion | Muslim | 189 | 73.0 |
| | Non-Muslim | 70 | 27.0 |
| | Total | 259 | 100.0 |
| Educational qualification | Less than graduation | 33 | 12.7 |
| | Graduation/Post graduation | 69 | 26.6 |
| | M.Phil./Ph.D. | 38 | 14.7 |
| | Professional qualification | 60 | 23.2 |
| | Madarsa[a] education | 59 | 22.8 |
| | Total | 259 | 100.0 |
| Occupation | Government service | 93 | 35.9 |
| | Private service | 101 | 39.0 |
| | Self-employed and business | 34 | 13.1 |
| | Any other | 31 | 12.0 |
| | Total | 259 | 100.0 |
| Age group | Below 25 | 31 | 12.0 |
| | 25 to 35 | 112 | 55.2 |
| | 35 to 50 | 34 | 13.1 |
| | Above 50 | 31 | 12.0 |
| | Total | 259 | 100.0 |

[a]Religious school or college for the study of the Islamic religion, though this may not be the only subject studied.

### *Customer Attitude and Demographics*

*Customer attitude with religion*: Variations in the dimensions of customer attitude with respect to religion is measured using independent sample *T*-test and proper inferences are drawn from '*t*' values and significance values obtained thus. Table 2 shows significant variations in all dimensions of customer attitude between Muslims and non-Muslims. In comparison to non-Muslims, Muslim customers have obtained significantly higher mean values in all dimensions of attitude towards Islamic banking.

### *Muslim versus Non-Muslim Attitude towards Islamic Banking*

Table 3 shows the mean values obtained by the respondents on the five dimensions of attitude towards Islamic banking. It has been found that on

*Table 2.* Results of Independent Sample *T*-Test.

| Dimensions | Mean Values | | *T* | Significance (2-tailed) |
|---|---|---|---|---|
| | Muslims | Non-Muslims | | |
| Awareness | 4.046 | 2.756 | 14.265 | 0.000* |
| Ideology | 3.889 | 3.233 | 8.370 | 0.000* |
| Implementation | 4.038 | 2.957 | 12.758 | 0.000* |
| Features | 3.784 | 3.053 | 10.418 | 0.000* |
| Institutions | 3.083 | 2.750 | 3.095 | 0.002* |

*Significant at 95% confidence level.

the whole in comparison to their non-Muslim counter-parts, Muslim customers have obtained significantly higher mean values in all the dimensions of attitude towards Islamic banking. In order to probe deeper into the findings, the mean values are also tabulated across different demographic characteristics considered for the study. Across demographic characteristics almost a similar trend has been noticed, that is Muslims have obtained high mean values as compared to the non-Muslims. It is surprising to note that the mean value on account of the institutions of Islamic banking is very low in the case of Madarsa educated Muslims, which may be redolent of a somewhat lower conviction of Madarsa educated Muslims in the existing institutional framework for Islamic banking in India. It has been observed that in most of the cases the mean value lies between a score of 3 and 4, which indicates that the overall customer attitude is favourable towards Islamic Banking.

Surprisingly, the non-Muslim customers who are professionally qualified, are doing private service and are in the age bracket of 35–50 years have shown higher mean values on account of the institutions of Islamic banking than Muslims in the respective demographic brackets. It may be attributed to their experience, better exposure to new developments in their private sector jobs and professional education. Further, the non-Muslim customers who are graduates and post-graduates have shown a higher mean value on account of the ideology of Islamic banking than Muslims in the respective demographic bracket. It may be inferred that education, experience and exposure to new ideas broadens the perspective of people which makes them appreciate and accept the good things offered by other religions. It appears that the educated non-Muslim customers view Islamic banking as an interest-free banking system based on ethics, risk sharing with an in built mechanism to control the exploitation of the masses.

***Table 3.*** Mean Values of Customer Attitude towards Islamic Banking across Demographic Characteristics.

| Dimensions of Attitude | Awareness | | Ideology | | Implementation | | Features | | Institutions | |
|---|---|---|---|---|---|---|---|---|---|---|
| Demographic Characteristics | Muslims | Non-Muslims | Muslims | Non-Muslims | Muslims | Non-Muslims | Muslims | Non-Muslims | Muslims | Non-Muslims |
| Below 25 years | 4.782 | N.A. | 3.881 | N.A. | 3.666 | N.A. | 3.540 | N.A. | 2.540 | N.A. |
| 25 to 35 years | 3.982 | 3.000 | 4.157 | 3.240 | 4.203 | 2.853 | 3.885 | 3.045 | 3.508 | 2.520 |
| 35 to 50 years | 4.159 | 2.620 | 3.964 | 3.229 | 3.441 | 3.014 | 4.135 | 3.058 | 2.608 | 2.877 |
| Above 50 years | 3.412 | N.A. | 3.127 | N.A. | 4.607 | N.A. | 3.367 | N.A. | 3.007 | N.A. |
| Government service | 3.693 | 2.739 | 3.600 | 3.303 | 4.238 | 3.171 | 3.716 | 3.102 | 3.150 | 2.727 |
| Private service | 4.341 | 2.779 | 3.928 | 3.294 | 3.916 | 3.215 | 3.610 | 3.132 | 2.750 | 3.264 |
| Self-employed and business | 4.006 | 2.76 | 3.904 | 3.066 | 3.857 | 2.383 | 4.437 | 2.906 | 3.250 | 2.350 |
| Any other | 3.948 | N.A. | 4.333 | N.A. | 4.064 | N.A. | 4.092 | N.A. | 3.782 | N.A. |
| Less than graduation | N.A. | 2.649 | N.A. | 3.020 | N.A. | 2.757 | N.A. | 2.950 | N.A. | 2.431 |
| Graduation/Post graduation | 3.437 | 2.892 | 3.256 | 3.317 | 4.569 | 3.063 | 3.283 | 3.131 | 3.088 | 2.761 |
| M.Phil./Ph.D. | 3.766 | 2.666 | 4.296 | 3.333 | 3.629 | 2.666 | 4.385 | 3.125 | 3.534 | 3.000 |
| Professional qualification | 3.952 | 2.815 | 4.166 | 3.595 | 4.195 | 3.309 | 4.008 | 3.169 | 3.375 | 3.446 |
| Madarsa education | 4.785 | N.A. | 3.937 | N.A. | 3.734 | N.A. | 3.650 | N.A. | 2.576 | N.A. |

The values which were not available have been indicated as a N.A.

Very much like the Muslims, the non-Muslims too are anxiously waiting the introduction of interest-free banking in India.

### *Customer Attitude with Educational Qualification*

Variations in the dimensions of customer attitude with respect to education are determined using ANOVA and proper inferences are drawn from *F* values and significance values. It has been found that there is a significant variation in all dimensions of attitude with respect to educational qualification (Table 4). The mean values indicate that the positive attitude of the customers increases with their education.

### *Customer Attitude with Occupation*

Table 5 shows that there is significant variation in the dimensions of customer attitude with respect to occupation. From the mean values it may be

***Table 4.*** Results of ANOVA (Educational Groups).

| Dimensions | Mean Values for Educational Groups | | | | | *F* | Significance |
|---|---|---|---|---|---|---|---|
| | Graduate | U.G./ P.G. | Research | Professional | Madarsa | | |
| Awareness | 2.649 | 3.271 | 3.708 | 3.687 | 4.785 | 101.995 | 0.00* |
| Ideology | 3.020 | 3.275 | 4.245 | 4.033 | 3.937 | 58.126 | 0.00* |
| Implementation | 2.757 | 4.111 | 3.578 | 3.988 | 3.734 | 27.053 | 0.00* |
| Features | 2.950 | 3.237 | 4.319 | 3.812 | 3.650 | 62.147 | 0.00* |
| Institutions | 2.431 | 2.989 | 3.506 | 3.391 | 2.576 | 21.683 | 0.00* |

*Significant at 95% confidence level.

***Table 5.*** ANOVA (Occupational Groups).

| Dimensions | Mean Values for Occupational Groups | | | | *F* | Significance |
|---|---|---|---|---|---|---|
| | Govt. service | Pvt. service | Business | Others | | |
| Awareness | 3.354 | 4.078 | 3.274 | 3.948 | 17.988 | 0.000* |
| Ideology | 3.494 | 3.821 | 3.411 | 4.333 | 21.444 | 0.000* |
| Implementation | 3.860 | 3.798 | 2.990 | 4.064 | 15.724 | 0.000* |
| Features | 3.498 | 3.529 | 3.536 | 4.092 | 9.311 | 0.000* |
| Institutions | 3.000 | 2.836 | 2.720 | 3.782 | 15.463 | 0.000* |

*Significant at 95% confidence level.

***Table 6.*** Results of ANOVA (Age Groups in Years).

| Dimensions | Means for Age Groups | | | | *F* | Significance |
|---|---|---|---|---|---|---|
| | <25 | 25–35 | 35–50 | 50 < | | |
| Awareness | 4.782 | 3.763 | 3.315 | 3.414 | 31.209 | 0.000* |
| Ideology | 3.881 | 3.952 | 3.561 | 3.127 | 21.716 | 0.000* |
| Implementation | 3.666 | 3.901 | 3.207 | 4.607 | 43.231 | 0.000* |
| Features | 3.540 | 3.697 | 3.544 | 3.367 | 3.089 | 0.028* |
| Institutions | 2.540 | 3.287 | 2.756 | 3.007 | 12.825 | 0.000* |

*Significant at 95% confidence level.

inferred that the service class (both government and private service) against business class is having a positive pre-disposition across all the dimensions of attitude towards Islamic banking.

### *Customer Attitude with Age Groups*

ANOVA results in Table 6 shows that customer attitude towards awareness, ideology, implementation, features and institutions of Islamic banking varies significantly across age groups. The mean values indicate that customer attitude towards awareness, ideology, implementation and features is relatively higher for younger customers, that is age groups of <25 years and 25–35 years. It may be attributed to the receptiveness and curiosity of youngsters towards new ideas.

## CONCLUSIONS

The focus of this study is to gain insight into the attitude of Indian Muslims and non-Muslims towards Islamic banking. Suitable hypotheses were formulated and tested in order to gauge the variations in the dimensions of customer attitude towards Islamic banking across demographic characteristics. The major findings of the hypothesis testing are mentioned as under.

There are significant differences in the attitude of Muslims and non-Muslims towards Islamic banking. However, both the groups have almost a similar attitude regarding the institutions of Islamic banking. Customer attitude towards Islamic bank significantly and positively varies with the educational qualification of the respondents. Awareness about the

Institutions of Islamic banking is relatively low across all sections of respondents. On the whole, the attitude of Madarsa educated Muslims towards Islamic banking is very much similar to that of other Muslims without Madarsa education. Ideology and implementation about Islamic banking varies significantly with the age groups which indicates that level of understanding and perceived operations of Islamic banking is different for the different age groups of Indian Muslims and non-Muslims. There exists a high level of awareness in Muslims about Islamic banking concept but at the same time they are less aware about features and institutions of Islamic banking.

The findings of the present study are in line with previous studies by Omer (1992) and Gerrard and Cunningham (1997) but deviate from the findings of Erol and El-Bdour (1989) and Bley and Kuehn (2004). This is may be because Erol and El-Bdour (1989) and Bley and Kuehn (2004) conducted their studies in Islamic nations like Jordan and Qatar with a Muslims majority, whereas Omer (1992) and Gerrard and Cunningham (1997) conducted their study in the United Kingdom and Singapore where Muslims are in a minority. Thus, the studies by Omer (1992) and Gerrard and Cunningham (1997) are closer in resemblance to the Indian context which also has a Muslims minority.

There is a clear indication that Indian customer's attitude towards Islamic banking is favourable. Most of the dimensions of customer attitude towards Islamic banking vary significantly across demographic characteristics. However, a large number of respondents were unaware of the specific features and functioning of Islamic banking which may be partially attributed to the fact that at present there are no Islamic banks operating in India. Therefore, the biggest challenge before the flag-bearers and advocates of Islamic banking is to create a general awareness about Islamic banking and its benefits among the masses. Further, this alternative system of banking needs to be de-linked from religion and should be simply referred to as interest-free banking.

## RECOMMENDATIONS AND MANAGERIAL IMPLICATIONS

Being a pioneering study in Indian context on customer attitude towards Islamic banking, this may serve a foundation for future research endeavours on the theme of Islamic banking and finance. Further, this study can help bank decision makers to identify the major factors that may shape the attitude of Indian customers towards Islamic banks. Such information should be of immense help to the managers of commercial banks in devising appropriate marketing strategies for reaching and attracting young customers.

Findings from this study show that the attitude of Indian customers can be classified into factors like awareness, ideology, implementation, features and institutions of banks. Therefore, such factors should be considered seriously by the Islamic banks in formulating suitable marketing strategies. It is increasingly being felt that descriptive studies on specific issues of customer attitude towards Islamic banking should be undertaken to develop insights into customer aspirations from Islamic banking.

If Indian organisations can build on their experience and reputation in the financial world, and can provide Islamic banking services in India, they can aim to gain a growing customer base of the Muslim population, especially those who abstain from dealing in interest based transactions of the traditional commercial banks. Furthermore, awareness about the Islamic banking is found to be very low. Therefore, not only the banks but other people involved in promoting the cause of Interest-free banking should work in the direction of creating awareness about Islamic banking through appropriate communication channels. In addition to academic seminars and conferences, regular interactions should be held between industry, government and academia in order to reach a consensus on the issue of formally introducing Islamic banking in India. Further, the general public should be made aware of the concept and rewards of Islamic banking by citing the examples of countries like Malaysia and Singapore where this system has been proved to be commercially viable. Islamic scholars can also play an important role in disseminating information about Islamic banking among Muslim population.

## LIMITATIONS OF THE STUDY AND FUTURE RESEARCH DIRECTIONS

This study surveyed the respondents of North India only, which represents a different culture and a high concentration of middle class.

This study also treats Indians as a single cultural entity. While this could be so at the macro level, however, cultural differences among the Indians could be an important factor at the micro-level. Therefore, it is necessary to carry out similar studies across different sub-cultures in India.

# NOTES

1. Crossing over to Islamic banking: Sharia'h compliant finance is prospering in Britain (*The Times*, 13 March 2009).
2. Jamaat-e-Islami Hind is one of the influential Islamic organisations in India.
3. Reliance Capital Limited (BSE: 500111, NSE: RELCAPITAL) is a financial services company and part of a Reliance Anil Dhirubhai Ambani Group. It is registered with the Reserve Bank of India under section 45-IA of the Reserve Bank of India Act, 1934, as a public limited company in 1986 and is now listed on the Bombay Stock Exchange and the National Stock Exchange (India).
4. Bajaj Allianz Life Insurance Company Limited is a joint venture between Allianz AG, one of the world's largest Life Insurance companies and Bajaj Auto, one of the biggest two- and three-wheeler manufacturers in the world.

# REFERENCES


Bley, J., & Kuehn, K. (2004). Conventional versus Islamic finance: Student knowledge and perception in the United Arab Emirates. *International Journal of Islamic Financial Services, 5*(4), 17–30.

Caragata, W. (July 21, 2000). Sharia'h lenders make headway in Indonesia. *Asiaweek*. Hong Kong.

Cronbach, L. J. (1971). Test validation. In R. L. Thorndike (Ed.), *Educational measurement* (Vol. 2, pp. 443–507). Washington, DC: American Council on Education.

Erol, C., Kaynak, E., & El-Bdour, R. (1990). Conventional and Islamic banks: Patronage behaviour of Jordanian customers. *International Journal of Bank Marketing, 8*(4), 25–35.

Erol, C., & El-Bdour, R. (1989). Attitudes, behaviour, and patronage factors of bank customers towards Islamic banks. *International Journal of Bank Marketing, 7*(6), 31–37.

Gerrard, P., & Cunningham, J. B. (1997). Islamic banking: A study in Singapore. *International Journal of Bank Marketing, 15*(6), 204–216.

Hair, J. F., Anderson, R. E., Tatham, R. L., & Black, W. C. (1998). Multivariate data analysis, upper saddle river. *Multivariate Data Analysis* (5th ed.). Upper Saddle River, NJ: Prentice Hall.

Hamid, A., & Azmin, N. (2001). A study on Islamic banking education and strategy for the new millennium: Malaysian experience. *International Journal of Islamic Financial Services, 2*(4), 3–11.

Haron, S., Ahmad, N., & Planisek, S. L. (1994). Bank patronage factors of Muslim and non-Muslim customers. *International Journal of Bank Marketing, 12*(1), 32–40.

Iqbal, Z. (1997). Islamic financial systems. *Finance and Development, 34*, 42–45.

Malhotra, N. K. (2007). *Marketing research: An applied orientation, 4/E*. India: Pearson Education.

Mannan, M. A. (1993). Ekonomi Islam: Teori dan Praktek. Penerbit Dana Bhakti Wakaf, Yogyakarta.

Metawa, S. A., & Almossawi, M. (1998). Banking behavior of Islamic bank customers: Perspectives and implications. *International Journal of Bank Marketing, 16*(7), 299–313.

Metwally, M. (1996). Attitudes of Muslims towards Islamic banks in a dual-banking system. *American Journal of Islamic Finance*, *6*(1), 11–17.

Naser, K., & Moutinho, L. (1997). Strategic marketing management: The case of Islamic banks. *International Journal of Bank Marketing*, *15*(6), 187–203.

Okumkus, H. Ş. (2005). Interest-free banking in Turkey: A study of customer satisfaction and bank selection criteria. *Journal of Economic Cooperation*, *26*(4), 51–86.

Omer, H. (1992). *The implication of Islamic beliefs and practice on Islamic financial institutions in the UK*. Unpublished PhD dissertation, Loughborough University, Loughborough.

Schuessler, K. F. (1971). *Analyzing social data: A statistical orientation*. Boston, MA: Houghton Mifflin.

The Economic Times. (2011). India may get its first foreign Islamic bank. *The Economic Times*, March 22.

Warner, R. M. (2008). *Applied statistics: From bivariate through multivariate techniques*. Sage.

Zainuddin, Y., Jahyd, N., & Ramayah, T. (2004). Perception of Islamic banking: Does it differ among users and non-users. *Jurnal Manajemen dan Bisnis*, *6*(3), 221–232.

# APPENDIX

KMO and Bartlett's Test

| | | |
|---|---|---|
| Kaiser-Meyer-Olkin measure of sampling adequacy | | 0.753 |
| Bartlett's test of sphericity | Approximate Chi-Square | 9191.186 |
| | Df | 435 |
| | Significance | 0.000 |

Total Variance Explained

| Component | Initial Eigenvalues | | | Extraction Sums of Squared Loadings | | | Rotation Sums of Squared Loadings | | |
|---|---|---|---|---|---|---|---|---|---|
| | Total | % of variance | Cumulative % | Total | % of variance | Cumulative % | Total | % of variance | Cumulative % |
| 1 | 9.931 | 33.103 | 33.103 | 9.931 | 33.103 | 33.103 | 6.655 | 22.182 | 26.182 |
| 2 | 3.388 | 11.293 | 44.396 | 3.388 | 11.293 | 44.396 | 4.525 | 15.084 | 39.266 |
| 3 | 3.237 | 10.791 | 55.188 | 3.237 | 10.791 | 55.188 | 3.577 | 11.922 | 54.188 |
| 4 | 2.329 | 7.764 | 62.952 | 2.329 | 7.764 | 62.952 | 3.036 | 10.121 | 69.309 |
| 5 | 1.849 | 6.162 | 69.114 | 1.849 | 6.162 | 69.114 | 2.941 | 9.805 | 82.684 |
| 6 | 1.495 | 4.982 | 74.096 | | | | | | |
| 7 | 1.390 | 4.634 | 78.729 | | | | | | |
| 8 | 1.186 | 3.952 | 82.681 | | | | | | |
| 9 | 0.821 | 2.738 | 85.419 | | | | | | |
| 10 | 0.801 | 2.671 | 88.090 | | | | | | |
| 11 | 0.653 | 2.177 | 90.267 | | | | | | |
| 12 | 0.487 | 1.622 | 91.889 | | | | | | |
| 13 | 0.475 | 1.584 | 93.473 | | | | | | |
| 14 | 0.387 | 1.291 | 94.764 | | | | | | |
| 15 | 0.282 | 0.942 | 95.705 | | | | | | |

| | | | |
|---|---|---|---|
| 16 | 0.227 | 0.758 | 96.463 |
| 17 | 0.186 | 0.621 | 97.084 |
| 18 | 0.168 | 0.562 | 97.645 |
| 19 | 0.129 | 0.431 | 98.077 |
| 20 | 0.125 | 0.417 | 98.494 |
| 21 | 0.104 | 0.346 | 98.839 |
| 22 | 0.078 | 0.261 | 99.100 |
| 23 | 0.063 | 0.210 | 99.310 |
| 24 | 0.051 | 0.170 | 99.480 |
| 25 | 0.040 | 0.133 | 99.613 |
| 26 | 0.034 | 0.113 | 99.727 |
| 27 | 0.027 | 0.090 | 99.817 |
| 28 | 0.024 | 0.081 | 99.898 |
| 29 | 0.017 | 0.055 | 99.953 |
| 30 | 0.014 | 0.047 | 100.000 |

Rotated ComponentMatrix

| | Component | | | | |
|---|---|---|---|---|---|
| | 1 | 2 | 3 | 4 | 5 |
| S1 | 0.189 | −0.101 | 0.296 | **0.726** | 0.089 |
| S2 | **0.769** | 0.058 | 0.385 | 0.066 | 0.199 |
| S3 | −0.046 | −0.045 | 0.555 | 0.352 | **0.535** |
| S4 | 0.160 | **0.651** | 0.118 | −0.255 | 0.058 |
| S5 | **0.935** | 0.126 | 0.036 | 0.130 | −0.062 |
| S6 | 0.137 | 0.067 | **0.563** | 0.325 | −0.363 |
| S7 | **0.858** | 0.124 | 0.203 | 0.057 | −0.129 |
| S8 | 0.056 | −0.172 | −0.098 | **0.642** | 0.006 |
| S9 | **0.595** | 0.090 | −0.013 | −0.216 | 0.447 |
| S10 | **0.791** | 0.341 | −0.138 | 0.187 | 0.201 |

*(Continued)*

| Rotated ComponentMatrix | | | | | |
|---|---|---|---|---|---|
| | Component | | | | |
| | 1 | 2 | 3 | 4 | 5 |
| S11 | 0.577 | **0.554** | 0.209 | −0.019 | 0.250 |
| S12 | 0.218 | **0.440** | 0.514 | 0.165 | −0.165 |
| S13 | 0.314 | −0.194 | **0.636** | −0.264 | 0.077 |
| S14 | 0.318 | **0.592** | 0.186 | −0.228 | 0.398 |
| S15 | 0.139 | 0.128 | **0.815** | 0.264 | 0.055 |
| S16 | 0.029 | 0.160 | **0.421** | −0.331 | 0.235 |
| S17 | 0.112 | **0.777** | 0.104 | −0.042 | 0.338 |
| S18 | 0.559 | −0.080 | −0.074 | −0.025 | **0.629** |
| S19 | −0.218 | 0.236 | 0.175 | **0.690** | −0.016 |
| S20 | 0.010 | **0.538** | 0.693 | 0.142 | 0.099 |
| S21 | **0.513** | 0.431 | 0.224 | 0.108 | 0.268 |
| S22 | 0.733 | −0.090 | **0.411** | −0.141 | 0.317 |
| S23 | 0.127 | **0.659** | 0.289 | 0.508 | 0.134 |
| S24 | 0.234 | **0.757** | −0.174 | 0.193 | −0.138 |
| S25 | 0.007 | 0.454 | 0.063 | 0.011 | **0.731** |
| S26 | **0.459** | −0.469 | 0.310 | 0.376 | 0.071 |
| S27 | 0.580 | **0.415** | 0.281 | −0.136 | 0.378 |
| S28 | 0.531 | 0.389 | 0.047 | **0.603** | 0.078 |
| S29 | **0.796** | 0.212 | 0.019 | 0.043 | 0.086 |
| S30 | 0.285 | 0.128 | 0.025 | 0.136 | **0.689** |

Factor Loading and Cronbach's Alpha Values

| S. No. | Dimensions | Statement | Factor Loading | Cronbach's Alpha |
|---|---|---|---|---|
| 1 | Awareness | In practice Islamic banking is not a roundabout way of looking at the conventional banking. | 0.769 | 0.886 |
| 2 | | Islamic banking is based on Sharia'h (Islamic Laws). | 0.935 | |
| 3 | | Islamic banking is at par with the present context of modern finance. | 0.858 | |
| 4 | | Islamic banking should be linked with religion and not taken as just an alternate system of banking. | 0.595 | |
| 5 | | Islamic banking provides a solution to financial problems. | 0.791 | |
| 6 | | Investments are more secure in Islamic banks. | 0.513 | |
| 7 | | Religious reasons are not the only reasons which motivate people to deposit their money in an Islamic bank. | 0.459 | |
| 8 | | Sharia'h scholars are qualified enough to give their inputs in development of Islamic financial products. | 0.796 | |
| 9 | Ideology | Islamic banking is strictly based on risk sharing model. | 0.535 | 0.695 |
| 10 | | Islamic banking restricts the uncontrolled expansion of financial markets. | 0.629 | |
| 11 | | If I put my money in Islamic banks, I am contended that my money will not be invested in unethical ventures like alcohol, gambling etc. | 0.731 | |
| 12 | | Successful implementation of Islamic banking in countries like Malaysia, Singapore, UK, Indonesia etc. indicates that it will successful in India too. | 0.689 | |
| 13 | Implementation | The rewards of Islamic banking are to be the same for all people irrespective of their religion. | 0.563 | 0.615 |
| 14 | | If more branches of Islamic banking institutions open up throughout India, more people will utilise the services provided by these banks. | 0.636 | |
| 15 | | Islamic banking is not an investment in religious activities. | 0.815 | |
| 16 | | Govt. should immediately allow Islamic banks to operate in India in order to mobilise funds from the liquidity rich middle eastern countries. | 0.421 | |
| 17 | | People should not keep financial matters and religion separately. | 0.411 | |

(*Continued*)

Factor Loading and Cronbach's Alpha Values

| S. No. | Dimensions | Statement | Factor Loading | Cronbach's Alpha |
|---|---|---|---|---|
| 18 | Features | Islamic banking is more than just interest-free banking. | 0.651 | 0.879 |
| 19 | | Financing on the basis of profit-loss-sharing between the lender and the borrower will be advantageous to both. | 0.554 | |
| 20 | | Islamic banking solves the problems related to loan recovery. | 0.44 | |
| 21 | | Islamic banking addresses socio economic issues like suicides committed by marginal farmers. | 0.592 | |
| 22 | | Granting of interest-free loans by Islamic banks is equivalent to helping the community in a just and efficient manner. | 0.777 | |
| 23 | | Islamic banking offers better value added services. | 0.538 | |
| 24 | | Islamic banking generates stable returns on my investments. | 0.659 | |
| 25 | | Customers are less prone to default risk in Islamic banks. | 0.757 | |
| 26 | | Islamic banks are more regulated form of banking as they are governed by regulatory bodies as well as by Sharia'h boards. | 0.415 | |
| 27 | Institutions | Islamic banking is a banking system for all not for Muslims only. | 0.726 | 0.696 |
| 28 | | Only profitability reasons motivate people to deposit their money at an Islamic bank. | 0.642 | |
| 29 | | Islamic banking institutions do not restricts the developments of new financial products and services. | 0.69 | |
| 30 | | Islamic Banking governing bodies like AAOIFI are fully equipped to develop new products and services. | 0.603 | |

# STRATEGIC REQUIREMENTS TO IMPLEMENT THE PRIVATIZATION PROGRAM IN IRAN

Mohammad Dolatabadi and Lotfollah Forouzandeh

## ABSTRACT

Purpose – *Privatization is one of the ways governments consider to dispense with the consequences of governmental economy in the economic reforms. One of the complex matters that governments face is decision-making in privatization and choosing policies and methods that move the country's economy toward more efficiency. Considering the importance and complexity of this issue, taking a comprehensive strategic perspective by the policy makers seems necessary for establishing successful privatization.*

Method – *Article 44 of the Islamic Republic of Iran's constitution is the foundation of its privatization program and this study specifies the strategic requirements in implementation of privatization based on the mentioned article and other legal documents. Iran Privatization Organization (IPO) is the single executor of the program and we surveyed all members of the statistical population of this study, including all experts, supervisors, managers, deputies, and senior advisers of IPO to collect the*

**The Developing Role of Islamic Banking and Finance: From Local to Global Perspectives**
**Contemporary Studies in Economic and Financial Analysis, Volume 95, 163–180**

**ISSN: 1569-3759/doi:10.1108/S1569-3759(2014)0000095018**

*required information by a questionnaire with some questions including strategic thinking, requirements, and results.*

*To analyze the data, at first, validity and reliability of the collected data, then the correlation between strategic thinking and requirements were tested and all strategic requirements of privatization were prioritized. We used tests such as Cronbach's Alpha, Pearson Correlation Coefficient, Linear Regression, and Friedman to perform the study.*

**Keywords:** Privatization; strategic requirements; strategic thinking

## INTRODUCTION

Globalization and its widespread changes made the private sector a serious necessity in economic development. Achieving all-around development is only possible under an efficient and capable private sector. Considering that a government with an extensive governing body and wide jurisdiction is the main factor of budget deficit, inflation, interference in allocating resources, and weakening competitiveness of the country on an international scale, it raises the need for economic liberalization. Despite Iran's constitution stipulating about public, cooperative, and private sector in economic matters, the public sector has always kept the other two sectors with a superior force under its unquestionable control. For an agile economy, there is no choice except transferring public companies to private sectors and developing them, which will provide major goals such as economic prosperity, social justice, poverty level reduction, and reaching the objectives of the 20-year development outlook.

## STATEMENT OF THE PROBLEM

In the early years after the Islamic revolution, government presence in the economy gradually grew and became exclusive in different and extensive areas such as industries, mines, and banking. Gradually signs of inefficiency in public sector activities appeared and there were trends toward privatization. In 1989 after the war, the privatization issue was mentioned in the text of policies of the first economic, social, and cultural development plan and reducing government size in economy was intended. In the next plans of economic, social, and cultural development of the Islamic Republic of Iran, the privatization organization became responsible for implementing the state privatization program. The range of privatization in Iran can be said to include "all shares belonging to ministries, institutions and government subsidiary companies which total or half of their shares belong to the state and includes shares of public companies in private firms that cover a wide range of government assets" (Document of Summary of Privatization Process, 2004). In 2003, the nation's 20-year development plan for 2025 and the Act for Policies for Privatization of Public Companies entitled "Policies for Implementation of Principles Article 44 of Constitution" was officially passed in 2005 by the supreme leader of the Islamic Republic of Iran, and the economic reform programs started in earnest.

Because of the requirement of strategic belief in management of organizations and observation of strategic requirements of privatization programs, evaluation of these items for an organization which undertakes such an important task is inevitable and can help the search for strategies and methods to reach the objectives of economic development. Thus, the following questions are answered in this chapter:

1. How much is the strategic thinking of the managers of the Iran Privatization Organization?
2. How much is the effect of managers' strategic thinking on determining strategic requirements of privatization implementation?
3. What are the strategic requirements of Iran Privatization Organization in performing privatization based on priorities?

## STRATEGIC REQUIREMENTS FOR IMPLEMENTATION OF IRAN'S PRIVATIZATION PROGRAM

James Robin Quinn has defined strategy as follows: "Strategy is a pattern which combines objectives, policies and operational chains of an organization to an integrated whole" (Ghafarian, 2008).

Mintzberg has divided the strategic management into two general schools of planning and learning. Strategic programming and strategic thinking which respectively result from the first and second schools form a combination of art and science of strategy. "Strategic thinking can determine a proper orientation for an organization and strategic programming can help the organizational momentum toward the designated direction" (Ghafarian & Kiani, 2005).

Thompson and Kay believe "privatization has various methods of changing the relationship of state and private sector such as anti-nationalization or sale of assets of government, deregulation or elimination of limiting terms of competition establishment in government monopoly and transfer of products and services that are managed by government to private sector" (Thompson & Kay, 1986).

Precise study of sources such as the constitution of the Islamic Republic of Iran, the state five-year plans for economic, social, and cultural development, the nation's 20-year outlook, internal regulations of the Expediency Discernment Council, and implementation policies of Article 44 of constitution, strategic requirements of implementing Iran's Privatization Program are as follows:

1. *Explaining the Basic Objectives Such as Efficiency and Justice*: It is essential to clarify the important objectives of privatization and resolving disagreements. When there is no clear understanding of the goals and agents of a reform program, earnest contribution and proper adherence to the principles and framework to reach the desired future may not be possible.
2. *Establishing Inner Belief in Managers*: Managers should believe in the objectives of the organization and purposes that the organization pursues so that the result appears as raising the indexes such as effectiveness, productivity, and possibility of reaching the objectives of privatization. Thus, clearly it is the duty of the senior management to stress the inner beliefs about the major goals of privatization in the senior and junior managers.
3. *Empowering the Private Sector*: For the private sector to set up trust and the ability to deal with dominant forces of state in the economy, they should come out of the current recession and depression and using experts and experienced individuals and advanced technologies, seriously engage in economic activities. "What weakens the private sector internally is lack of experts with high experience, job experience with no high productivity, interaction with foreign investors and the like" (Anonymous, 2005). And "As long as the private sector is not empowered, it cannot buy block shares of large companies" (Fouladgar, 2009).
4. *Making Supportive Policies*: The state should be aware of the basic difference in strategic drive of companies in private and public sectors

because all efforts of a manager of a private sector are to increase effectiveness; this leads to a behavior which probably is different from behaviors in a public institution. If social insurance can offset the negative consequences such as workforce reduction, similar cases will be accepted as a natural part of economic development. "The state competes with private sector in many fields. Such competition is not on fair basis because authority of government is far beyond that of the private sector and such unequal competition leads practically to the bankruptcy of the private sector" (Anonymous, 2005). Moreover, only with proper supportive policies the investors will be encouraged to participate. "Investor seeks profit. Wherever it is more profitable, so there will be more investment and one of the main factors of profitable and higher investment is operating and supporting guarantee in that field" (Ahmadigorji, 2008).

5. *Making Regulatory Policies*: The supreme leader's important notification about implementing Article 44 of the constitution, the principled acceptance such as competitiveness of economic in policies indicates the ever-increasing need for transparency in the regulatory system. "It is the right of people that transferring all the business establishments are conducted by state law and observing the rights of the applicants. Meanwhile, economic corruption causes violations of social and economic rights of many people and development of poverty" (Maghami, 2009).

   In Article 31 of internal regulations of the expediency discernment council, supervision on implementing the overall policies and following the implementation of approvals are considered the duties of the secretary of expediency discernment council (Aminimehr, 2002). Simultaneous with enhancement of the private sector and changing of the duties of government from operator to a supervising organization, it can be hoped that a more realistic monitoring will be applied from the state over the government's privatization and private sector services and in all involved bodies, especially inside the privatization organization it is to be defined as direct supervision on performance accuracy and activities of organization.

6. *Establishing a Foundation for Public Ownership*: Respecting the needs and rights of private sector through establishment of real competitive condition should be in a way that private companies can compete with the public companies and micro-investors can invest their capital in secure economic environment. "In a monopoly conditions, either consumer or producer will incur the loss. This is also true about hidden

monopoly conditions that will be presented so that it would look like without monopoly" (Danaei, 2004).

7. *Using Standard Methods of Transferring*: Every state has a different method for transferring the companies under their ownership with regard to various factors, and presenting a fixed transferring formula is difficult. The most effective factor in selection of a specific method for privatization is: "objective of state, current structure of the company, financial condition and performance of the company, ability to mobilize the resources of private sector, degree of capital market development and social factors" (Matlabi Asl, 2004). Nonetheless, in the policies of state privatization, one of the points to be considered is adequate consideration of reputable methods of transferring so that any dispute and corruptions can be avoided.
8. *Establishing a Clear and Unbiased Information System*: One of the threats in each area is lack of useful information. In private economy, that there is no common support of the state's economy, lack of adequate information and accurate statistics on the various work processes will jeopardize the economy and drive investors from investing.

> Having information about producing of goods, number of competitors, amount of exports, characteristics of consumption market, smuggled imports, to name but a few, is necessary for an investor and public and private sectors in Iran are in strained circumstances in this regard. (Anonymous, 2005)

Establishing a public acceptance of economic reforms in the community for increasing public participation and understanding the requirements of privatization is required so that society understands that "implementing privatization program is not in harmony with groups and large internal companies or foreign companies' aims and their role and participation in privatization is specific and limited" (Momeniha & Alavi, 2008). Because mass media are considered public organizations in supervision and have a significant role in the promotion of culture and general belief, they have the ability to conduct and mobilize thoughts and social beliefs in investment and supervision on performance of authorities by applying public pressure to prevent bribery and state the value of investing to the people.

9. *Creating Equal Opportunities for Public Investment*: This is one of the requirements that should be considered by government. It is obvious that unequal conditions of opportunities will disappoint the investor. Dr. Mahmoud Salahi, advisor of president in economic and free zone areas, in his speech in the conference entitled "supervision on

implementation of overall policies of Article 44 of constitution" in 2008, states "providing legal agents for investment, state support, commercial policies, strong and stable monetary and financial market, other state regulation, geographical, political and economical conditions and political factors" (Salahi, 2008) as the fields for discovering financial security and removing obstacles of investment.

10. *Empowering Human Resources*: One of the most important challenges in modern management in organizations is applying intellectual resources and capacities of human resources. "Empowering the human resources means making required capacities in employees to enable them to create value and perform their responsibility in organization efficiently" (Bazazejazayeri, 2003). In many organizations, employees' abilities are not used and the managers are not capable of applying their potential capacities. This is especially seen in public organizations. However, the ability of individuals will directly affect the intellectual and practical value that they consider for their work and it is expected that higher capability of individuals will help the organization achieve the goals and implementations of intended strategies.
11. *Government Decision Makers Not Being Beneficiary in Transferring*: Another important factor is the accuracy in the performance of authorities and "not being beneficiary in the transferring, whether it is government decision makers or those involved in transferring" (Internal Regulations of Expediency Council, 1997). There is information in any organization that distinguishes the ordinary people from those dealing with such information. This is information rent, which is defined as gaining access to the valuable economic and political information and misusing it for personal, group, and party purposes. Economical activities of politicians, decision makers, and government policy makers, even with no source of incorruption, lead the economic liberalization program to corruption. One way to limit the renting and monopolization is to prohibit or restrict the economic activities of public authorities.
12. *Preparing Firms before Transferring*: Considering the high costs of non-productive and less productivity in costs and human resources in the public sector, one of the success factors of a privatization program is changing the structure of firms before privatization. "Some consider it as the duty of the government because they believe that new owners of organization are following the profitability and neglect of this important. Others consider it as duty of private sector because cost of reconstruction is high and out of power of state" (Katouzian, 2008).

Nevertheless, reconstruction of companies before transferring is necessary because of its potential to reduce the negative consequences of privatization.

13. *Standard Methods of Pricing*: Correct methods of pricing are considered explicitly in policies of Article 44 of the constitution. In this regard, higher council of implementation of overall policies of Article 44 of the constitution approved the executive regulations of the firms' pricing practices and how to apply these techniques in the framework according to the transferring board in a session dated September 15, 2009. One of the problems until approval of this regulation in pricing method of firms is "not specified rate of return of capital and investment" (Anonymous, 2008b). In this regulation, four main methods such as "market method (applying stock prices), profitability, the current value of net assets of the company and determining the component stocks" (Anonymous, 2008a) are provided and notified to determine the price of the shares.
14. *Preventing the Monopoly of Private Sector*: Creating a competitive environment and decentralization means that all the departments should undertake their costs of failure. Thus, creating an atmosphere of anti-monopoly is an important requirement for the privatization of public companies.

> "Decentralization and foreign competition of government agencies in transferring process before privatization of public firms and facing them with competitive pressure are basic principles in this field" (Momtazuddin, 2003). One of the principles which should be observed is codification of law about the competitiveness in economy bound and observing accurate implementation of these rules in transferring process. "Subject of the competition law is important. There should be a legal and disciplinary environment to prevent abuse and monopoly of private institutions and to assure, some decision should be taken so that real competitive & private markets established." (Zare, Kouaroei, & Ghadami, 2008)

15. *Preventing Foreign Influence on State Economy*: Liquidity supply problem in our country is the main assignment of shares to the private sector and according to the primary estimation by the research center of Islamic Consultative Assembly in recent years, assigned volume subject to paragraph (j) of Article 44 of the constitution is about one thousand and two hundred trillion Rials. When according to the official statistics, "the liquidity of society is less than one thousand trillion Rials" (Tavakoli, 2007). To encourage domestic and foreign investors to buy public firms, the government is obliged to establish a secure environment for investing and "comply with objectives of policies of article 44,

investment will be raised by domestic and foreign source" (Momeniha & Alavi, 2008), In paragraph 8 of the 20-year outlook of Islamic Republic of Iran, "Iran is a country with constructive and interaction with world based on dignity, wisdom and advisable principle" (Anonymous, 2008a). In paragraph 2 of implementation policies of Article 44, "Governance practices, preventing from monopoly, influence and foreign domination of the national economy" (Internal Regulations of Expediency Council, 1997) are emphasized.

## RESULTS OF PRIVATIZATION PROGRAM

Habibi and Khoshpour consider the privatization interests as "growth of national product through productivity enhancement, privatization effect on finance & budget, increase efficiency and privatization effect on income distribution" (Habibi & Khoshpour, 1998).

National production will be changed by privatization through "two ways of transferring financial funds from private sector to government and ownership and institution control transfer from state to private sector" (Aryanmenhr & Iji, 2008) and the rise in national product will increase the economic growth. "Few but growing studies which evaluate privatization effect on macroeconomic and financial requirements show the positive financial benefits and strong correlation between privatization and economic growth" (Kikeri & John, 2004).

One of main subjects of privatizing public firms is their efficiency resulting from privatization which is mainly estimated more than public firms. Boubakri et al. have stated according to two different studies on 79 firms in 21 developing countries and 230 firms during 1980 to 1999 that "privatization leads to profitability, efficiency and output enhancement" (Mathur & Banchuenvijit, 2007). Galal et al. have studied the profitability and stated that "average growth after privatization is 2.49% and 69% of all the firms have profited by privatization" (Smith, Andrew, & Trebilcock, 2001). But despite much research, it is considered without any impact. Villalonga has experimented with 24 Spanish companies in different industries and came to the conclusion that "privatization has no effect in efficiency enhancement of these companies" (Okten & Arin, 2006).

One of the claims of advocates of privatization is motivations. "Lack of competitiveness and profit motive in public sectors will lead to inability to decrease the cost" (Anonymous, Investment Dictionary). Another interest is competitiveness in private market between counterparts. "One of the factors for improving the profit motive in private sector is strong competitiveness and elimination of monopoly rules that public companies have" (Smith, Andrew, & Trebilcock, 2001). In the viewpoint of Vickers and Yarrow, "managers of private companies are suffering from lack of strong motivation and right supervision" (Okten & Arin, 2006).

Another reason of defending the privatization is workforce productivity. "Although private sector pays lower salary and benefits to its personnel, the main reason of cost difference in private sector in comparison with public sector is productivity of employees" (Anonymous, Investment Dictionary). Earle and Telegdy in their investigation of different companies and inconsistent of Romania understood that "privatization will increase the productivity of workforce" (Okten & Arin, 2006).

In addition, its effect on income of the state is a method for earning in low-income countries. Companies earn money by selling their owned companies. If they are profitable, higher prices will be put on them and if they are not, each year the losses of keeping of these companies will be removed from the government and in case of future profitability in the government tax revenue increases from private companies. "Privatization with sharing the government's commitment with private sector reduces the costs, increases incomes, improves the structure of the economy and reduces pressure even in complex economic perspectives" (Starr, 1988). "Benefits from the program in examined 18 countries are more than 2% of GDP" (Kikeri & John, 2004). This debate has an important place, especially in the Third World economies. "One of the objectives of firms and institutes in privatization is significant reduction in their budget requests. This incentive is considered more by authorities because of the reason that Third World countries has often budget deficit" (Aryanmenhr & Iji, 2008).

If supportive policies of government from private sectors performed well, the influence of politicians in decision-making of state managers will be reduced. "Shleifer and Vishny emphasize on interference of politicians in companies affairs such as too much hiring, inappropriate selection of products and situation of production, lack of investment and inappropriate definition of motive for managers" (Okten & Arin, 2006).

Mathur and Banchuenvijit believe that some reasons for priority of private sector firms are presenting services in "1 – business and explicit management objectives, 2 – more supervision of shareholders, 3 – more competitive and higher performance of market to control the business and 4 – emerging more competitive markets" (Mathur & Banchuenvijit, 2007).

One of the debates of governments is equitable distribution of income among the population, which has opposing opinions. Income distribution in less-developed countries that are faced with serious financial problems is challenging and privatization even with submission of the raised profitability should proceed with many cautions. In confirming the role of government as a factor in holding prices down, Shapiro and Wiling (1990) believe that public companies can solve the issues of market with operating an effective pricing system on social costs and production profitability and stated that the objective of a private company is maximizing the profit while a public firm wants to increase its social benefits (Okten & Arin, 2006). Moreover, these two researchers stated that a study reported in Mexico that after privatization the prices increased: "by analyzing different Mexico companies from various industries, La Porta and Lopez-de-Silanes (1999) found out that privatization boosts the prices" (Okten & Arin, 2006). "Saal and Parker (2001) with analyzing the water and sewerage companies of England and Wales understood that output price increases and in addition, their total performance will indicate that output price will grow more than input costs" (Okten & Arin, 2006).

On the one hand, some experts consider justice as a secondary result of economical growth and liberalization and believe that direct government intervention in this regard would only result in restrictions of competitive market. Sharifzadegan believes that preference of economic growth to redistribution of income and vice versa is not a good strategy: "social justice cannot be settled without having a flourish and empower economic. Social justice is result of economic growth" (Charbalesh, 2009). He believes that economic growth strategy with income redistribution is optimal: "economic growth will support the economy and will be accomplished along with economic and income redistribution" (Charbalesh, 2009).

On the other hand, justice advocates believe that this market economy will remove the appropriate distribution achieved among the community: "in 1995 in England, only 10% of richest people have owned the half of wealth of country" (Sloman, 2000) and also: "20% of the richest people of the world have consumed 45% of animal protein" (Anonymous, 2005). Advocates of a justice government in market mechanism believe that without income redistribution, many people will be deprived of social blessings: "Injustice caused by the free market system functions is not acceptable anywhere in the world. So in all capitalist countries, government interferes in income distribution" (Tavakoli, 2007). With this viewpoint, the plan called the Justice Shares Distribution proposed to increase the level of low-income households and some of its objects are "equal distribution of wealth and income in the country, increasing the wealth and permanent income for households in need and reduction of direct liabilities of state and supportive organizations" (Anonymous, 2006).

Another challenging item is the effect of privatization on employment. "Privatization has always been a concerning factor for workforce. Because in cases, it causes firing of a large number of public workforces" (Anonymous, 2002). And "fear of job instability and being deprived of the power of collective haggling leads to disagreement of public firms or unions with privatization programs" (Anonymous, 2005). Governments with methods such as granting stock and incentive benefits to employees, retirees and retraining of fired workers in order to use them in other areas, attempt to compensate damages of workforce reduction. This problem is larger in densely populated countries which are slightly proportional between economic capacity and the population of job seekers. For instance, in Bangladesh, "results of a research performed by ILO in 1999 indicate that after privatization, employment reduced 25% in 11 active companies (total of 13 privatized manufacturing companies during 1991 to 1996)" (Momtazuddin, 2003). In this regard, legislators' and operators' performance is very decisive and if no legal supervision on performance of privatized industries and required support of vulnerable existed, the social phenomenon of unemployment will cause everyone to suffer.

Overall, we can see the summary of all the above as the expected results of privatization in the official notice of the supreme leader of the Islamic Republic of Iran as the overall policies of Article 44 of the constitution, as the following:

1. Reducing the monopoly of government and increasing share of private sector.
2. Increasing effectiveness and productivity.
3. Encouraging social justice and proper distribution of wealth.
4. Increasing the rate of economical growth.
5. Increasing GDP with reliance on domestic resources.
6. Establishing competitive environment.
7. Increasing government revenue.
8. Increasing public welfare.
9. Increasing capability of country in production of technology and knowledge.
10. Interacting constructively in international relations.
11. Achieving first place in economy and science in the region.
12. Increasing the general level of employment.

13. Enhancing the private sector.
14. Promoting public confidence in private sector.
15. Promoting motivation for managers of transferred companies.

## PROPOSED RESEARCH MODEL

The proposed research model with considering the results and legal documentation are seen in Fig. 1.

## RESEARCH METHOD

This research is a descriptive – survey research. Two methods applied for collecting data: library and field studies (questionnaire). The research is performed on Iran privatization organizations and in terms of scientific technique, it is required that all the information is obtained from professional and higher categories, additionally, 45 experts of organization which are considered as statistical population of research measured. More than 97% of this population has academic education and in addition, more than 62% have completed their graduate's course. Therefore, after a conceptual analysis of the raised issues, the questionnaire was designed and distributed among the experts. This questionnaire is comprised of 40 questions which includes 10 questions about strategic thinking, 15 questions about strategic requirements of privatization, and 15 questions about results of privatization and it was scored by Likert scale from 1 to 10.

To calculate reliability coefficient of questionnaire, Cronbach's alpha method with SPSS 17 applied. The results were respectively 0.944, 0.974, and 0.964, which all show high reliability.

## RESULTS

Considering the results of the binominal test, it can be said that with 99% confidence level that strategic belief and thinking in organization is 0.84. After performing the Pearson correlation test between strategic thinking as independent variable, strategic requirements of privatization as dependent variable with correlation of 0.636 and significant number of 0.001, linear

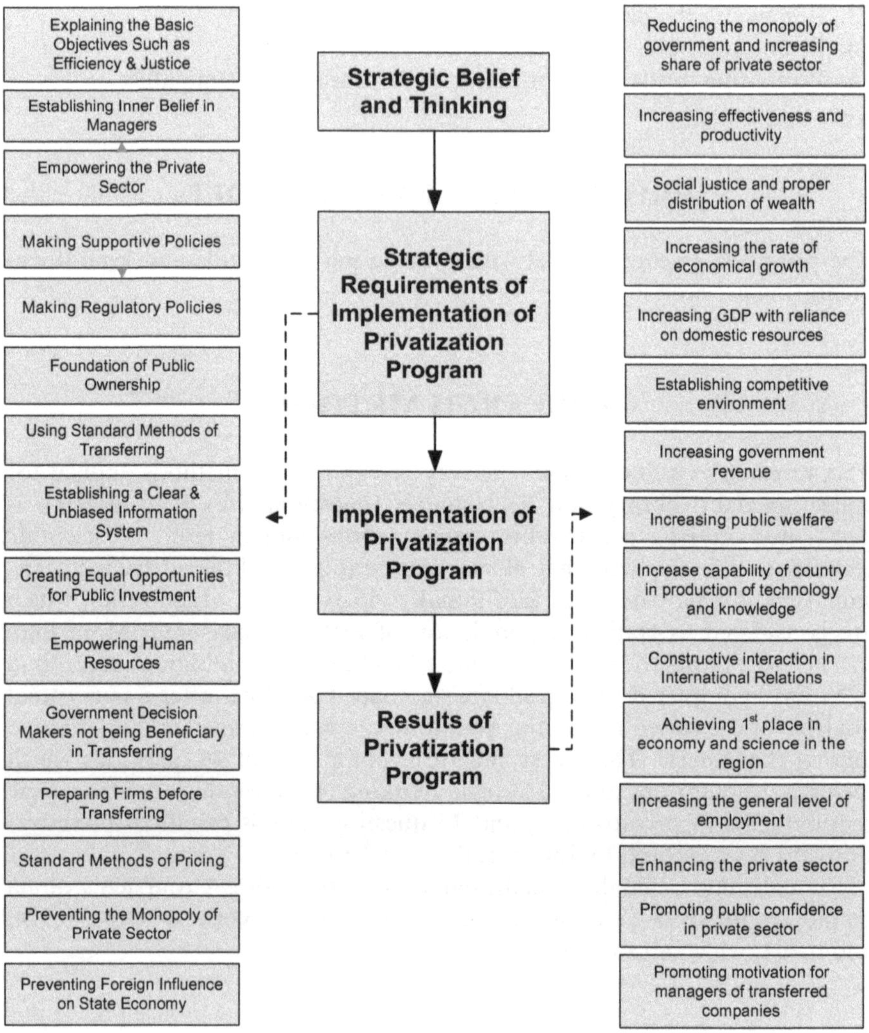


*Fig. 1.* Proposed Research Model.

regression test was used to determine the relationship; and as a result, relationship of these two variables is 0.64. So, the result of the Pearson correlation test between strategic thinking as an independent variable and result of privatization as dependent variable was 0.682 with significant number of 0.001 and the result of linear regression test for determining this

***Table 1.*** Priority of Strategic Implications of Privatization.

| Strategic Requirements | Average | Priority |
|---|---|---|
| Empowering the private sector | 8.2 | 1st |
| Making supportive policies | 7.36 | 2nd |
| Foundation for public ownership | 7.27 | 3rd |
| Making regulatory policies | 6.89 | 4th |
| Preparing firms before transferring | 6.88 | 5th |
| Preventing the monopoly of private sector | 6.82 | 6th |
| Establishing a clear and unbiased information system | 6.42 | 7th |
| Creating equal opportunities for public investment | 6.33 | 8th |
| Explaining basic objectives such as efficiency and justice | 6.25 | 9th |
| Government decision makers in transferring not being beneficiary | 6.1 | 10th |
| Standard methods of pricing | 5.87 | 11th |
| Establishing inner belief in managers | 5.69 | 12th |
| Preventing foreign influence on the state economy | 5.49 | 13th |
| Empowerment of human resources | 4.96 | 14th |
| Using standard methods of transferring | 4.84 | 15th |

relationship was 0.68. The Friedman test was used for priority ranking of strategic requirements and the results are found in Table 1.

## FINAL ANALYSIS AND RECOMMENDATIONS

For the Iran Privatization Organization to achieve a successful transfer as it stipulated to its duties, it needs to consider the requirements of privatization which are affected by independent variable of strategic thinking that is fairly reasonable in the organization. As a matter of fact, managers and economical experienced experts who are familiar with strategic management are very effective in the success of the organization in succeeding transfers. It will be more important to analyze the results of strategic thinking questionnaire because according to the experts, there is 84% strategic thinking and belief in organization, which is considered as one of the valuable assets of organization that must be diligently maintained.

The strategic requirements of privatization prioritized by experts lead us to the fact that the most essential requirements for the success of privatization programs in the country are summarized in support of the private sector of the country. Presenting technical education and comprehensive and targeted management to private economical firms, making the supportive rules of private investment, performing educational and propagator private property at the national level programs are respectively the highest priorities of strategic requirements in privatization. The lowest priorities are dedicated to the requirements that are focused on the country's regulations and are not considered a concerning factor for experts. The lowest level in Table 1 uses the Reputable Method of Transferring, Empowerment of Human Resources & Preventing from Foreign Influence on the State Economy.

## RECOMMENDATIONS

1. Considering proper foundation of strategic thinking in organization, advanced skills of strategic managements in economic development should be established in an organization with proper education and promoting workshops attended by experts.
2. The role of organization as the entity that is aware of the impact of corporate restructuring on assignment success is very important. Furthermore, organizations should endeavor to improve structure of companies and provide standards for enhancing the qualitative level.
3. Considering the most important priority requirements, it is considered that one of the most required plans of the organization with representatives of the government should be support of investors of private sector in scientific, financial, and executive areas to principally confront the common problems of privatization such as employment.
4. Performing a comprehensive strategic planning such as providing organizational and functional level strategies by considering strategic thinking and requirements is suggested in this study.

## SUGGESTIONS FOR FURTHER STUDIES

1. It is recommended that a study should be performed on the methods of amending companies' structure subjected to assignment with modeling of successful countries.
2. It is necessary to perform research to evaluate the success of the Islamic Republic of Iran in the implementation of privatization of justice-oriented based on the topics of management of Islamic economy and its methods of implementation in Islamic countries.

# REFERENCES

Ahmadigorji, H. (2008). How to support safe investment in monitoring organizations. *Conference of supervision on implementation of overall policies of Article 44 of constitution.*

Aminimehr, A. (2002). Privatization. *Payame Irankhodro Journal*, No. 69.

Anonymous. (1998). The report of human development of UNDP 1998. *Tadbir Journal*, No. 88.

Anonymous. (2002). *Encyclopedia of small business.* Retrieved from www.findarticles.com

Anonymous. (2005). Another view to privatization, *Tadbir Journal*, No. 164.

Anonymous. (2006). *The goals and pillars of justice share plan.* Justice Share Website. Retrieved from http://www.vase.ir/index.aspx?siteid = 81&pageid = 372

Anonymous. (2008a). *Executive regulations of pricing.* Iran Privatization Organization.

Anonymous. (2008b). *Sarmaye Newspaper*, No. 851. Retrieved from http://www.sarmayeh.net/ShowNews.php?18061

Anonymous. *Investment dictionary.* Retrieved from http://www.investopedia.com

Aryanmenhr, N., & Iji, M. (2008). Requirements to implement and monitor of privatization process. *Conference of supervision on implementation of overall policies of Article 44 of constitution.*

Bazazejazayeri, S. A. (2003). Management based on human resource empowerment. *Tadbir Journal*, No. 162.

Charbalesh, M. (2009). Social justice is the result of economic growth. *Tadbir Journal*, No. 203.

Danaei, M. (2004). Ready for new round of privatization. *Bank and Economy Journal*, No. 51.

Document of Summary of Privatization Process. (2004). Iran Privatization Organization.

Fouladgar, H. (2009). *Khorasan Newspaper*, No. 17446. Retrieved from http://www.khorasannews.com/news.aspx?10_17446_10_2146.XML

Ghafarian, V. (2008). *Strategy: 360 degree view.* Publication of Industrial Management Organization.

Ghafarian, V., & Kiani, G. (2005). *Five commands for strategic thinking.* Fara Publication.

Habibi, Ali, & Khoshpour, H. (1998). Performance evaluation of public sector privatization policies in Iran (1989–1995). *Plan and Budget Journal*, No. 7.

Internal Regulations of Expediency Council. (1997). Retrieved from http://www.irec.ir/Contents.aspx?p = b7528411-f439-4e06-a64c-66bc8eca4e7d

Katouzian, M. (2008). Study on the role of supervision parts in the pre, post and during the process of privatization of governmental companies with the approach of human resources. Conference of supervision on implementation of overall policies of Article 44 of constitution.

Kikeri, S., & John, N. (2004). Privatization in the competitive sectors: The record of date. World Bank Policy Research Working Paper No. 2860.

Maghami, A. (2009). Implementation of convention of combating corruption during privatization. *Conference of supervision on implementation of overall policies of Article 44 of constitution.*

Mathur, I., & Banchuenvijit, W. (2007). The effects of privatization on the performance of newly privatized firms in emerging markets. *Emerging Markets Review*, *8*, 134–146.

Matlabi Asl, S. (2004). Management of privatization of banking system. *Tadbir Journal*, No. 175.

Momeniha, A., & Alavi, H. (2008). Nation's inspectorate organization, rentier government and main policies of Article 44 of constitution of Islamic Republic of Iran. *Conference of supervision on implementation of overall policies of Article 44 of constitution.*

Momtazuddin, A. (2003). *Privatization in Bangladesh.* Iran Privatization Organization.

Okten, C., & Arin, K. P. (2006). The effects of privatization on efficiency: How does privatization work? *World Development, 34*(9), 1537–1556.

Salahi, M. (2008). Safety of investment. *Conference of supervision on implementation of overall policies of Article 44 of constitution.*

Sloman, J. (2000). *Economics* (4th ed.). UK: Pearson Education.

Smith, C., Andrew, D., & Trebilcock, M. J. (2001). State-owned enterprises in less developed countries: Privatization and alternative reform strategies, Netherlands. *European Journal of Law and Economics*, No. 12.

Starr, P. (1988). The meaning of privatization. *Yale Law and Policy*, Review No. 6, pp. 6–41, USA.

Tavakoli, A. (2007). *Public finance for social science.* Organization of Research and Writing of Social Science Books (SAMT).

Thompson, J. A., & Kay, J. A. (1986). Privatization: A policy in search rationale. *Economic Journal*, No. 96.

Zare, R., Kouaroei, M., & Ghadami, M. (2008). Article 44 of constitution and privatization: Requirements and challenges, conference of supervision on implementation of overall policies of Article 44 of constitution.

# ANNEXES

## ANNEX 1

**The Accounting and Auditing Organization for Islamic Financial Institutions**

The Accounting and Auditing Organization for Islamic Financial Institutions (AAOIFI) is an Islamic international autonomous non-for-profit corporate body that prepares accounting, auditing, governance, ethics and Shari'a standards for Islamic financial institutions and the industry. Professional qualification programs (notably CIPA, the Shari'a Adviser and Auditor "CSAA", and the corporate compliance program) are presented now by AAOIFI in its efforts to enhance the industry's human resources base and governance structures.

AAOIFI was established in accordance with the Agreement of Association which was signed by Islamic financial institutions on 1 Safar, 1410H corresponding to 26 February, 1990 in Algiers. Then, it was registered on 11 Ramadan 1411 corresponding to 27 March, 1991 in the State of Bahrain.

As an independent international organization, AAOIFI is supported by institutional members (200 members from 45 countries, so far) including central banks, Islamic financial institutions, and other participants from the international Islamic banking and finance industry, worldwide.

AAOIFI has gained assuring support for the implementation of its standards, which are now adopted in the Kingdom of Bahrain, Dubai International Financial Centre, Jordan, Lebanon, Qatar, Sudan and Syria. The relevant authorities in Australia, Indonesia, Malaysia, Pakistan, Kingdom of Saudi Arabia, and South Africa have issued guidelines that are based on AAOIFI's standards and pronouncements.

*Source*: http://www.aaoifi.com/aaoifi/TheOrganization/Overview/tabid/62/language/en-US/Default.aspx

**Objectives of AAOIFI**

The objectives of AAOIFI are:

1. to develop accounting and auditing thoughts relevant to Islamic financial institutions;
2. to disseminate accounting and auditing thoughts relevant to Islamic financial institutions and its applications through training, seminars, publication of periodical newsletters, carrying out and commissioning of research and other means;
3. to prepare, promulgate and interpret accounting and auditing standards for Islamic financial institutions; and
4. to review and amend accounting and auditing standards for Islamic financial institutions.

AAOIFI carries out these objectives in accordance with the precepts of Islamic Shari'a which represents a comprehensive system for all aspects of life, in conformity with the environment in which Islamic financial institutions have developed. This activity is intended both to enhance the confidence of users of the financial statements of Islamic financial institutions in the information that is produced about these institutions, and to encourage these users to invest or deposit their funds in Islamic financial institutions and to use their services.

*Source*: http://www.aaoifi.com/aaoifi/TheOrganization/Overview/tabid/62/language/en-US/Default.aspx

# ANNEX 2

**The Islamic Financial Services Board (IFSB) Role**

Background

The Islamic Financial Services Board (IFSB), which is based in Kuala Lumpur, was officially inaugurated on 3rd November 2002 and started operations on 10th March 2003. It serves as an international standard-setting body of regulatory and supervisory agencies that have vested interest in ensuring the soundness and stability of the Islamic financial services industry, which is defined broadly to include banking, capital market and insurance. In advancing this mission, the IFSB promotes the development of a prudent and transparent Islamic financial services industry through introducing new, or adapting existing international standards consistent with Sharī'ah principles, and recommend them for adoption.

To this end, the work of the IFSB complements that of the Basel Committee on Banking Supervision, International Organization of Securities Commissions and the International Association of Insurance Supervisors.

As at April 2013, the 187 members of the IFSB comprise 57 regulatory and supervisory authorities, eight international inter-governmental organizations and 122 market players, professional firms and industry associations operating in 43 jurisdictions.

Malaysia, the host country of the IFSB, has enacted a law known as the Islamic Financial Services Board Act 2002, which gives the IFSB the immunities and privileges that are usually granted to international organizations and diplomatic missions.

**Adoption of Standards and Issuance**

Since its inception, the IFSB has issued nineteen Standards, Guiding Principles and Technical Note for the Islamic financial services industry. The published documents are on the areas of:

1. Risk Management (IFSB-1)
2. Capital Adequacy (IFSB-2)
3. Corporate Governance (IFSB-3)
4. Transparency and Market Discipline (IFSB-4)

5. Supervisory Review Process (IFSB-5)
6. Governance for Collective Investment Schemes (IFSB-6)
7. Special Issues in Capital Adequacy (IFSB-7)
8. Guiding Principles on Governance for Islamic Insurance (Takâful) Operations (IFSB-8)
9. Conduct of Business for Institutions offering Islamic Financial Services (IIFS) (IFSB-9)
10. Guiding Principles on Sharī'ah Governance System (IFSB-10)
11. Standard on Solvency Requirements for Takâful (Islamic Insurance) Undertakings (IFSB-11)
12. Guiding Principles on Liquidity Risk Management for Institutions offering Islamic Financial Services (IFSB-12)
13. Guiding Principles on Stress Testing for Institutions offering Islamic Financial Services (IFSB-13)
14. Recognition of Ratings on Sharī'ah-Compliant Financial Instruments (GN-1)
15. Guidance Note in Connection with the Risk Management and Capital Adequacy Standards: Commodity Murâbahah Transactions (GN-2)
16. Guidance Note on the Practice of Smoothing the Profits Payout to Investment Account Holders (GN -3)
17. Guidance Note in Connection with the IFSB Capital Adequacy Standard: The Determination of Alpha in the Capital Adequacy Ratio for Institutions (other than Insurance Institutions) offering only Islamic Financial Services (GN-4)
18. Guidance Note on the Recognition of Ratings by External Credit Assessment Institutions (ECAIS) on Takâful and ReTakâful Undertakings (GN-5)
19. Development of Islamic Money Markets (TN-1)

The standards prepared by the IFSB follow a lengthy due process as outlined in its Guidelines and Procedures for the Preparation of Standards/Guidelines which involves, among others, the issuance of exposure draft and, where necessary, the holding of a public hearing.

Awareness Promotion

The IFSB is actively involved in the promotion of awareness of issues that are relevant or have an impact on the regulation and supervision of the Islamic financial services industry. This mainly takes the form of international conferences, seminars, workshops, trainings, meetings and dialogues staged in many countries.

*Source*: http://www.ifsb.org/index.php

**IFSB last conference on Future of Islamic Financial Services**

Final Sessions of the 10th IFSB Summit to Conclude the Future of Islamic Financial Services Industry Moving Forward

Date posted: 17 May 2013

Kuala Lumpur, 17 May 2013 – On the second day of the 10th IFSB Summit, key leaders in the Islamic financial services industry (IFSI) deliberated on the role of innovation and inclusion to further develop the industry and support economic growth. Themed, "The Future of the Islamic Financial Services Industry: Resilience, Stability and Inclusive Growth", the Summit took place on 16 and 17 May 2013 at Sasana Kijang, Kuala Lumpur. Bank Negara Malaysia is the host of the Summit.

The fourth session, themed, "Islamic Finance: Innovation and Inclusive Growth", was chaired by Andrew L.T. Sheng, Chief Adviser to the China Banking Regulatory Commission and President, Fung Global Institute Ltd, Hong Kong. The speakers in the session included Professor Dr. Azmi Omar, Director General of Islamic Research and Training Institute, Islamic Development Bank Group, Abayomi Alawode, Manager Financial Systems Global Practice, The World Bank Group and Professor Dr. Volker Nienhaus, Visiting Professor, University of Reading, United Kingdom. Mr. Sheng in the opening of the session emphasised the roles of product innovation and risk-sharing principle in Islamic finance to help promote financial inclusion and support economic growth.

Professor Dr. Azmi Omar elaborated on the role of Islamic microfinance as one of the products that can help to reduce poverty levels among Muslim populations, increase financial inclusion and contribute significantly towards achieving economic growth. Meanwhile, Mr. Alawode shared how Islamic finance serves as an advocate of inclusive economic growth as it helps to reduce irregularity and improve financial sector development, has a direct impact on business growth, and enhances sustainability of economic growth. Meanwhile, Professor Volker Nienhaus stressed the importance of innovation. He suggested that financial engineering should also focus on developing risk-sharing financial instruments for small- and medium-sized enterprises (SMEs). The speakers concurred that for Islamic microfinance and SMEs to succeed, this requires certain policies to be put in place, which include a comprehensive approach to address financial inclusion, legal, regulatory and supervisory frameworks, capacity building and training to macro-entrepreneurs and SMEs, to be further supported by a credit guarantee scheme and a business and credit information bureau.

The fifth session, themed, "Panel Discussion on Lessons Drawn: Prospects for the Future", was chaired by H.E. Dr. Zeti Akhtar Aziz, Governor, Bank Negara Malaysia. The speakers in the session included H.E. Sultan Bin Nasser Al Suwaidi, Governor, Central Bank of the United Arab Emirates, H.E. Dr. Ishrat Husain, Dean and Director Institute of Business Administration, Pakistan, Former Governor, State Bank of Pakistan and Professor Rifaat Ahmed Abdel Karim, Chief Executive Officer, International Islamic Liquidity Management Corporation. The speakers shared their views on the lessons learnt by the IFSI following the global financial crisis, the roles of the IFSI in promoting economic development and stability in emerging economies, as well as the prospects of the industry moving forward.

H.E. Dr. Zeti Akhtar Aziz highlighted that Islamic finance will continue to serve the economy in an effective manner and that its internationalisation will also continue due to interconnectedness and high interlinkages. However, she also warned that key prospects for Islamic finance would depend upon how the IFSI evolves. She also mentioned that the implementation of the IFSB standards is key in promoting the stability and resilience of the IFSI. H.E. Sultan Bin Nasser Al Suwaidi was of the view that Islamic finance can play an important complementary role in economic development and it can provide key support to the vulnerable society through financial inclusion, which will allow access to Islamic finance. He also stressed the need for strengthening the micro prudential framework including strengthening the regulatory and supervisory framework covering buffers, liquidity, collateral, risk cultures, and contingency plans.

H.E. Dr. Ishrat Husain stated that the inherent nature of Islamic finance will stabilize the global economy and that in many jurisdictions Islamic finance has become the preferred choice of financial intermediation. He remarked that the asset-backed nature of Islamic finance, avoidance of speculation in financial transactions, and giving access to financial inclusion, will help to contribute towards the resilience and stability of the global financial system.

Professor Rifaat Ahmed Abdel Karim highlighted issues of legal risk, recommending an international court consisting of judges and scholars. He felt there was a policy challenge that was best addressed by transforming the Islamic Financial Stability Forum into a more deliberative and policy making body perhaps along the lines of the Financial Stability Board. He also emphasised the need for conducting more research and awareness in the IFSI and there is strong need for standardisation of the Sharī'ah with common guidelines across the industry..

*Source*: http://www.ifsb.org/preess_full.php?id = 225&submit = more

- Reports / Research / Proceedings

May 2013

Islamic Financial Services Industry Stability Report 2013

March 2011

Revised Compilation Guide on Prudential and Structural Islamic Financial Indicators

Note: This document is the revision of the Compilation Guide on Prudential and Structural Islamic Finance Indicators: Guidance on the Compilation and Dissemination of Prudential and Structural Islamic Finance Indicators for Banking and Near-Banking Institutions offering Islamic Financial Services published by the IFSB in November 2007.

April 2010

IFSB-IRTI-IDB Islamic Finance and Global Stability Report.

May 2007

Islamic Financial Services Industry Development: Ten-Year Framework and Strategies

August 2006

Issues in Regulation and Supervision of Takâful (Islamic Insurance) by IFSB and International Association of Insurance Supervisors.

ISLAMIC FINANCIAL SERVICES INDUSTRY DEVELOPMENT

**TEN-YEAR FRAMEWORK AND STRATEGIES**

A joint initiative of the Islamic Research & Training Institute, Islamic Development Bank and Islamic Financial Services Board and Islamic Research and Training Institute

## VISION

Facilitating sustainable economic development and just social progress through a sound, efficient, progressive and resilient Islamic financial services industry.

## MISSION

Development of a dynamic, comprehensive and innovative Islamic financial services industry, which closely supports real economic activities and is well integrated within the international financial system.

*Source*: http://ifsb.org/docs/10_yr_framework.pdf

## EXECUTIVE SUMMARY

This document, which will be revised and updated periodically by its initiators, aims to provide a general framework that national authorities may find beneficial for designing Islamic financial services industry (IFSI) development initiatives and integrating these in their national financial sector development policies. The document also aims to offer an integrated basis for promoting international policy

Dialogue among stakeholders and fostering the orderly development of an efficient, sound, resilient and sustainable IFSI in the rapidly changing global market, technological and regulatory environments.

The fundamental precondition for development of a robust financial services industry is the existence of conditions that are conducive to the operations of free, fair and transparent markets. The critical issues of poverty alleviation and improvements in important socio-economic aspects of life such as health and education, reduction in child mortality, providing safe and secure future for youth etc., are top of the public policy agenda of our societies. A sound, vibrant and market-driven financial services industry can play a vital role in creating opportunities and therefore addressing human development challenges of our societies by efficiently and equitably channeling financial resources towards productive opportunities and employment generation. Islamic law protects private property, safeguards the free, fair and transparent operation of market forces and offers other significant guidance in the domain of economic, financial and commercial activities. Ensuring the compliance of financial services with these guidelines is necessary for the services to be relevant for use by Muslims and hence broadening the public's access to financial services. The IFSI caters to this special need of society. Simultaneously, it is also possible to capture demand beyond the Muslim population through the provision of innovative and high-quality Islamic financial service (IFS). Therefore, by adding another alternative in an array of choices of financial services, IFS can foster healthy competition. Promotion of the IFSI is also part of the efforts being made to gradually replace informal markets with organized and regulated ones and to enhance the overall development of the financial sector. The contemporary IFSI has just passed through its 30th anniversary year. During those years, it has come a long way in providing a range of financial services in a variety of segments, including banking, non-bank financial services, insurance and capital markets. Given its inherent features, the IFSI has the potential to concurrently achieve the goals of sustainable economic development and just social progress, supported by sound and stable financial institutions and markets. However, the IFSI also faces significant challenges as a result of having its own special risk characteristics and unique governance requirements, on the one hand, and operating in a tax, legal and regulatory environment originally designed for conventional financial services, on the other hand.

*Source*: http://ifsb.org/docs/10_yr_framework.pdf

**Published Standards**

December 2005: IFSB-1: Guiding Principles of Risk Management for Institutions (other than Insurance Institutions) offering only Islamic Financial Services (IIFS)

[ENGLISH | ARABIC]

December 2005: IFSB-2: Capital Adequacy Standard for Institutions (other than Insurance Institutions) offering only Islamic Financial Services (IIFS)

[ENGLISH | ARABIC]

December 2006: IFSB-3: Guiding Principles on Corporate Governance for Institutions offering only Islamic Financial Services (Excluding Islamic Insurance (Takâful) Institutions and Islamic Mutual Funds

[ENGLISH | ARABIC]

December 2007: IFSB-4: Disclosures to Promote Transparency and Market Discipline for Institutions offering Islamic Financial Services (excluding Islamic Insurance (Takâful) Institutions and Islamic Mutual Funds.

[ENGLISH | ARABIC]

December 2007: IFSB-5: Guidance on Key Elements in the Supervisory Review Process of Institutions offering Islamic Financial Services (excluding Islamic Insurance (Takâful) Institutions and Islamic Mutual Funds)

[ ENGLISH | ARABIC]

December 2008: IFSB-6: Guiding Principles on Governance for Islamic Collective Investment Schemes

[ ENGLISH | ARABIC]

January 2009: IFSB-7: Capital Adequacy Requirements for Sukûk, Securitizations and Real Estate investment

[ENGLISH | ARABIC]

December 2009: IFSB-8: Guiding Principles on Governance for Takâful (Islamic Insurance) Undertakings

[ENGLISH | ARABIC]

December 2009: IFSB-9: Guiding Principles on Conduct of Business for Institutions offering Islamic Financial Services

[ENGLISH | ARABIC]

December 2009: IFSB-10: Guiding Principles on Sharîah Governance Systems for Institutions offering Islamic Financial Services

[ENGLISH | ARABIC]

December 2010: IFSB-11: Standard on Solvency Requirements for Takâful (Islamic Insurance) Undertakings

[ENGLISH | ARABIC]

March 2012: IFSB-12: Guiding Principles on Liquidity Risk Management for Institutions offering Islamic Financial Services

[ENGLISH | ARABIC]

March 2012: IFSB-13: Guiding Principles on Stress Testing for Institutions offering Islamic Financial Services

[ENGLISH | ARABIC]

**Guidance Notes**

March 2008: GN-1: Guidance Note in Connection with the Capital Adequacy Standard: Recognition of Ratings by External Credit Assessment Institutions (ECAIs) on Sharî'ah-Compliant Financial Instruments

[ENGLISH | ARABIC]

December 2010: GN-2: Guidance Note in Connection with the Risk Management and Capital Adequacy Standards: Commodity Murâbahah Transactions

[ENGLISH | ARABIC]

December 2010: GN-3: Guidance Note on the Practice of Smoothing the Profits Payout to Investment Account Holders

[ENGLISH | ARABIC]

March 2011: GN-4: Guidance Note in Connection with the IFSB Capital Adequacy Standard: The Determination of Alpha in the Capital Adequacy Ratio for Institutions (other than Insurance Institutions) offering only Islamic Financial Services

[ENGLISH | ARABIC]

March 2011: GN-5: Guidance Note on the Recognition of Ratings by external Credit Assessment Institutions (ECAIS) on Takâful and ReTakâful Undertakings

[ENGLISH | ARABIC]

**Technical Notes**

TN-1: Technical Note on Issues in Strengthening Liquidity Management of Institutions Offering Islamic Financial Services: The Development of Islamic Money Markets

*Source*: http://www.ifsb.org/published.php

# ANNEX 3

**Strategic Planning**

Basis for Planning, Strategy and Terminology

An organization's strategy is the approach it takes to survive and succeed. It will usually be explicit.

Subsidiary strategies

The group of individual strategies which support the strategic plan, such as the Risk Management strategy, Investment strategy or the Human resources strategy.

**Strategic plan**

Also known as the corporate plan. The strategic plan provides an overarching framework for the institution's strategies. It is an output of the strategic planning process.

Strategic planning

Strategic planning is that part of the strategic management process concerned with identifying the long-term direction of Financial Institution, generating ideas and choices, taking the necessary steps to achieve the stated goals, and monitoring progress or non-achievement in order to adapt the future strategy.

Activities

These are the activities or processes which are undertaken to fulfil the aim. Activities result in outputs.

Inputs

These are the resources used to achieve an aim. Examples of inputs are staff time, facilities and equipment

Operating statement

Also known as the operating plan. The operating statement describes the action to be taken to implement the strategic plan in the foreseeable future, usually taken as one or two years. It is an output of the strategic planning process.

Outcomes

These concern the benefits (or otherwise) arising from outputs, and have qualitative and quantitative aspects. In evaluating performance against aims, output and outcome measures are complementary.

Outputs

These are products of activities and are normally tangible (for example, the number and value of projects financed.

The strategic plan

The strategic plan for any institution normally includes the following elements:

An introduction to the organization which explains why the plan has been produced at this time.

A mission statement which condenses the generic strategy into a few words.

A set of high-level aspirations and long-term aims.

A schedule of the main objectives over the duration of the plan, specifying where responsibility for implementation rests and the timescale for completion. This schedule leads to the annual operating statement, which is discussed below.

Summaries of integrated strategies for key activities and resource

Financial and other data to demonstrate the feasibility of the plans.

**The vision** is designed to depict the long-term aim in a succinct way.

It is an expression of leadership, and often provides an interpretative framework which can guide decision making. Some institutions amplify their mission and vision with a statement of strategic aims, policies or values

A long-term plan, referred to as either the strategic or corporate plan, which includes the overall strategy and sets out the long-term objectives and how these are to be achieved

Operating plan or statement which distils the actions required in the year ahead;

Actions necessary to effect implementation

Here is no virtue in sticking doggedly to a plan which has been overtaken by events. It is essential for all institutions to retain the flexibility to adjust as circumstances change, so that they can exploit unexpected opportunities and respond to unforeseen threats.

Planning is made up of four elements: 'scanning', 'analysing', 'generating ideas' and 'enabling' are stages to the process, while 'enabling' refers to the underlying requirements for the process to be effective.

Finance and resource plans.

The financial and resource aspects must be integrated with the strategic plan to secure practicality, flexibility and value for money. A financial strategy can assist institutions with integration process.

**Responsibility for monitoring**

Senior management teams are generally responsible for monitoring progress in the implementation of the strategic plan, at least through a regular review of the operating statement and summary management accounts Businesses are increasingly taking advantage of opportunities to utilize advances in technology to enhance the efficiency and effectiveness of their businesses.

*Source*: http://www.hfrp.org/publications-resources/browse-our-publications/strategic-planning-process-steps-in-developing-strategic-plans

See also: Beseiso, F. H. (2010). Manual on the management of economic financial and banking crisis – The conceptual and practical basis (pp. 510–514). Published by Arab Banks Union (Arabic).

# ANNEX 4

**Developing Role of Islamic Banking in Europe**

Islamic Banking in the U.K

Non-Muslims turn to Islamic Bank as a safe option

Oct 3 2008 by Anna Blackaby, Business Staff

Growing numbers of non-Muslims are turning to Islamic banking as customers spooked by turmoil in the Western banking system increasingly see the sector as a safe haven.

The Birmingham-headquartered Islamic Bank of Britain said it had seen significant growth in non-Muslim customers since the onset of turbulence on financial markets as Islamic banks, bound by strict religious principles, are largely seen as insulated from the credit crisis.

Islam's prohibition on the charging or paying of interest – riba – as well as rules on the kinds of investments they can make is among the reasons Islamic banks are coming through the crisis unscathed.

Islamic Bank of Britain head of marketing Steven Amos said: "Our core business will always be Muslims but the numbers of non-Muslims are really picking up.

"We've had massive interest and it's down to the number of reasons why we're insulated from the credit crunch.

"There were two reasons for the credit crunch. The first is liquidity – banks lending to each other on the money markets – but Islamic banks do not borrow or lend on money markets because interest is not allowed.

"The second reason Islamic banks are insulated is to do with assets – everything has to involve an underlying asset or service and if you are going to trade in an asset you have to own it first."

The explosion in complex derivative products over the last few years has left Western banks reeling from exposure to toxic assets often far-removed from their everyday activities.

In contrast the more risk-averse Islamic finance system did not embrace this kind of deal.

"Conventional banks didn't know what they were buying in these derivatives but we have no exposure to subprime as we just don't deal in it full stop.

"That is one of the fundamental reasons we are insulated."

Stipulations that you must own the asset you are trading in also mean practices such as short-selling are not a feature of Islamic banking.

Mr Amos also said the principle of partnership underlying Islamic finance means banks would never enter into the subprime-style agreements behind the current crisis.

"For the benefit of the customers and the bank themselves, we enter into a partnership agreement. "Islamic banks don't just enter into any agreement; we make sure the agreement is right for both partners."

The growth in ethical investment in the UK over the last few years has also spelled an increase in interest from non-Muslims attracted by the strong ethical tenets of Islamic banking.

"We guarantee you we won't invest customers' funds in alcohol, tobacco, pornography or in any form of gambling.

"These factors are often in keeping with the ethical products that we've seen growing in the UK over recent years," said Mr Amos.

The Islamic Bank of Britain is the UK's only stand-alone fully Shariah-compliant retail bank.

In July it launched its Home Purchase Plan, billed as "the mortgage alternative," which enables customers to purchase their homes in an ethical and Shariah-compliant manner.

The plan is based on the Islamic financing principles of Ijara, which means leasing, and Diminishing Musharaka – partnership.

For example, the bank contributes 80 per cent of the purchase price and the customer puts in 20 per cent.

Over a period of up to 30 years, the customer will make monthly instalments buying back the bank's share of the home and with each instalment paid the bank's share decreases.

Many of the big conventional UK banks have entered into the Islamic finance market in recent years, with big names such as Lloyds TSB offering a Shariah-compliant home finance product.

*Source*: http://www.birminghampost.net/birmingham-siness/birmingham-business-news/other-uk-business/2008/10/03/non-muslims-turn-to-slamic-bank-as-a-safe-option-65233-21962049/

**Cooperation on Islamic Banking with Europe**

Malaysia-based Islamic Financial Services Board and ECB conducting study on Islamic finance based Islamic Financial Services Board (IFSB) are conducting a joint study on policies affecting Islamic finance in Europe, the IFSB's top official told Reuters.

"We are doing a joint study with Europe's central bank which brings together European scholars and regulators to examine a broad set of policy and regulatory issues in relation to Islamic finance in Europe," said IFSB secretary-general Jaseem Ahmed.

The IFSB is one of the main bodies setting standards globally for Islamic finance.

"What we are seeing is a strong public policy stance emerging, which I think is essential for Islamic finance to flourish on the continent. This is happening both within and outside the euro zone," Ahmed said.

An ECB spokesman confirmed to Reuters that the study was underway at the level of a research paper. He did not give an expected release date.

The study will be complemented on April 9 by the IFSB's annual forum, which will be hosted by the Bank of Italy in Rome. The forum attracts regulators and market players from the Islamic finance industry, which grew to $1.55 trillion in assets globally in 2012, according to consultants Ernst & Young.

The last time the 184-member IFSB held a forum in Europe was in Paris in 2009; since then the euro zone crisis has increased interest in Islamic finance, which follows religious principles such as a ban on interest and pure monetary speculation.

"There is broad recognition that relying only on an excessively leveraged and debt-fuelled financial system has great risks. There is a corresponding stress on equity financing in the post-crisis environment," Ahmed added.

"I think the global crisis has really brought Islamic finance to the front, if not yet the center, of the stage."

In November 2009 Mario Draghi, then governor of Italy's central bank and now president of the ECB, called the growth of Islamic finance a "welcome development", adding that it raised some "intriguing questions" for financial markets.

Draghi's successor at the Bank of Italy, Ignazio Visco, will be joined at next month's IFSB forum by officials from the ECB, Italy's finance ministry and other central bankers to discuss the "European challenge", according to the forum's schedule.

## REGULATORY SUPPORT

Partly because it has the support of cash-rich Islamic funds from the Gulf, Islamic finance fared relatively well during the global financial crisis, and it is expected to keep growing; 150 new Islamic financial institutions will be needed globally by 2020 to satisfy demand, according to consultancy Oliver Wyman.

The IFSB has taken steps elsewhere to win regulatory support for Islamic finance. In October, it signed an agreement with the Asian Development Bank, which would see the ADB encourage member countries to adopt IFSB standards.

The Italian central bank doesn't have a specific standing group studying Islamic finance, but it follows industry trends and developments on a regular basis, according to a Bank of Italy spokesman.

The Bank of Italy's research department noted in a paper in 2010 that the industry could be hampered by problems including governance structure, regulation, a lack of monetary policy instruments and liquidity management.

The experience of Medio factoring, a fully owned subsidiary of Intesa Sanpaolo, Italy's biggest retail bank, which explored Islamic financing options but did not go ahead with a deal, shows that companies in Europe can find Islamic transactions uneconomic without regulatory support.

"We have tried but it was very difficult to put in place a structure that was fiscally efficient," Mediofactoring's chief executive Rony Hamaui, who will be a speaker at the forum, told Reuters.

"Unfortunately in Italy very little is being done in Islamic finance. We talked to the Treasury regarding sukuk (Islamic bonds), but for the government it is not a major focus."

**Sukuk** will be one of the major themes in the IFSB forum; Islamic bonds have gradually moved into the mainstream as a viable funding option for both governments and corporates. Over $121 billion worth of sukuk were issued around the world in 2012, according to Thomson Reuters data, up from around $85 billion in 2011.

So far, the closest which Europe has come to issuing a sovereign sukuk was in 2009, when Britain prepared it's first-ever issuance, which would have been a rare AAA-rated issue in the industry.

"Four years ago we worked on structuring the UK's sukuk issuance, but the UK postponed the issue due to a view that the transaction would not provide value for money," said Farmida Bi, European head of Islamic finance at Norton Rose in London.

"The UK Treasury has made it clear they are not going to revisit this issue for now."

But British regulators have introduced legislation facilitating Islamic finance, which could serve as a reference for other European countries.

"Where the UK's approach to Islamic finance is helpful is in creating a level playing field, where there is no tax or regulatory incentives or penalties for Islamic transactions, thus creating a pragmatic way of dealing with it," Bi said. (Reuters)

*Source*: http://www.thestar.com.my/Business/BusinessNews/2013/03/12/Malaysiabased-Islamic-Financial-Services-Board-and-ECB-conducting-study-on-Islamic-finance.aspx

**WORLD ISLAMIC ECONOMIC FORUM**

Press release

Embargoed 1000 Wednesday 3rd July

PRIME MINISTER OF MALAYSIA BRINGS WORLD ISLAMIC ECONOMIC FORUM TO LONDON

The Prime Minister of Malaysia, the Honourable Dato' Sri Mohd Najib Tun Abdul Razak, the Mayor of London, Boris Johnson, and Lord Green, Minister for Trade and Investment, will today launch the 9th World Islamic Economic Forum.

The forthcoming Forum, entitled 'Changing World, New Relationships', will be held at Excel in London later this year – the first time the event will meet outside the Muslim world.

More than 1,500 government leaders, captains of industries, academic scholars, regional experts, professionals and corporate managers from 100 countries will come together at the 9th World Islamic Economic Forum in October to boost trade partnerships between Islamic and European markets, and explore London's future as a global hub for Islamic Finance.

Speakers from the world of politics will include the Prime Minister of Malaysia, the Honourable Dato' Sri Mohd Najib Tun Abdul Razak, the British Prime Minister, David Cameron, the Mayor of London, Boris Johnson, the Governor of the Bank Negara Malaysia, Tan Sri Dato' Sri Dr. Zeti Akhtar Aziz, President of the Islamic Development Bank, H.E. Dr Ahmed Mohamed Ali, the Malaysian Minister for International Trade and Industry, Dato Sri Mustapa bin Mohamed, Minister of State at the Foreign and Commonwealth Office, Baroness Warsi, Minister for Trade and Investment, Lord Green, Financial Secretary to the Treasury, Greg Clark, and Minister of State for International Development, Alan Duncan.

Business leaders from banks, infrastructure, technology, design and media companies from countries including China, UAE, Malaysia, USA, UK, South Africa, Japan, and Indonesia, as well as health and education experts will take part. Organisations represented include Islamic Development Bank, the Aga Khan Development Network, Abu Dhabi Commercial Bank, World Health Organisation, Thomson Reuters, Halal Food Festival, Saudi Economic and Development Company (SEDCO) Capital, JS Comsa Corporation, Japan and BDA China with strong support from Malaysian based corporations as Khazanah Nasional, Maybank Islamic Berhad and Bank Negara Malaysia.

The Forum aims to deliver tangible investment. At last year's 8th WIEF, deals worth an estimated RM28 billion (£5.8billion) were struck.

The 9th WIEF in London comes alongside the recent acquisition of the iconic Battersea Power Station site. The £400m Malaysian consortium investment is the largest of its kind in the UK. With a development value of around £8bn, it is expected to create 15,000 new jobs and 3,500 new homes.

The Islamic Finance sector is estimated to be worth £1.2 trillion, and is expected to grow to £1.6 trillion by 2015.i Islamic nations account for nearly 25% of the world's total population.

London will seek to extend its role as a western hub for Islamic finance, building on the £22.3

*Source*: http://wief.org/wp-ontent/themes/twentyeleven/cms/uploads/images/press/download_49.pdf

BUSINESS

29 October 2013, Last updated at 15:17 GMT

**London's role in growing market for Islamic finance**

By Andrew Walker BBC World Service Economics correspondent

The global Islamic finance market is forecast to be worth £1.24tn ($2tn) next year

The World Islamic Financial Forum is in London and the UK Prime Minister David Cameron has taken the opportunity to announce some initiatives to raise the financial district the City of London's profile in this growing business.

The government has been keen to promote London and attract a wide range of financial activity.

It is consistent with the recent efforts of the Chancellor of the Exchequer George Osborne to promote the City as a centre for trading in China's currency, the renminbi.

Mr Cameron says the UK Treasury is working on an Islamic bond that will raise about £200m ($320m) and which is likely to be launched next year.

Selling bonds is the routine method that governments use to borrow money in the world's financial markets.

Scholarly debate

The distinctive feature of these Islamic financial products – known as sukuk – is that they are intended to get round the prohibition on paying or receiving interest.

They are usually described as investments rather than lending.

It is usually done by making the initial payment – in this case, from an Islamic investor to the British government – an investment in some asset rather than loan.

The return to the investor comes as profit or rent rather than interest.

The British government's bonds are likely to make use of property – buildings or land – as the asset into which the investments would go.

This approach does have its critics, with some Islamic scholars arguing that it does not really avoid interest payments.

This is because fixed returns and a fixed repayment when the investment matures do look rather like a loan with interest.

But there is a vigorous debate among Islamic scholars about exactly what is and is not acceptable, and the details of the British government's bonds have not yet been settled.

Several governments in the Islamic world do use this method to raise funds, with Indonesia, Malaysia and Turkey being among those who have adopted this approach.

Britain would, says Mr Cameron, be the first country outside the Islamic world to use this approach.

He also says the London Stock Exchange is launching new stock indexes of firms whose business is consistent with Islamic principles.

That would make it easier for Muslim investors to decide where to put their money.

**Growing niche**

Islamic finance is certainly a growing business, and the Prime Minister has said it is currently expanding at a 50% faster rate than conventional banking.

However, it is still something of a niche.

Conventional borrowing with interest still dominates for governments in the Islamic world that need to get funds from the markets, or from agencies such as the IMF or the World Bank.

And many of them hold interest-bearing investments, such as US government bonds.

Nonetheless, global Islamic investments are forecast to reach £1.24bn ($2tn) by next year according to accountants EY – which makes it quite a substantial niche.

*Source*: http://www.bbc.co.uk/news/business-24728409

BUSINESS

**Cameron unveils Islamic bond plan**

The prime minister is keen to make London an international centre of Islamic finance

Prime Minister David Cameron has announced that the UK will become the first non-Muslim country to issue an Islamic bond.

At the World Islamic Economic Forum (WIEF) in London, he also announced plans for a new Islamic index on the London Stock Exchange.

It is intended to attract more Islamic investors by making it clearer which companies match their criteria.

Under Islamic rules, no interest on business dealings can be charged.

Transactions must also be based on a real trade or business activities and they must not involve anything forbidden under Sharia law, such as gambling or alcohol.

Mr Cameron believes that Islamic finance is a good opportunity for the UK's financial services industry as Islamic investments have soared by 150% in the past seven years and are expected to be worth £1.3 trillion next year.

"I don't just want London to be a great capital of Islamic finance in the Western world, I want London to stand alongside Dubai as one of the great capitals of Islamic finance anywhere in the world," he told delegates of the WIEF.

"There are some countries which naturally look inwards, pull up the drawbridge and refuse to recognise that the way the world is changing affects their future success. But Britain will not make that mistake," he added.

The Treasury hopes to launch an Islamic bond – called a sukuk – worth £200m as early as next year. It will be structured to bring in a fixed return from a tangible asset or service, and without charging interest, in accordance with Islamic financial principles.

*Source*: http://www.bbc.co.uk/news/business-24722440

# AUTHOR INDEX

# SUBJECT INDEX